The
Management
of
Purpose

The
Management
of
Purpose

Lewis Anthony Dexter

Martín Sánchez-Jankowski
and Alan J. Ware,
editors

Routledge
Taylor & Francis Group

LONDON AND NEW YORK

First published 2010 by Transaction Publishers

2 Park Square, Milton Park, Abingdon, Oxfordshire OX14 4RN
711 Third Avenue, New York, NY 10017

Routledge is an imprint of the Taylor & Francis Group, an informa business

First issued in paperback 2017

Library of Congress Catalog Number: 2009016357

Library of Congress Cataloging-in-Publication Data

Dexter, Lewis Anthony.
  The management of purpose / Lewis Anthony Dexter ; Martin Sanchez-Jankowski and Alan J. Ware, editors.
      p. cm.
  Includes bibliographical references and index.
  ISBN 978-1-4128-1034-0 (alk. paper)
    1. Social psychology. 2. Organization. 3. Dexter, Lewis Anthony.
  I. Sanchez-Jankowski, Martmn, 1945- II. Ware, Alan J. III. Title.

HM1033.D49 2009
302.3'5--dc22

                                                        2009016357
ISBN 13: 978-1-4128-1034-0 (hbk)
ISBN 13: 978-1-138-51629-8 (pbk)

Contents

Part III: Practicing Social Sciences

Preface

It was a warm autumn day and we were walking separately from the Dalhousie University campus in Halifax, Nova Scotia toward an area of the city called "the arm," named for its particular geographic location. The two of us meet at a corner where there is a stop light and exchange greetings. As we continue to walk in the same direction we ask each other a series of questions that leads to the conclusion that we are going to the same place—Professor Lewis Dexter's residence for a seminar on politics and public policy. The class is small, ten students, and Dexter serves cookies and tea in a room that overlooks a picturesque view of the Halifax shoreline. We both agree that the course will be interesting, that Dexter is demanding, and there will be little time to enjoy the picturesque scenery because he continues to randomly ask each student questions like a Supreme Court judge asks questions of the lawyers presenting their respective cases. Further, we both agree that what he chooses to have us read seems odd, and that he personally seems extremely eccentric. For three more months, we both trek down and back once a week to the Dexter seminar, and we continually complain there and back about Dexter and the course. When we are finished we are delighted that we no longer have to deal with either the material or Dexter, but we also agree that it is the best course we have taken and we have learned a great deal. It is safe to say that Dexter was a gifted teacher and researcher, but his impact was slow to mature because it was not easy to see the connections in the social world that he was engaged in making, not to mention trying to reproduce what he did. Many years later one of us would build a career that used history to understand political organizations and change in the United States, and one of us would carve out a career combining economics, political science, and sociology to understand various aspects of people living in poverty. The irony is that despite all our complaining we both would use the analytic tools that Dexter introduced to us in that course. Little did we realize during that first encounter on the way to the Dexter seminar how important the interactions with him and his work would be for our own research careers. Thus, it is only appropriate that we have used the title to the seminar we took so many years ago to introduce in this book Dexter's thought, method, and work. It certainly captures the core of what he was about.

We would like to thank some people that have helped us gather information on Dexter and his family. First, we would like to thank Lewis Dexter's niece and nephew, Mary and Robert Pennington (Dexter). Mary Pennington was particularly helpful in providing information on the Dexter and Anthony familial backgrounds. Also, Dr. Holly Snyder, North American History Librarian at Brown University's John Hay Library, where she is responsible for the Library's "Robert Cloutman Dexter and Elisabeth Anthony Dexter Autograph Collection, 1757-1942" (Ms. 77.3) was very helpful in providing us needed information, and we certainly would like to thank her. Finally, we would like to thank Professor David Braybrooke who was a long-time friend and colleague of Lewis Dexter at Dalhousie University for giving us information about various writings that Dexter had published.

Last, but not least, a number of graduate student research assistants aided us in finding various articles that were published in some obscure and out-of-print journals. They were Maria Hollowell-Fuentes, Manata Hashemi, and Corey Abramson.

Martín Sánchez-Jankowski
Berkeley, California

Alan W. Ware
Oxford, England

Introduction

I

Lewis Anthony Dexter, who died in 1995 at the age of seventy-nine had a varied, productive, and successful career as a political scientist, sociologist, and consultant. He may well have been one of the better known and least appreciated political scientists of his time, and yet it is the power of his thought on practical issues that makes his work of continued relevance for the 21st century. Hence, within this introduction, we hope to provide the reader with answers to why Dexter remains important, some suggested reasons for him being underappreciated, the reasons for researching the topics he did, and a guide to his thought and analyses. In this way, we will highlight the reasons we have chosen the writings included in this volume and what "gems" the reader will discover as they engage them.

Nelson Polsby, one of the most prominent political scientists of U.S. Congressional politics and a great admirer of Dexter once remarked with sincere conviction: "Dexter is so smart and insightful, but he is a bit of a nut! Don't you think!?" Polsby's comment about an eminent political scientist that he so admired (he published a significant number of Dexter's articles in books he edited and was in continual correspondence with him) is not as peculiar as it might seem. He no doubt reflected the sentiments of a great many academics of the time that read and met Lewis Dexter. Part of the reasons for this view was that Dexter overstepped disciplinary boundaries in answering social questions, used evidence that was new or unorthodox to answer these questions, wrote in an antiquated idiomatic style, and exhibited an interpersonal style that was idiosyncratically uninhibited. Each of these can in some way be traced to biography, which we will briefly turn to next.

Lewis Anthony Dexter was born in Montreal, Quebec on November 9, 1915, and his sister Harriet Anthony in 1917, where their father had recently accepted the position of General Secretary of the Montreal Charity Organization Society. Lewis Dexter's career was influenced by a number of events, but his mother and father, and their family histories, was certainly one of them. Dexter's father, Robert Cloutman Dexter, was both a Canadian and American citizen having been born in Shelburne, Nova Scotia to a father that was Canadian and a mother who was American. He was educated at Colby Academy in New London, New Hampshire, and graduated from Brown University with an A.B. in 1912 and an A.M. in 1917. He received his Ph.D. in sociology from Clark University in 1923. Robert C. Dexter taught sociology on the faculty of Skidmore College from 1923-27, but after being ordained as a Unitarian minister he pursued a career in administering agencies that provided direct services to people in need, particularly children. He was to become Director of the American Unitarian Association's Department of Social Relations that provided humanitarian programs for refugees; Executive Director of the Unitarian Service Committee, which worked to help Jews escape Nazi persecution in Europe; attaché in charge of refugees at the U.S. Embassy in Lisbon, Portugal; Representative of the Church Peace Union; and Director of Massachusetts Council of Churches, National Council for Prevention of War, Massachusetts Branch of the League of Nations Association, and the World Affairs Council of Rhode Island. Robert Cloutman Dexter wrote a number of books in the general area of social work, the most significant being *Social Adjustment*.[1] He also published scholarly articles in such journals as *American Journal of Sociology*, *Social Forces*, *Educational Review*, *Journal of Statistics* and *Journal of Social Psychology*; and lectured widely. He died in October, 1955 at the age of 68.

Lewis Dexter's mother, Elisabeth Williams Anthony came from a long line of New England clergy and mill owners. Her education was impressive, even more so given the time in which it occurred, with a B.A. from Bates College in Maine, an M.A. from Columbia, and a Ph.D. in History from Clark University in Massachusetts; and additional study at Brown, Oxford, and Radcliffe. Mrs. Dexter met and married Robert Cloutman Dexter in 1914. In 1915 she accompanied him to Montreal where he assumed the position as Director of the Montreal Charity Organization Society. After the First World War, Mr. Dexter accepted a social worker position in Worcester, Massachusetts, which allowed him and Mrs. Dexter to take graduate courses at Clark University. Both would receive their Ph.D. degrees from Clark, his in sociology and hers in History in 1923. Upon completion of their degrees, she accompanied her husband to Saratoga Springs, New York where she taught history at Skidmore College and Mr. Dexter became the head of the sociology department.

She would go on to teach history at Radcliffe College and publish two books: *Colonial Women of Affairs* in 1924 and *Career Women of America* in 1950.[2] Although teaching and scholarship were important throughout her life, most of her career consisted of working with her husband in providing social services to people in need and the maintenance of world peace. She died in 1971 at the age of 84.

Lewis, the first child of Robert and Elisabeth Dexter, would no doubt have been considered eccentric and a child prodigy. He learned to type before learning to write longhand, attended the University of Chicago and received his A.B. degree in 1935 after only fifteen months of study, roughly doing four years of work in little more than a year. Quite a remarkable accomplishment, though the renowned sociologist David Riesman, a fellow student at Chicago during this period, thought that it hampered Dexter's personal experiences during a particularly important developmental time and may well have contributed to his social awkwardness that his colleagues would often refer to. However, he proceeded on to Harvard where he finished his joint M.A. in Political Science, Anthropology, and Sociology in 1938, writing his thesis on "Anthropological Theories of Imperialism." He returned to the University of Chicago for a Ph.D. in Political Science, but never finished. He was a student of Morton Grodzins who was one of the leading political scientists in America, but he was never able to pass his general exams. In fact, he was very proud of the fact that he failed them seven times and would write that on the syllabi he handed out to his students. What made him most pleased was the reason for failing. He was constantly trying to integrate political science with sociology at a time when both disciplines were working to create separate academic subject matter for the purposes of disciplinary boundaries and credentialing. Morton Grodzins would plead with Dexter to simply drop the sociology part of his answers and he would pass with flying colors, but Dexter never would compromise. Dexter finally left Chicago frustrated that he was not allowed to integrate the two disciplines, though it is unclear who was the more frustrated, Dexter or Grodzins. After a few years of doing consulting, Dexter enrolled in the Ph.D. program at Columbia University and studied with Paul Lazersfeld, another icon, this time in sociology. Here again Dexter would insist on integrating sociology with political science, and yet again he would encounter resistance. As fortune would have it, Lazersfeld gave in and Dexter was allowed to write a dissertation entitled "Congressmen and the People They Listen To." His Ph.D. in sociology was awarded in 1960. This preoccupation with attempting to integrate sociology with political science was a direct result of his father and mother's efforts to solve social problems. Through his family's vocation, he had learned that social problems, which often manifested themselves in conflict and war, required political solutions and thus both disciplines were required for societies to benefit.

Upon completing his dissertation he commenced a career that was productive, but unorthodox. There is no question that his career path was also the result of the confluence of his mother and father's family background and careers. His career can be divided into the categories of a practicing public intellectual, educator, and scholar; each of which was engaged in with a uniqueness worth commenting on.

Lewis Dexter's interest in being a practicing public intellectual was clearly influenced by his father's career as an administrator of a number of public aid programs throughout the world. As his father Robert had done, Lewis Dexter was determined to provide expertise to organizations engaged in the public good. He was a consultant to the President of the University of Puerto Rico on issues to improve educational opportunities to the citizens of that island. He actively advised a number of political campaigns, including the 1956 presidential campaign of Adlai Stevenson, and Foster Furcolo's (Democrat) 1956 and John Volpe's (Republican) 1960 runs for governor of Massachusetts. It was Dexter's belief that politics was one, if not the highest, calling to public service and as such was equivalent to the work that his father had done in administering to the social needs of people experiencing hardship. Dexter once remarked that his parents had to constantly interact with governments in their efforts to aid refugees and all those who need assistance, and from that he realized the importance of being active in providing information and analysis to politicians and government officials. He believed that government played a very important role in improving everyone's lives and addressing social prejudice and inequities was an important part of that effort. Thus, he advocated that intellectuals should be actively engaged in politics and public policy.

Along with education and governmental policy, Dexter was actively involved in both when consulting on issues related to mental retardation. His interest was stimulated by family. His mother's family, the Anthonys, had members that were politically active in social issues and problems. They had members who were active in the anti-slave abolitionist movement. Further, his mother's great aunt was the famous suffragette Susan B. Anthony, whose work, along with those of his other abolitionist relatives, Dexter once said made him aware that injustices and inequities must be addressed within for a democracy to evolve. This belief was instrumental in his work on mental retardation, which it might be added was supported by his relative Kate Jackson Anthony and the Kate Jackson Anthony Trust that was devoted to the subject. In his lectures, he often mentioned that the social issues surrounding mental retardation reinforced in him the principle that governments must assist the most in need in society; and confronted by James Madison in the *Federalist Papers*, particularly paper number 10, when he insisted that governments must adjudicate the interests and needs of both the majority and minority if they were to build and maintain a healthy democracy. It should also be mentioned that he occasionally noted that his father being a minister in the Unitarian Church also influenced his ideas about providing assistance and protection to the most vulnerable in society.

Teaching was another important aspect of his career. Dexter considered education a fundamental part of democracy and something that was critically important to improving both the individual and society. He often referred to his teaching career as being that of an "itinerant visiting teacher." This is because he never accepted, for any significant period, a tenured professorship at a university. Many who knew of him thought this very odd indeed. His scholarship alone would have earned him a tenured position at one of the top universities in the United States, but he was not terribly interested in that and he was not the most congenial person that endears one to other faculty members of a department. By this I mean he was a principled person who was honest and willing to take unpopular and principled positions, at least to him, that would often stimulate strong reactions. The upshot would be the development of a committed opposition to his presence as a member of that department. This never bothered Dexter, because he was independently wealthy having been financially successful in the stock market where he engaged in the high risk, high return of "puts and calls." Thus, when he felt his presence was not productive to the students and faculty he would simply leave to assume a visiting professorship at another university.

His commitment to education can be seen in the places he chose to teach. As indicated, there is little doubt that he could have been on the faculty of a number of top universities, and he did teach at a number of them including Harvard, MIT, California-Berkeley, and Johns Hopkins to name a few; but he also chose to teach at places considered "lesser status" schools. Some of these schools were traditional African-American colleges like Howard and Talledega and others were simply campuses where the students were from predominantly working-class families like the University of South Florida, University of Massachusetts at Boston, and University of Maryland at Baltimore. Dexter considered teaching very important and he invested a great deal of time and energy into it. He believed education was the key to supporting democracy because it enlightened people and provided them with skills to improve both theirs' and their fellow citizens' lives. Education, to him, was not for the rich and privileged, and it was necessary that students from all backgrounds be given the opportunity to be taught at the highest level. His uncompromising effort to provide the highest quality instruction regardless of prior background is what he brought to students no matter where he taught, though that was often interpreted by students as him being pompously difficult.

Research formed the basic foundation of his career. There was never a time that Dexter was not engaged in research. Information and understanding he thought composed the cornerstones for the creation and maintenance of a vibrant democratic society. Thus, it was the responsibility of scholars and institutions to provide this resource to a public that needed it even if it was rarely acknowledged and sometimes ignored, snubbed, and rejected. He understood the roots of American anti-intellectualism and saw the need to persevere despite it. He once commented to a number of his colleagues after a particularly hostile and misguided demonstration of anti-intellectualism, that he "had reconsidered the virtues of participatory democracy, but found no reasonable means for withdrawing it." By which he meant that he was more inclined to see the benefits of having a system much like that of the early American republic where an educated and propertied elite would be the principled citizens allowed to engage in governing the political system.

As has been consistently mentioned, the research that he would devote his life to was indeed influenced by his family, most notably his mother and father. From his father he would research sociology questions, particularly those having to do with social problems. His father, trained as a sociologist, focused on that part of sociology that dealt with social problems and organizational responses to them. Lewis Dexter would also focus on the very same issues through his research and this can easily be seen in his work on mental retardation, education, civil defense, and the policy management of the professional and non-professional activists. Yet from his mother, who was a professional historian, he would focus on history in both the analytic and decision-making process, and see the importance of morals in the social and political judgments of public life. It would be these two substantive and methodological concerns that would befuddle his professional colleagues in political science. They would see him as a compatriot sympathetic to the development of a behavioral approach to politics, but clearly a deviant because he would include things that were inconsistent with the prescribed orthodoxy of behavioralism, which wanted to analytically separate empirical data from historical evidence. This befuddlement on the part of his professional colleagues provided Dexter with the evidence that he had indeed become the generalist he had always intended to make of himself.

II

It is more than a fair question to ask why one should invest in reading articles that were written so many years ago. What contemporary relevance might they have for the current scholar? The answer to this query is that Dexter was one of those scholars whose writings came from a career that afforded him a vantage point to provide insights of complex phenomena that have withstood the test of time. As such, the reader will be able to both better understand many of the issues and mechanisms that remain a part of the American political landscape, and the analytic tools to make their own contributions toward further understanding.

Lewis Dexter's contributions were many, and while they can be organized around the large categories that comprise the three headings in this volume, there are at least three constituted themes. The first of these was his integration of sociology and anthropology into political analysis. Of course his notions of what constituted sociology and anthropology were a mixture of antiquated understandings of each and practical concerns for using them to illuminate political matters. For sociology, he concentrated on social problems and the role of the individual in group relations; and for anthropology his focus was on the role of morals, beliefs, symbols and culture in the foundations of society, and how that impacted the means by which social issues and problems were addressed.[3]

The study of society's response, particularly government's, to social problems was an area that he made significant contributions. His use of multiple types of evidence, most notably history and logic, should be seen as a standard for increasing both causal explanations and more general understanding. This approach provided conclusions that contributed to behavioralism's quest (and its epistemological parent logical positivism) for generalized social laws, and phenomenology's design for understanding. Thus, from a methodological perspective, his admittedly "generalist approach" to the study of social and political problems would prove particularly effective in describing how and why various organizations and institutions worked the way they did.

From a sociological perspective, Dexter was important in the development of what would become known as "Labeling Theory." Labeling theory is generally associated with the sociologist Howard Becker, but Lewis Dexter was clearly working with the concept at the same time, or even a little before Becker. His paper "On the Politics and Sociology of Stupidity in Our Society" appeared in Becker's often cited book on deviance, *The Other Side* and is reprinted in the present volume.[4] His findings on both the mentally "retarded" and "gifted" was that there was a power with social labels which transcended and distorted reality for the interaction of the labeled and those doing the labeling. In essence, Dexter's work showed the difficulties that democratic societies have with groups of individuals that lie within the outer tails of a society's normal population distribution where the policies are designed to support the middle of this distribution while forcing the "deviants" to conform. In his book *The Tyranny of Schooling* this argument was more fully developed, showing that democracies like the United States try to establish a social equilibrium by making the majority of its citizens "average" because that maximizes regime governability.[5] This important book never had the impact that it might have had because it was published shortly after Paul Goodman's *Growing Up Absurd*, which covered some of the same issues (although treated quite differently) and became a perennial best seller, commercially pushing important books like Dexter's into public anonymity.[6]

Another sociological legacy was Dexter's work in the area of organizational behavior. It was here that his interests in sociology and political science met and meshed. Dexter argued that organizations tend to compartmentalize and specialize just as Weber had theorized and that within government this limited the ability of elected officials to represent the interests of their constituents and those of the larger society. This situation made for a tension in "the management of purpose" for both the individual politician and government bureaucrat. Within this predicament of trying to balance the interests of the individual's patrons (i.e., the politician's constituents and the bureaucrat's clients) and all of society's citizens, there was the dilemma between professional judgments commensurate with establishing equilibrium between the greatest good for the whole and meeting the specific needs of those who were their immediate responsibility. For Dexter, a democratic citizen, politician, and bureaucrat needed to utilize practical judgments in pursuit of their objectives and this "management of purpose" required the political vision exemplified by George Savile, the 1st Marquis de Halifax (1633-1995), and the "prudence" advocated by Edmund Burke (1729-1797). It can safely be said that both of these statesmen had the greatest intellectual influence on him. He was committed to a Halifaxian and Burkean notion of governance because it was focused on the political virtues of inclusion, compromise, and prudence, which he believed had historically been shown to be most economical in effectively governing democratic societies.

Before concluding this introduction we would like mention that all but one of the readings in this volume were previously published. Those interested in the full citations for these papers should consult the Selected Bibliography in the back of this book which is arranged by the year they were published. The citation for the unpublished work, "Toward a Sociological Analysis of Policy," can be found in the note section at the end of that chapter.

Notes

1. See Robert Cloutman Dexter, *Social Adjustment* (New York: Alfred A. Knopf, 1927).
2. See Elisabeth Anthony Dexter, *Colonial Women of Affairs: A Study of Women in Business and the Professions in America before 1776* (Boston: Houghton-Mifflin Co., 1924); and *Career Women in America, 1776-1840* (Boston: C.M. Jones, Co., 1950).
3. In addition to some of the readings presented in this volume, for sociology see his, *The Sociology and Politics of Congress* (Chicago: Rand McNally, 1970); and for anthropology see *Representation Versus Direct Democracy in a Fighting about Taxes: Conflicting Notions of Sovereignty and Civility* (Cambridge, MA: Schenkman Books, 1982).
4. Howard S. Becker, *The Other Side: Perspectives on Deviance* (New York: The Free Press of Glencoe, 1963).
5. See Lewis A. Dexter, *The Tyranny of Schooling: An Inquiry into the Concept of "Stupidity"* (New York: Basic Books: 1964).
6. See Paul Goodman, *Growing Up Absurd: Problems of Youth in the Organized Society* (New York: Random House, 1960).

Part I

Sociology

1

"Be Not the First"

What price unorthodoxy? "There is nothing more bothersome ... than to alter entrenched habits. That is what the innovator wants done when he advocates a new ritual in the church, a new technique in the file department, a new labor saving device in the factory."[1]

Spoonfuls of salt should always be poured on one of the favorite beliefs of the folklorists of self-help. It is simply not true that ingenuity, inventiveness, and a perception of new needs and new devices smooth the way to promotion and pay. In fact, a readiness to recommend reforms is one of the greatest handicaps under which an ambitious apprentice can labor.

The sophist might maintain that the belief, though false, is socially beneficial. Taking the thesis that "the blood of the martyrs is the seed of the church" as his text, he could point out that, although those who first introduce innovations usually succumb to the slings and arrows of outraged public opinion, sooner or later the more desirable new departures are adopted, precisely as a consequence of the sufferings of their early advocates; and, since no modern man deliberately chooses to be a martyr, it is fortunate indeed that the superstition about the rewards of originality exists, for it causes men to become martyrs in spite of themselves.

However, in fact, the most that one can say with accuracy is that the blood of some martyrs may have been the seed from which some churches have sprung. By the world's standards, at least, such martyrs as the Albigenses of Languedoc, who fell before the orthodox and covetous crusaders of Northern France, during the era of St. Louis, died in vain; and it is open to grave doubt whether the ultimate success of Quakerism is attributable to the willingness of early Quakers to suffer the stake. As Max Weber has suggested in his work on the Protestant Ethic and the Spirit of Capitalism, perhaps Quakerism really grew in esteem because of the congruence of its doctrines with business-mindedness.

Pure logic, on the other hand, will demonstrate the fallacy, as a general counsel for everybody all of the time, of the old rhyme:

Be not the first by whom the new is tried,
Nor yet the last by whom the old is laid aside.

But, under what circumstances is it wise to try the new first? As things go, it is often the most intelligent young people who see something that needs to be done and try to do it. They find themselves thrown against stone walls; and, according to temperament and experience, become cynical or embittered.

Perhaps some instruction in the sociology of reform might lessen their sufferings and benefit society through making possible more ready acceptance of new contributions. On the principle, "Forewarned Is Forearmed," potential reformers would study the history of inventors and innovators. They would be told of Semmelweiss who valiantly tried to explain to fellow-physicians how elementary hygiene would reduce deaths at childbirth; and they would be shown how as a consequence, he was ostracized to the point where he sacrificed career, sanity, and life itself. They would study the case of Jonas Hanway, who first introduced the umbrella into England, and have it explained to them why he was mobbed. They would hear of eminent scientists who joined with the lay public in deriding the pioneers of aviation. They would see Servetus, the forerunner of Unitarianism, burned at the stake, and Priestley, scientist and religious thinker, in effect exiled two centuries later by public opposition. They would learn to understand why Roger Williams' "inconvenient questioning of land titles and his views on the Massachusetts charter" led to his banishment into the wilderness where he was "sorely tossed ... in a bitter winter season, not knowing what bread or bed did mean."

Cost of Unorthodoxy

And, lest they gather the impression that these are matters of far away and long ago, there would be those to instruct them in the cost of unorthodoxy today. It would be explained that although in the western democracies resort to physical violence is infrequent, the pressures to conformity are intense. Case studies to document this generalization would be made, case studies, not chiefly from the lives of those now considered heroes, but from the experience of men who, whether rightly or wrongly, are trying to advance the cause of human decency and efficiency today. These case studies would permit them to answer such questions as: What happens to the Negro dentist in some backward areas who tries to dissuade his patients from getting gold teeth if they do not need them? What is the fate of the worker who complains that his trade union's leadership is autocratic? What happens to the little street vendor who sells a magazine, which influences, close to the Commissioner of Licenses, distrust? What are the chances of promotion for a private who was formerly a publicist and lets ex-colleagues know of some scandalous situation which has developed in his camp?

Instruction could be carried well beyond the bounds of what we ordinarily think of as civil liberties. Tables might be prepared of the average number of articles accepted by the more reputable academic journals from persons using orthodox scientific methods and terminologies and of the average number accepted from those who utilize a new (and afterwards accepted) method or style; similar tables might be made of the salaries of the former group, as compared with the latter, at the same ages. Studies might be made of certain organizations to see who is promoted when and why; and these will demonstrate that those who accept the accustomed methods of doing business on the whole rise to the top. The careers of physicians who adopt *new and soundly-based* treatments might be examined to see whether they lag behind less progressive men in income; it will be shown that poets who write in a new idiom are retarded in winning recognition.

If these facts are accepted simply as facts, the curriculum just outlined might serve only to discourage potential innovators. But, wisely handled, the insistent question will be: Why did these new ideas meet with so much opposition? How could that opposition have been avoided?

In each case, presumably, the answer will be somewhat different; but certain general conclusions will probably emerge from a study, directed towards answering such questions.[2]

Innovators Are Nuisances

First, students will come to see that most innovators lack completely the ability to see themselves as others see them—which is to say as nuisances. There is nothing more bothersome in the entire world than to alter entrenched habits. That is what the innovator wants done when he advocates a new ritual in the church, a new technique in the file department, or a new labor saving device in the factory. There is nothing more insulting than to imply that the man who does the job does not do it as well as it could be done. This is what the bright employee does when he suggests that the manager employ a new technique of administrative analysis or that statisticians scrap conventional methods of analyzing costs. There is nothing more dreadful than to run the risk of losing prestige. And any significant change in any organization means that some people are likely to be less influential and prominent than they were.[3] When two churches are merged, then there will be only one chairman of a standing committee instead of two; when the United States joins a League of Nations, perhaps individual United States Senators (and especially the Chairman of the Committee on Foreign Relations) will feel less important.

The typical inventor appreciates none of these things. He is obsessed with the particular kind of improvement which he can offer; and he regards those who stand in his way as reactionaries or dunderheads.[4] For the most part, to be sure, his opponents disguise their opposition behind well-sounding arguments about the merits of the new proposal. Its sponsors will then waste time in attempting to destroy the rationalizations put forward instead of striking at the real issues. For instance, not one man in ten thousand who cites George Washington's words about "no entangling alliances," is in any sense convinced by them or cares what Washington really means. Some deeper motive of habitual patriotism, or dislike of foreigners, or suspicion of the British, or desire to see the Senate continue free to reject treaties, is almost surely at work when that immortal cliché is trotted forth. Nor will argument convince the real Jew-baiter that the Protocol of the Elders of Zion is a forgery. He believes in it because deep within him is a need to hate something, and the Jew is a convenient target for the hostilities of which he is especially aware.

Mere awareness of the factors creating opposition to a plan may at least make reformers more charitable towards their opponents, more able to meet them on grounds of genuine tolerance, more perceptive to answer what they mean, and less quick to ridicule what they say. And, in some cases, forethought may enable inventors to see who will lose what in the way of prestige, profit, and entrenched habit, if the proposed plan be adopted; and consequently to have ready some method of allaying fears and soothing injured feelings. A chairman of a standing committee who fears for the loss of his position may be assured that the two churches which merge will back him for a post in the state conference; suggestions for the introduction of labor saving devices, or the elimination of conductors on buses, may be accompanied by schemes for retaining ousted men.

There is another motive, frequently present in resistance to change, of which the typical innovator is unaware. Schiller has expressed it thus:

For, of the wholly common is man made
And custom is his nurse. Woe then to them
That lay irreverent hands upon his old
House furniture, the dear inheritance
From his forefathers, for time consecrates
And what is gray with age becomes the sacred.

The typical innovator has no sympathy with such sentiments. Accordingly, to those who have grown up in some old fashioned way of doing business, reform seems to be (and in fact sometimes is so handled that it really is) nothing but an excuse for more or less refined sadism. Anthony Trollope in *The Warden* presents an extremely touching picture of the sufferings, which a reform may impose upon those who have grown into the old order of things.

Few innovators see, either, that frequently they suffer not so much because of their good ideas as because of their total personalities. That is to say, the kind of man who develops something new is apt to be relatively insensitive to customary courtesies in many respects. For personalities tend to be more or less integrated; and unorthdoxy in one field is apt to be accompanied by unorthodoxies in others. It is characteristic that several potential donors to a project for reducing the chances of war were unwilling to give anything when they observed that the leading advocate to the idea had dirty fingernails. He himself was not aware of this; he does not care about appearance. But they could not judge his ideas; they could judge his cleanliness. And so they refused to support his plan. So, in larger matters too, the man with a new vision is apt to be unconventional. Priestley was born an original scientist and a deviant religious thinker; had he confined himself to one occupation or the other he might have been safer than in fact he was. Veblen was not only a scoffer at classical economics; he was personally sarcastic.

Innovations and Military Planning

It is imperative that embryo innovators realize that the chances are they are wrong in any original suggestion which they advance. This does not mean that original suggestions should not be advanced. It does mean, however, that men should make sure they know why things are done the way they are done before they propose different procedures.[5] Amateur strategists who ignore problems of supply and transport can always evolve paper-brilliant plans because they do not recognize that effective planning must be *organismic*. That is to say, a new proposal or innovation must fit both into the limitations imposed by the attitudes and values of those who have to adopt it. Military critics, like Winston Churchill and Liddell Hart, have justly pointed out that the Allied commanders in the last war made a great mistake in not using the tank intelligently; but there *had* to be a change in the cautious, infantry-minded thinking of the high command, before they could use the tank properly. It is, in fact, almost axiomatic that no genuinely new weapon will be used effectively because it takes time for generals to readjust their conceptions of military propriety to its possibilities.

Similarly, it might be desirable in the United States to adopt many features of Russian or German military organization; but, in fact, such adoption would presuppose a change in the attitudes and values of American officers and men. Or, in every congregation, and in every university, one may notice many, many needed changes; but always, always, the man who first tries to introduce such changes "fails," because he tries to *impose* them upon persons whose attitudes and values are adjusted to the previous situation. Sometimes a leader who recognizes the necessity for a democratic educational process can, more or less slowly, get people to alter their attitudes and values. Corey, in a brilliant article on the nature of educational leadership,[6] which should be carefully considered by all would-be innovators, has shown how this may be done; but in other cases it is probably necessary to admit that, without a total reorganization of society, it is inconceivable in a measurable period of time, that one's proposals can be effectuated.

Finally, there should be emphasis upon the fact that no new approach can stand on its own merits. The use of influence and pressure are just as important in getting inventions and reforms accepted as in anything else. Kelvin started his academic career by trying to obtain publication for a paper which offended one of the leaders of his profession; but Kelvin's father, himself a well-known scholar, succeeded in smoothing the matter over. Mendel, on the other hand, undertook experiments which are basic to the whole science of genetics; but, published as they were, obscurely, they lay unnoticed until his methods were rediscovered about thirty years later.

This suggests that the apprentice innovator should learn not to come forth with proposals until he has undertaken an analysis of the situation and prepared a plan of campaign. An isolated article or act will either be ignored or considered scandalous, according to its nature, and will but rarely lead to any wider understanding. The innovator must know—after the first shot is fired—what is to be done next; who in relevant professions or organizations can expected or persuaded, for whatever motives, to support the new departure? Who can understand what is actually being attempted? What alternative means of winning a livelihood are open to those who take the risks? What friendships may they expect to lose, what temptations to unhappiness and bitterness must they be prepared to avoid?

Were such insight into the sociology of innovation widely provided, there might be fewer mute, inglorious Mendels, fewer potential Semmelweisses, hindered so completely by popular or professional disapproval, that they make no effective contribution to human progress at all.

Notes

1.   The major theme of this article might be stated somewhat differently. It could read: Statesmen, ministers, scholars, and citizens, are continually faced with the problem of compromise. This does not mean that they must resolve a general abstract dilemma: To compromise or not to compromise? On the contrary, in any concrete instance the question which they must answer is: What is the optimum degree of compromise in this particular situation? (Note, please, that the possible range of compromise is from 0 percent to 100 percent.)

When confronted with practical problems, political theorists, church social action leaders, scientific administrators, etc., tend to analyze them caustically; but when they discuss social action theoretically, they are apt to be dogmatic. Note, for example, the scholar who asserts that he will let *nothing* interfere with complete freedom of research, publication, and teaching. Among political theorists, in particular, there has been a continuing tradition of revolt against the futility of such absolutism.

Among the outstanding critics of conventional political theory, one might name Machiavelli, Hobbes, and Lord Halifax, the author of the *Character of a Trimmer* (flourished 1690). An outstanding modern example is E. Pendleton Herring's *Politics of Democracy* (New York, 1940).

As a student of Herring's, the writer found himself forced into a position where James. A. Farley became more admirable than Senator Norris, or Governor Bricker than Wendell Willkie.

This means that one sacrifices moral considerations in evaluating political realities, or that one relies with Herring upon some unformulated limitation, which enables the honest man to distinguish between legitimate compromise and illegitimate opportunism. J. H. Hallowell, taking T. V. Smith, whose position is entirely analogous to Herring's, as his target, has given a largely antithetical criticism of the philosophy of compromise in *Ethics*. The present article attempts rather to synthesize the sense of reality, which is to be found in the works of Halifax and Herring, with the vivid awareness of such moralists as William Lloyd Garrison and John Haynes Holmes that compromise can all too often be used simply as an excuse to avoid trouble and to let evil flourish unchecked.

This article arose too out of the writer's concern with a related problem, well illustrated in David Lindsay Watson's *Scientists Are Human.* Watson demonstrates that the original thinker—the scholar who looks for new methods or utilizes new techniques—is likely to handicap himself in terms of his own career as compared with his conventionally-minded brethren. But science taken as a whole will grow precisely because of unorthodox discoveries and to known truths. What then is the obligation of the young scientist if he finds himself interested in borderline topics or unfamiliar methods?

2.   Such a work as William F. Ogburn's, *Social Change*, New York, 1922, might be used as a major text here. (The most explicit criticism of Ogburn is furnished by Gunnar Myrdal, *An American Dilemma,* New York, 1944, especially appendixes 1 and 2.)

3.   The fact that administrative analysts and industrial engineers are not often aware of the sociological factors in change makes them (and such ecclesiastical equivalents as commissions of appraisal) extremity impotent, in many situations.

4.   A prig has been defined as one who judges other people, not by their standards, but by his.

5.   Students should of course learn that there is a danger of developing the academic attitude, which consists of delaying action until all the facts are in, knowing that all the facts never will be in. In other words, they must learn to set a time limit upon the period for reflection and analysis.

6.   Stephen Corey, "Cooperative Staff Work," *School Review,* 52 (1944) 336-345. See also Marshall Dimock, "Bureaucracy Self-Examined," *Public Administration Review*, 4, 1944, 197-207, for an analysis of the way in which the executive is limited by his subordinates' preconceptions and preferences. A comprehensive discussion of the organic nature of society is to be found in Ruth Benedict's *Patterns of Culture,* New York, 1934.

It should not be concluded from the above statement that it is necessarily an error to try to impose a new arrangement upon a group or institution. It may be that this is sometimes the best way to educate them; but the innovator should undertake an advance analysis of the different possible ways of proceeding, and decide whether it is likely to be more effective to go so far as to have to retreat, or to proceed more slowly and comprehensively along the line suggested by Corey.

2

A Dialogue on the Social Psychology of Colonialism and on Certain Puerto Rican Professional Personality Patterns[1]

In the field of culture-in-personality, hypotheses should be ordinarily put forward with considerable tentativeness. Ordinarily, the analyst is unable to undertake systematic, detailed investigation, which permits him to attach a high degree of probability to his assertions. Therefore, he should not overlook propositions about a culture made by sophisticated or insightful laymen, even though they do not accord with his own observations.

It seemed to me that it would help convey the mood of tentativeness attaching to my impressions about Puerto Rican professional personality types if, instead of writing in conventional academic form, I used the dialogue technique to suggest various hypotheses. This technique has the additional advantage of permitting me to record suggestions which I have heard put forward by other people who know Puerto Rico well, even though I do not happen to accept them. Every statement made by any character hereinafter has been, implicitly at least, made in my hearing by two or more persons; although I have evidently been forced to make systematic and explicit what was hinted at by an anecdote or a phrase.

In order that the reader may allow for the advantages and disadvantages of my perspective, an account of my own experiences in Puerto Rico may be in order.

I was in Puerto Rico from July 1944 to July 1945, appointed as Visiting Professor of Sociology and Political Science, with the understanding that my primary responsibility was the organization of a social science general course to be offered in 1945-46. Accordingly, much of my time was spent in studying available material about Puerto Rico, the West Indies, and the Caribbean; I also taught a year-long course for sophomores in introductory sociology, and two upper-class semester courses in political theory and techniques of research, respectively.

11

During November I was assigned by the Chancellor to prepare a history of the University during his administration, 1942-45, a period of great expansion. In consequence, I was given a number of other administrative duties, which threw me into contact with insular politics. In particular, I planned the organization of a research center in social sciences, involving the expenditure of $360,000 over three years. I projected two major studies, one in population, which Warren Thompson planned for the University, and the second in personality type and social structure, along the lines of work done by Kluckhohn, Leites, Keskjemiti, and Gorer (2, 5, 7).[2] I also received a separate grant for the study of suicide in the island; although I was able to collect preliminary data for this, and to prepare a schedule, pressure of time prevented my undertaking any field work. This study was oriented to test the Durkheim-Halbwachs hypotheses (6). The population study has since been carried out, chiefly under the direction of Kingsley Davis of Princeton.

A series of changes in executive decisions about the research center placed me in a position where I either had to assume responsibility for several actions with which I was then unwilling to concur, or to resign; so I resigned. I now believe I was mistaken in so doing.

My chief weaknesses in analyzing Puerto Rican professional personality types were: (1) a lack of familiarity with Spanish and Spanish-American literature, (2) the fact that my contacts were predominantly with supporters of one political party (the *Populares).* I have not lived in any other Hispanic area, although I have lived outside the English-speaking countries at several times. I have also lived in the Southern regions of the United States, which economically are colonial as Puerto Rico is, and I have taught at two continental American schools, which were administered entirely for minority members.

The original version of the present paper was written in 1945, about three months after I left Puerto Rico. Of some relevance is my (semi-popular) essay on independentism and economic planning in Puerto Rico: "Puerto Rican Puzzle", (4).

Since writing the dialogue I have become aware of the possibility that recent analyses of basic personality structure have failed to make a sufficiently rigorous distinction between "personality type" and "social type" or between the basic personality structure and what W. Bagehot calls "the style and tone of national character," in his *Physics and Politics* (1). Were I to undertake any further studies of this sort, I would find it necessary to systematize this distinction.

CHARACTERS (in order of appearance)

Harriett: a Jewish physiologist, born and educated in the United States.

Eleanor: an intellectually curious and alert woman, wife of a continental business man, who has lived in Puerto Rico for the last six years.

Maria: a Puerto Rican teacher of Spanish and English.

Norman: a continental (North American from the United States), who has taught at the University of Puerto Rico for the last year as a visiting professor.

Edward: an American Negro lawyer, active in interracial groups.

Blanca: a Puerto Rican home economist, interested in cultural problems.

Thomas: a continental social psychologist, who has travelled widely, but has never been in Puerto Rico or any Hispanic country.

Lewis: a sociologist, interested in culture and personality, who has spent a year in Puerto Rico.

Jack: a graduate student in sociology, much interested in mathematical biophysics and symbolic logic.

Harriet: It seems to me that all you people here, talking about Puerto Rico, are doing something, well, very dangerous. I know nothing about it except what you tell me. But you all talk as though Puerto Ricans just naturally are different from Americans, as though ...

Eleanor: But, my dear girl, of course they behave differently from Americans. Whoever heard an American worry about his dignity? Yet, sooner or later, in Puerto Rico, they talk about independence, and when they talk about independence, they talk about *dignidad,* and ...

Maria: And you here on the continent, you love statistics so. In Puerto Rico we hate objectivity.

Harriett: But the point which you seem to forget is—well, you know when we took psychology in college we learned to beware of stereotypes. Now, aren't you talking in terms of stereotypes? Pretty soon, you'll be saying "Jews" do such-and-such and "Negroes" do such-and-such, just like the worst reactionaries, won't you?

Edward: Yes, I would like to add to that point. It seems to me that this is very dangerous. My race has spent centuries trying to teach people to treat us not as "Negroes," but as "human beings." S. I. Hayakawa in his column in the *Chicago Defender* points out for us very frequently that that is our real problem—to teach people to think of us as *men,* not as

Negroes or as Japanese or Jews. And you, in the name of psychology and sociology which ought to help us, aren't you forging new chains with which to keep us down?

Norman: Well, I am Jewish, you know, and it seems to me that Jews, by and large, are a little bit different from Yankees.

Edward: Didn't Klineberg prove that there isn't any difference in intelligence between us and white people? Didn't he ...

Thomas: Wait, wait. What Klineberg proved was that granted similar training and education, intelligence test scores fall within the same ranges when opportunities are the same. In other words, he demonstrated that the differences, which do exist between Southern sharecroppers and Northern mechanics in intelligence test scores are socially created rather than biologically produced. So far, so good. But he certainly did *not* show that these differences do *not* exist. In fact, we know that they do exist. Now, what we here have been talking about this evening is the existence of differences, which are socially created. Blanca told us how she could tell, better than by chance, simply by seeing a person's gestures, whether he's a Puerto Rican or not; and sometimes, whether he's speaking Spanish or English. Now, maybe she cannot do this as well as she thinks, but these differences in gesture certainly exist and certainly are not biological. They are social in origin. If you put a Puerto Rican with a group of Americans, it is probable that his gestures would somehow be affected—he would emphasize more by way of contrast or less in imitation. On the other hand, if you brought a Puerto Rican child up with Yankee children, no doubt he'd behave like them. But, bring him up as a Puerto Rican and a difference exists; that is what we maintain. Now on this point of gesture we have a very good point, an evident, significant difference.

Lewis: Yet, Tom, it isn't exactly what we could call a neutral point. In fact, it shows in a way the trouble with our discussion of all such things. A good many continental Americans laugh at the way in which Puerto Ricans gesture, and so some Puerto Ricans are sensitive on the point. And there are many occasions when Puerto Ricans complain about continental rudeness, of course, too. But it's the continental laughter that's more important now to think about. We just can't get away from the fact that every aspect of Puerto Rican life is somehow or other related to the evaluation which Puerto Ricans make of themselves, and that the evaluations which they make of themselves are influenced by the evaluations which they believe continentals make of them. For instance, many "Anglo-Saxons" think of themselves as imperturbable and regard gesticulation as un-American and slightly ridiculous, and Puerto Ricans are well aware of this attitude. We would have similar difficulty in finding it possible to discuss cockfighting, sex behavior, efficiency, punctuality, cleanliness, politics, excitability, or race relations without implying that we thought one group or the other is superior. Some Puerto Ricans want to be like continental Americans and hence resent any imputation that they are different; others want to be different and regard any statement by an American on the differences as a potential slam. Or, more accurately, I guess, most Puerto Ricans have an ambivalent attitude on these issues.

Race relations is particularly interesting. It shows the whole complex question of colonial attitudes very neatly. Here is an area of behavior where, by continental American standards, Puerto Rican practices are higher than our own. Juan Barbosa, the first important political leader, was a Negro; Ramos Antonini, one of the most important men in the present political set-up, is a Negro; Negroes are accepted *almost* everywhere, but, still and all, there is some discrimination.

Eleanor: Yes, but it's pretty minor, you know. You remember what Doctor ... oh, what is her name?... that visiting teacher found out when she asked the girls in her class whether a woman should marry a Negro. After a long discussion, they said, "Well, yes, if she's getting to be around twenty or thirty and can't get anybody else." *And* they thought that even at that age a girl should not marry a really poor man, a *jibaro.*

Maria: But don't forget, it's you Americans who make all this discrimination for us. It is because of you that the tables at the restaurants have "reserved" signs so that waiters can chase dark-skinned people away and let your naval officers dine in white peace.

Eleanor: But, my dear, wasn't it you who told me about the dances of the upper class people, years ago, to which nobody was admitted if he was not pure white?

Maria: That would have all died out, if it hadn't been for the Americans, though.

Blanca: Well, my dear compatriot, I wonder. In my village nobody in the upper class married a Negro, except one who was very rich. And in Santo Domingo and Cuba, which are something like us, there is still discrimination.

Lewis: Yes, Rogler makes the same point in his study of Comerio (11). Class differences tend to be racial. But the crucial point here, the thing that makes this business of discussing cultural differences so painful to many people, is that Puerto Ricans will not, most of them, admit in front of continentals that there is any sort of flaw in their treatment of

Negroes. They insist that there is *absolute* equality. And, when one of my students in class pointed out that there was not, a perfect storm of agitation burst out.

They seemed to feel he was betraying the group to admit to me, a continental, that inequalities exist in Puerto Rico. It was not enough to say truthfully that Puerto Rico is an awful lot better than the continental U.S.A. It had to be perfect.

Thomas: Two points: first, I remember very clearly a discussion at International House in which a group of Latin-Americans participated, and I had the feeling that all of them reacted on this race relations issue just as you describe Puerto Ricans doing—they were claiming perfection where all they can legitimately point to is superiority.

Second, doesn't it seem that the attitude of Puerto Ricans is something like the attitude of immigrant groups in the United States, who resent it bitterly if their behavior is discussed in terms of the old country and resent it bitterly, too, if their behavior is judged in terms of old-line Yankee values?

Edward: Well, I guess I'm changing my mind a little, but to be perfectly honest, isn't that true of all cases where one race or group condemns another to be inferior and at the same time the so-called inferior group is struggling to be equal and alike? Certainly, Negroes at one moment will criticize a white man for being too stiff and the next for being too friendly. We don't know where we belong in relation to you people; and I expect Puerto Ricans wonder whether they are "second-class citizens" or not, too. Don't they?

Maria: We are second-class citizens. Why, we are not even a real territory, so the Supreme Court decides we aren't all under the Constitution—and in the army, our soldiers are given a treatment entirely different from anybody else. Why, one general came to Puerto Rico, and I heard him say, "You know, I don't think these what-do-you-call-them—Puerto Rican *jibaros*—are really human beings like you and me."

Eleanor: Let's wait a while before we talk about independentism, Maria.

Thomas: Yes, there is a big problem of colonial social psychology, which nobody that I know of has tackled. There should be a systematic, comparative analysis of the processes of ambivalence in different colonial societies. There may be a fairly general pattern of superordinate-subordinate group relationships wherever industrial Western Europeans have colonized, regardless of the past of the particular culture which is subordinate. My inclination is to believe that a whole series of problems, which *appear* isolated can in fact be understood in terms of ambivalence and in terms of the consequent assimilation of Western cultural values *while* at the same time denying that they are being assimilated. We could start perhaps with the Irish patriots of the early nineteenth century; how much they borrowed from their British "oppressors"! We would roam as far afield as the Indians in Bolivia who now object to Spanish as the language of the school, just as the Puerto Ricans objected to English. We would concern ourselves with nativism, bilingualism, "Uncle Tommism," the writing of "Babu" English in India ...

Lewis: One thing in Puerto Rico along that line, which you find in many of these areas in one form or another, is the romanticization of the "authentic"—that is, the relatively unindustrialized—Puerto Rican peasant. I believe the social function of this attitude is the same as that of the revival of Welsh in Wales. Busy, professional Puerto Ricans in many cases regard impoverished, tubercular *jibaros* as something authentic, something genuine. Again and again one hears about their peculiar virtues. But the *jibaro* isn't like the inland Indians of Yucatan or some such group, which truly has a way of life distinct from and perhaps more coherent than that of the dominant people. He is rather an extreme type of our own stranded lumber cut-over people whose culture has become impoverished because of cultural and economic destitution.

Pedreira in *Insularismo* (10) looks back with nostalgia to what he regards as the flourishing culture of the Puerto Rico of seventy-five years past. He is talking about culture in the humanistic sense of the term, of course. I suspect that he was factually wrong, and that he really yearned for the easygoingness of the old days, when there was no conflict between old ways and new ones. I find a certain serenity in Davila's poems (3), which, I think, is absent from modern Puerto Rico; and Pedreira, like our own medievalophiles, coveted such serenity. But serenity is not art and it is not intellectual achievement. In every exploited region and among every exploited group, I imagine, those not wishing to face the problems created by exploitation or conflict of roles and status, look romantically down at the lower classes in the community or back to the old, golden days, because then the problems, which they face had not arisen—so they fancy there were no problems.[3]

Jack (who arrived late): Well, as far as I've heard you, you're talking and talking without getting anywhere. Let's stop telling anecdotes and prove something, show something. Give us some meaty, rigorous hypotheses.

Lewis: O.K., O.K., I will. But let me explain what I mean. And I admit this is not as rigorous as Newton; but it will compare not unfavorably with organic science, I think. My summary formulation is: There is a typical Puerto Rican professional male type, a man who behaves as if playing a dramatic role, centering around the acquisition of prestige value by flamboyance—that isn't the *mot juste* but I don't know of one—for personal *immediate* gratification. Now, first, there are plenty of other personality types in Puerto Rico. But this one is of importance because it is predominant in the newer leadership; I imagine it was predominant in the old leadership, too, but I don't know. I suspect it's pretty important in many other Hispanic countries, too. By "professional" I mean political, business, academic. There are women who conform to the type also, but I believe, it is less common among them; and there is an important type among the women, lacking among the men, which might be characterized by such adjectives as reliable.

This summary is valuable, because it puts together a great many things, which are otherwise just isolated incidents and observations. I myself have found it led me to "understand" a good deal, which I did not understand when I was actually in Puerto Rico. Had I thought it out while I was there, I would have been a much better teacher and administrative analyst than I was—I would have avoided lots of mistakes I committed. And my suicide study would have been better planned.

Jack: But that's not a hypothesis.

Lewis: Well, we could argue about that—I'd call it a kind of leading or master hypothesis. But that's not important. You're right. It's not perfect. Let me give you an example. It has often been pointed out that the Puerto Rican will not typically give to philanthropies; but it would offend his pride to refuse to give to any undeserving rascal who asks of him. More generally, I think this formulation could be related to a lot of things, which are important in Puerto Rico: so-called Spanish individualism, the high suicide rate, the interest in *gestures* of planning, the extremely rapid speaking speed of Puerto Ricans, the generosity to beggars and the like.

Blanca: How about the physical gestures which we use? And the difficulty in getting good morale in Puerto Rican organizations?

Eleanor: And independentism?

Jack: That's a whale of an hypothesis—only it isn't an hypothesis.

Lewis: Well, I called it a summary. Now as to hypotheses—well, I'll go ahead and describe *things*—observations which I've made—and then give you some hypotheses later. That isn't as neat and nice, but I think, in the present stage of the study of culture and personality, it's more revealing. For there are really two different propositions: first, that these facts are related; second, that they are related in the way that I say they are related. I feel much surer of the first than of the second.

Thomas: That phrase your friend quoted, "The Puerto Rican is a lion who walks alone in the streets." Isn't that related to this and Spanish individualism?

Maria: That means that we don't pay any attention to other people, driving or walking. You should see our *publicos* on the mountain roads.

Eleanor: Yes, they say that the motorcar companies used to put in special kinds of noisy horns for cars to sell in Puerto Rico.

Lewis: That's one aspect of Spanish individualism. That's the assertive side. Another side is the failure to realize in a way that other people exist. Persons, who, in many respects, seem sophisticated professional people have no sense at all of other people's motives or reactions. Typically, I have heard someone point to a man who had been divorced under rather embarrassing circumstances, and was a good friend, and explain to the company how unlucky he had been in losing his first wife, and how fortunate another unmarried man, a continental, was, who could now have a chance to marry the first wife—all with the utmost good humor, very little evident malice, in front of casual acquaintances. I have seen a number of cases where a man has irritated or exasperated a friend by repeated shortcomings, and finally was irritated or amazed or amused by some particularly vehement protest, without the slightest idea of what really happened.[4]

Blanca mentioned this business of morale. An important aspect is the constant making of criticism with the greatest frankness by some men. They do not realize that the criticisms are apt to be irritating or disheartening to the objects thereof, because they do not really see other people as persons. It is hard to say this accurately. I have the feeling that much of the literature, which is popular in Puerto Rico as tragedy would be by our standards melodrama—it has the aspects of what I might call slapstick tragedy. The definition of tragedy which I learned in high school, "the downfall of a good character," would be utterly alien to this culture.

A good deal of the inefficiency and unpunctuality, which constantly worries continentals is related to the same factor. Puerto Ricans do not see other people in full dimension as being worried, alarmed, dismayed, by being made to wait.[5] Of course, the Puerto Rican does not have the compulsive dependence on time, which many of us do, so it isn't *as* important there as here—but, in many cases, for example medical appointments, of course it is important.

By the way, Jack, here is an important methodological point. Analytically we can, as I shall do in a minute, split these elements up into hypotheses. Concretely, in particular instances, the different factors work together. For instance, Puerto Ricans do not have a high suicide rate just because of one factor, such as the breakdown of the old order under the influence of industrialization, or the emphasis on high prestige values, but because a number of different factors are present.

Blanca: This Spanish individualism, that is at the root of our troubles. We try and try to get people to cooperate, to work together—but it is so much harder in Puerto Rico than here. I saw some of your rural health and welfare services and they have all sorts of groups through, which they can operate. We do not have such groups.

Eleanor: Sometimes, you know, I wonder whether a lot of Muñoz [6] present —and probable future—difficulties do not trace back to this same problem of which you speak. He tries so awfully hard to be democratic, he lets all the boys have their say, he doesn't impose any decision, and things get into a mess, until finally he has to impose a decision, because there is no other way. If he just said at the beginning, "This is the way I want it," it would be simpler.

Blanca: Well, Puerto Ricans don't very much like to have anybody tell them what to do, not even Muñoz-Marin.

Maria: But Muñoz is the leader of the people, Blanca. Eleanor may be right.

Thomas: Let me see if I state your point correctly or rather let me restate it pedantically. What happens is that Muñoz tries to apply ideas about democracy, which come from the United States or Northern Europe and are not really indigenous to the Spanish tradition and to a society, which is still essentially Spanish. In other words, at the ideological level, there's been a good deal of cultural diffusion. But, in practice, this comes bang up against a whole set of behaviors, which are Spanish or Spanish-Colonial, and which do not provide for deliberation and discussion in the sense in which Yankees, for example, practice these arts in town-meeting. That raises a question about, which I've often wondered; how far can democracy adapt itself or be adapted to the character structures of those who are being democratized? And isn't it likely that an ideology will diffuse when supported by those possessing status and power, faster than the set of habits within which that ideology can really be practiced?

Here, of course, I am getting back to my general theme of colonial social psychology—what happens to ideologies, anyhow, as they get diffused into groups possessing different social patterns?

Norman: You know, several of my students, very intelligent boys, said and I don't believe they themselves know if they were joking or not that one reason for Puerto Rican independence was so that Muñoz could be dictator. Puerto Rico of course is a long way away already from the other Hispanic countries in the area, but I've wondered sometimes whether dictatorship isn't a much more normal phenomenon in Santo Domingo than it is, say, in the Adirondacks?

Jack: Well, I thought we were discussing social science, not political theory.

Lewis: O.K. First hypothesis: *the type, which we are discussing has a very high degree of striving for deference.* Second: *its techniques of obtaining deference are active and dramatic, as contrasted, say, with the relatively reserved deference-obtaining tactics of a Japanese or a Puritan.* Third: *the struggle for deference is a struggle, which is carried on between ego, the person, and a number of other individuals who are only vaguely envisaged in full personal richness.* The struggle might, of course, be rather to master the other person by thoroughly understanding him, by being tactfully sympathetic, *et cetera.* Fourth: *the struggle creates or is created by a number of personalities who are quick to resent, but resent more like fire than like ice.* Fifth: *in many cases—and this explains the suicide phenomenon—the high valuation attached to oneself makes it easy to seem to avenge oneself upon others by hurting oneself.*

Jack: "Like fire and ice" sounds more like poetry than science to me.

Lewis: I communicate something somewhat organized and semi-systematic by it. That's progress. On the fourth point, I might point out that there is a Puerto Rican habit of saying a person knows enough about something or other "to defend himself." I imagine this business of the automobile horns fits in there too. Much of the reckless driving is protective, it seems to me—and this is an hypothesis, only, Jack—rather than expansive. Puerto Ricans drive recklessly, in a word, but they aren't dare-devils with the connotation that word has of challenging the universe for fun. On the third point, Puerto Ricans do say "our" country, but I expect that the ratio between "my" country and "our" country there is quite different from what it is in many other areas. My hypotheses could be put another way; here are actors who walk alone; they talk much and rapidly in order to protect themselves from such things as interruption; they gesture to enhance the act.

Harriett: Granting all you've said, how do they get this way? Certainly, their parents don't deliberately—couldn't deliberately—teach them all these things.

Lewis: No, there we get a little beyond what I can talk about. But, at a guess, a reasonable guess, checked with some people who know something about the matter, and confirmed by questions to a couple of shrewd Puerto Rican observers, I imagine what happens is this: Puerto Ricans, especially Puerto Rican men, are inordinately fond of children. They "spoil" them by continental standards—that is, they fondle, caress, and admire. Boys are "spoiled" much more than girls; they're encouraged to show off. But there's nothing persistent or consistent about this treatment; let the children go away, they're forgotten, let the father be in a bad humor, they may be ignored. Cleverness is about the only way to win the attention of the environment for certain—that is, verbal cleverness. There's a lot more which should be studied—relatively low emphasis on toilet-training, I suspect, irregular, sometimes very affectionate, sometimes hurried, irritable, and inadequate nursing, *et cetera*. Of course, really, Jack is right, none of us should study these problems until we have a complete theory of the dynamics of character formation—but in the meantime we must do the best we can in full consciousness of our ignorance.

On this matter of democracy, there's one point, which I might add. You know I've been associated chiefly with progressive schools and colleges. Accordingly, I prefer discussion or seminar methods. I tried to use them in Puerto Rico. I bewildered my students at first. After a while, they were willing to try them; but they literally didn't know how to discuss. Everybody always interrupted everybody else; except for me, the teacher, authority. More precisely, if one student was giving a report, there might be silence, until one interrupted or I asked a question; then there would be a tremendous amount of noise and irrelevance. The students were usually interested in the questions we treated in introductory sociology; in fact they were far more alert to the philosophical implications of social theory than any group I could have collected up here.[7] But they didn't know how to listen. I had assumed previously that the important part of discussion is knowing how to express oneself; these students taught me that knowing how to listen is just as important. Again and again and again, I would find that a dozen students were interrupting, each trying to give a speech, and that not one of them had really heard what had been said before.

Harriett: There are plenty of people in the United States like that.

Lewis: Sure, there is an overlap. But listen to a group of Puerto Rican professionals talking for just a few minutes and you know there is on the average a substantial difference nevertheless. Ortega y Gasset says here (9) about his classes in Spain: "For a number of years, I have had to find a room outside the university buildings because the habitual shouting of our precious students, standing around in the halls, makes it impossible to hear oneself talk in the classroom." There were many times, especially in the law school building at Puerto Rico, when I wished I could have found such a room.

Now, I am sure there are places, plenty of them, in the United States where this could happen. But listen to these groups of students in Puerto Rico, and you hear speeches, punctuated by interruption, growing increasingly more oratorical. The speeches tend to be set off, not by the propositions uttered by someone else, but by the particular nouns, which a person uses. That is to say, A is listening to B. They do not argue about the revision of, say, the organic act under which Puerto Rico is governed. But B happens to use the word "colony." So A gives a vehement speech about his reactions to that word, perhaps quite unrelated to what B said. There are no quantitative studies of difference, no ways of proving that my sample wasn't biased, so I have to say, Jack, simply, "I was there and I saw." The relative probability of any one of these observations is, I think, increased by the fact that the hypothesis explains a large number of the observations. It even made me conscious of some things I hadn't noticed before. For instance, I had a pleasing degree of success in my classes in teaching my students to listen. When I thought of this character-type hypothesis, I checked through and noted that *all* the students who showed any marked improvement were men, conforming on other ways to the personality pattern I have described. (There were, of course, some men, not conforming to this pattern, who already, at the beginning of the year, knew how to listen.)

Norman: There's a good deal that could be added about the way Puerto Ricans speak. They talk with shoulders, hands, torso, neck; they emphasize and emphasize and emphasize. *El Mundo,* the biggest newspaper, uses superlatives, which, in translation, sound ridiculous. Puerto Ricans interested in literature say this is not good Spanish, but the point is it's characteristically Puerto Rican Spanish. You heard Maria, herself, and her English is just as good as mine, tell you it was a "torture" for her to speak English my most intelligent students habitually referred to the American tyranny and our difficulty there is one of emotional translation, not because Puerto Rican evaluations of the situation are different from mine, but because they emphasize so much. Muñoz, who before he was a political leader was a journalist, said in the shrewdest article ever written about Puerto Rico (8), "In an island where nothing grand ever happened, everything happens in a grand manner," and points out how fond Puerto Ricans are of adjectives like sublime, delirious, grandiose.

Lewis: Muñoz in a way, I think, suggested my general approach in the same article when he said: "We love to strut in a falsely epic atmosphere..."

To get back to this immediate matter of discussion and democracy; Puerto Rican committee meetings are, I judge, again, and naturally, on the average, more full of oratorical speeches than those on the English-speaking sections of the continent. I have been told that there is the same difficulty at the regular meetings, which the governor holds with the heads of the various agencies as in my classes at the beginning—that nobody listens and everybody speechifies.

Eleanor: I have a feeling that the spirit of *mañana* is somehow related to all this.

Lewis: I wish that word would be abolished, because I think it conveys a false connotation. Florence Kluckhohn, in the best study of Hispanic-Americans, which I know (7) points out that *mañana* does not really mean that people are thinking of or even looking forward to tomorrow; rather it refers to unwillingness to do something today which will give you gratification tomorrow. (Tom, you'll recognize a relationship to pleasure and reality principles.) I think Kluckhohn hit the nail squarely on the head; but the trouble is that we "Anglo-Saxons," I am sure, and the Hispanic peoples, I think, usually interpret mañana to refer to actual laziness, to the attitude "God will provide if we wait." So Puerto Ricans and others, sensitive to our criticism, try to avoid laziness, try hard to be energetic. But that isn't the real difficulty; I would bet that the typical Puerto Rican professional spends more ergs in a day than the typical continental professional; he does this, that, the other thing. But he doesn't get the thing done that he started out to do. The continental assumes this failure is due to laziness; this explanation is very acceptable to Puerto Ricans, basically, because any individual Puerto Rican knows that he, personally, isn't lazy, so he goes ahead, rushing more and more, but not accomplishing any more.

Take this matter of unpunctuality. It seems to be more characteristic of Puerto Rico than of the continent, but, most assuredly, the Puerto Rican isn't unpunctual because he's lazy, but because a thousand-and-one things happen about which he has to do something, and ...

Thomas: A possible interpretation along another line, which would fit some things you've said, is a kind of unconscious hostility, a resentment at being made to do things, a desire to show, by God, that one is master of the situation, and doesn't have to work.

Lewis: That might be. The immediate point, however, that the Puerto Rican accepts the mañana explanation cheerfully because it isn't a valid explanation, still stands. One point, which is related, and about which we ought to think more, is the fact that the difference between continentals and Puerto Ricans in such matters is much greater in writing letters, sending checks, returning books, *et cetera,* than in direct, personal appointments or engagements. That is, the continental feels less obligated in a non-business situation, the Puerto Rican more.

Thomas: That seems to me to substantiate my point.

Lewis: One other thing, Puerto Rican men are far more unpunctual than women.

Eleanor: There are, of course, quite a number of men whom we know who are just as conscientious as continentals of the most conscientious sort, but they always seem awfully hag-ridden (except for some of the older men, who lived some time in the States). They aren't the kind of people one remembers, Alfonso or Herminic or Ernesto Ibanez, afterwards, whereas those who are damnably unpunctual are striking personalities, a lot of them.

Norman: Remember, by the way, Herminic's favorite saying, "I must kill my conscience or it will kill me."

Lewis: I don't know whether Herminic, who has always puzzled me, fits into it, but there certainly is a type that has just failed to be dramatic and aggressive, along the lines of my summary, and hence is full of self-criticism and self-doubt and depends very much on a stronger, although less able, personality. Here, Jack, is a case where this sort of discussion gets into difficulties—I could not cite examples for this or for a lot of other statements I've made without seeming to betray friends, students, or colleagues, but, I assure you, I could cite an example for every statement made this evening.

Blanca: You know, that article of Muñoz has another comment which is very true of us I hope it may not be true of the plans of the *Populares*—"We are always contemplating what we never carry out. Some paved approach to hell ought to be named for Puerto Rico. Visions that burst forth magnificently and take impetus as plans cool off as calculations and generally peter out." (8) There is the tragedy of my country.

Eleanor: And now, Lewis, how about independentism?

Lewis: Well, I have written an article on this (4). But there are some things I didn't say there, which fit into our present discussion. When Professors Rheinstein and Johnson of Chicago, returning from Puerto Rico, spoke to graduate students at the University of Chicago from Puerto Rico, pointing out the tremendous economic costs of independence, one rather typical reaction was, "I would rather starve in the streets and be free than be a slave of the United States." Remember my quotation from Muñoz a few moments ago: "We love to strut in a falsely epic atmosphere; we know it's a sham; and we catch not ourselves, but each other," at it. I had a number of presumably independentist students, who would speak dramatically against the American tyranny. But each one in private conversation would tell me that he, personally, was a sensible person, and knew all the difficulties in the path of independence, but so-and-so or so-and-so were stupid oafs who really believed in absolute independence.

Don't get me wrong; I think the United States has treated Puerto Rico with a callous disregard of the sensibilities of the Puerto Rican people. I should not be surprised to learn that such federal regulations as the coastal shipping laws have been manipulated to hurt Puerto Rico. I believe Puerto Rico should be given an honest choice of political alternatives. I sympathize deeply with the Puerto Ricans in the tragic destiny, which geography and population have imposed upon them.

Norman: I think the story of the Cuban students and independence is worth telling at length. Of course, everybody had his own story; but this is probably substantially correct. Some Cuban students arrived at a Puerto Rican military field, assertedly on a mission from the University of Habana student body to that at Puerto Rico. Despite lack of credentials or papers, they were admitted. They visited a number of people before coming to the University; allegedly, they boasted they would shoot or have something to do with shooting Muñoz. It was believed that they had some connection with the Puerto Rican terrorist leader recently released from Atlanta, Albizu-Campos. When they reached the University, the University information officer suggested that they would do well to get credentials and check with immigration authorities. They did not do so. But they spoke at a meeting of pro-independence students, attacking both the United States and Roosevelt violently. Then the immigration authorities looked them up and kicked them out.

Consequently, the greater part of the student body went on strike. At first, they received permission from the Chancellor to hold a meeting if they didn't disturb other students in class. Well, they banged the doors of classrooms and harangued those who stayed in to come out; I shouted fiercely at my visitors and they went away. A meeting was held at 9, which lasted and lasted and when some students tried to walk out to go back to classes at 10, independentist members of the faculty forbade them to leave. At 10, there were only five students out of the normal thirty-odd in my class. They didn't know whether to stay or not. We agreed to hold class, with the understanding that if the Dean thought it fair, the same material would be covered again for the benefit of absentees.

Around 11 there was an outdoor meeting at which a member of the student council told about a book he was writing, called, I think, "Fourteen Who Have Betrayed Puerto Rico," and indicated that the University information officer, and other university officials, were among the guilty fourteen. Both the information officer and the Dean of the Social Sciences, formerly, and perhaps at the time, independentists, were accused of having reported the Cuban students to the immigration authorities. Later on, after the strike, there was great dissension in the student council about responsibility for starting the strike and its propriety. The President of the Student Council resigned. The Dean of the Social Sciences was indignant about the aspersions cast at him, denied he had had anything to do with the matter, and demanded and got a hearing before the Council, which voted that it considered him "not guilty."

This very month, "riots closed the University," to quote the headline in the *New York Times*. "After a week of demonstrations by striking Nationalist students ..." according to the United Press, "thirty-five students have been arrested" and "there are unconfirmed reports that martial law will be declared if student disorders continue." Of course, this was only two weeks before the intermission; but nevertheless, apparently 40 percent of the students struck. The manifesto issued by a group of student leaders against the Chancellor declared: "The University crisis remains very grave. Academic despotism has reached its limit. The despot lives upon cowardice, indolence, ignorance, and the defeated spirit of the slave," and concluded, "For the grandeur of the heroic fight! For the noble consecration of youthful impetuousness! For the glory of a University of free men! For liberty!" Later a group of students invaded the Chancellor's anteroom, in effect held him and his staff prisoners, and threatened to hang him and throw him out of the window.[8]

Another thing, which happened to one of our continental colleagues, and seems to me psychologically similar to the independence movement: a student aged nineteen, came to see him, protesting, saying, "You require that we work or else not participate in class discussions. This is an insult to us. In the United States college students are boys, and you can tell them to work. Here we are men and need not work. We are accustomed in all our classes not to work until the last week of the semester and we want you to understand this. All of us who are prelegal students were going to the Dean to protest; but we thought we'd tell you first." The professor explained that he'd made a personal promise to the Chancellor that he'd make the students work, that he had to keep that promise, that he was a stranger in a strange country, and maybe didn't belong there at all, but, as long as he was here, he'd have to keep the promise. After a lot of dramatic conversation, the student said, now he saw the professor's viewpoint, he'd try to persuade his fellows. There was no further trouble.

Harriett: Well, this is all very interesting, but I'm not convinced.

Lewis: Neither am I. But I think it's a hopeful way of proceeding. I think it can be practically useful. Had I formulated these hypotheses six months or ten before I did, a lot that looked to me like caprice would have become comprehensible, and I would have known how to deal with it. I doubt, too, whether planning programs can be very effective until we have developed work along this line. And perhaps many of the difficulties in group adjustment are due to differences in personality types; for instance, the characteristic Irishman, the characteristic Jew, the characteristic Yankee, are different in character structure from each other, and hence suspect each other.

Of course, there's much more I would need to know about Puerto Rico and Hispanic countries and about colonial areas before I could consider any hypothesis verified, even if the general approach is right. It would be extremely valuable to make detailed studies of Puerto Rican behavior patterns of the sort we contemplated; but I would like to see these studies carried on by people who know, for example, Santo Domingo and/or Manila and/or Central Chile and/or Cuba and/or Costa Rica and/or various non-Hispanic colonial areas, where there is a professional class, trying to accommodate itself to the requirements of an industrialized society.

Notes

1.   I am grateful to Natan Leites whose questions and comments led me to write this article. Neither he, nor any of the numerous others who have advised me on its preparation and to whom I am also indebted, are in any way responsible for anything I may say.
2.   See References.
3.   The wide sale of F. Lundberg and M. Farnham, *Modern Woman: The Lost Sex,* New York: Harper's, 1947, is an instance of the same phenomenon, women who are bothered by problems of reconciling the conflicting demands of our culture upon

them, and who are too intellectual to find much solace in the movies, can conjure up a vision of a "normal" woman who does not have to *try* hard at anything.

4.   A continental reader looking this statement over thought it was literally unbelievable. How, he asked, could organizations operate in Puerto Rico? They do not operate with the same degree of order as in other parts of the world. Many continental Americans become completely disheartened by the Puerto Rican situation for this reason. However, Puerto Rico represents a great modification of traditional difficulties, which Americans have had with Spanish officials. A number of anecdotes about Franco Spain could be recited to indicate the point; or consult Dean Worcester, *The Philippine Islands*, New York: Macmillan, 1899, for an account of difficulties, which he had with Spanish colonial officials, pp. 44-56, 86-93, 123, 126, 146, 191-192, 211, 265, 292-295, 303, 318-323, 339-342, 485.

5.   I did not get any clear picture of typical Puerto Ricans' reactions to being made to wait. I have an impression that they are more likely to be displaced against some irrelevant target, without any notion of the process of displacement that is taking place occurring to any participant in the situation, than is the case in Anglo-Saxon culture.

6.   Luis Munoz-Marin, President of the Senate of Puerto Rico, is the much-beloved leader of the popular Democratic party, which won two thirds of the island's votes in the general elections of 1944. Munoz is worshipped by the people in a way that no contemporary North American leader is.

7.   Generally speaking, Puerto Ricans are interested in speculation, as distinguished from system building. It is characteristic that several students, sent up on government scholarships to study empirical subjects at the University of Chicago, have shifted to work under the Committee on Social Thought, and exert considerable pressure on their fellow scholarship holders to do the same thing. Indeed, Hispanic-American sociology is evidently different from sociology elsewhere precisely in the presence of this speculative element, especially speculation about: What are we as Argentinians or Venezuelans or Puerto Ricans, etc.? A profitable analysis might well be made of the works on national sociology cited by Alfred Povifia in *Historia de la Sociologia en Latino-America.* Mexico City: Fonda de Cultura Economica, 1941.

8.   The United Press story upon which I rely for the first half of this account is dated May 8, 1948. The account of the manifesto and the invasion of the Chancellor's offices is taken from a statement by Chancellor J. Benitez to the Faculty of the University of Puerto Rico, published in *Los Sucesos del dia 14 de Abril en la Universidad de Puerto Rico,* 1948, 47 pp. (translation mine).

Addendum

Puerto Rico was, to the Spaniards, for several centuries, perhaps the least glamorous of their colonies. For two and a half centuries the overwhelming majority were illiterate, and records are very sparse. We do not know what influence the Indians or Negro slaves have had; and relatively little is known to me, at least, about the provenance of Spaniards or Negroes. Puerto Rico's population grew greatly during the nineteenth century by immigration. What proportion of the immigrants were Spaniards I do not know; but, apparently, the overwhelming majority fit into prevailing patterns of culture. Corsicans, Yankees, Italians, Loyalists from Venezuela, Russians, and Lebanese are observable elements in the population.

Probably Santo Domingo is the closest to what Puerto Rico would have become without the Americans; it remained a Spanish colony longer and had the same economic bases. Cuba has many similarities, also, but is and was very much richer, and is thinly populated. Chile would be the most extreme contrast with the Hispanic world, being, so to speak, the area in Latin America where the Protestant ethic would probably be least alien. Venezuela is perhaps in many respects similar to Puerto Rico culturally; Colombia is extremely different in some factors of social organization. The church, for instance, which is a negligible affair in Puerto Rico, is reportedly very important in Colombia. The population of Puerto Rico has doubled, through natural increase, since 1898; no other Spanish area has suffered a similar fate, although, reportedly, the coffee-growing sections of El Salvador face the problem of overpopulation in somewhat similar form. The Philippines have probably increased at a slightly faster rate, but they happen to contain many times the amount of arable land. Economically and population-wise, some of the British West Indies are closer to Puerto Rico.

An excellent book, in fact, for the understanding of Puerto Rico, is that by Professor Simey, *Welfare and Planning in the (British) West Indies.* (12).

Various points, which did not arise in the discussion may also profitably be noted:

1.   Puerto Ricans in St. Thomas and St. Croix are regarded by many continentals and Virgin Island residents as hard, grasping, and unreasonably efficient. To hear people talk about them, they sound like the Japanese in California. In St. Croix, perhaps the poorest place beneath the United States flag, several impressively clean stores are run by Puerto Ricans.
2.   Kluckhohn refers to *"los costumbres"* (tradition) as an important element in New Mexican society. I have never met a group as completely oblivious of tradition as the professionals whom I knew in Puerto Rico. There is, to be sure, considerable agitation for the teaching of Puerto Rican history; but no one has any sense of historical continuity. Indeed, as one trained in New England, I found this absence disheartening. There is very little, too, of telling stories about "when I was a girl ... "
3.   It is important to recognize that simple impulsiveness, if such a thing exists, is not an important element in the type, which I am trying to describe. I have seen a substantial number of professional Puerto Ricans intoxicated; I do not remember much amorousness of the sort fairly common in many drunken groups in the United States.

References

Bagehot, W., *Physics and Politics.* New York: Appleton, 1873. pp. 30-40.

Benedict, R., *The Chrysanthemum and the Sword: Patterns of Japanese Culture.* Boston: Houghton Mifflin, 1947.

Davila, Virgilio., *El Pueblito de Antes, versos criollos.* San Juan: Fernandez and Co., 1917.

Dexter, Lewis A., Independentism and Economic Planning in Puerto Rico. *Puerto Rican Puzzle. Forum,* 1946, 105. pp. 780-785.

Gorer, G., *The American People: A Study in National Character.* New York: Norton, 1948.

Halbwachs, M., *Les Causes du Suicide.* Paris: Alain, 1930.

Kluckhohn, Florence, *Los Atarquenos.* Radcliffe College, Ph.D. Thesis MS., 1941.

Muñoz-Marin, Luis., *Porto Rico* in *These United States* edited by Ernest Gruening. New York: Boni and Liveright, 1934, Vol. II. pp. 373-393.

Ortega Y. Gasset, Jose, *Mission of the University.* Princeton: Princeton University Press, 1944. P. 42.

Pedreira, Antonio., *Insularismo: Ensayos de Interpetacion Puertoriqueno.* Madrid: Tipografia artistica, 1934.

Rogier, Charles, *Comerio: A Study of a Puerto Rican Town.* Lawrence: U. of Kansas Press, 1940.

Simey, T. S., *Welfare and Planning in the (British) West Indies.* Oxford: Clarendon Press, 1946. Esp. pp. 101-105, 138-143, and 150-160.

3

Heredity and Environment Reexplored: Specification of Environments and Genetic Transmission*

Geneticists nowadays generally accept in principle some such formulation as the following: "A trait is an abstraction…. What is actually inherited is a dynamic pattern of developmental processes which directs the course of the body…. Development at any stage is a function of the environment in which the process has taken place." (1)

But the *application* of this approach to such psychogenic phenomena as schizophrenia, mental deficiency, neurosis, accident-proneness, and allergy is very unusual. Geneticists mislead non-technical readers by falling back on such phrases as "The Inheritance of Personality" to quote the title of a recent article in the *American Journal of Human Genetics,* (2) which then goes ahead to discuss the so-called "inheritance of neurosis"; and of course we are all familiar with attempts to trace the pedigrees of schizophrenics (4) and mental defectives (5) and draw rather sweeping conclusions from them.[1] There is every reason to trace such pedigrees, but reason also to express caution in drawing conclusions from them.

The difficulty we face is that we have only vague and general bases for specifying the "existing variety of environments." There is therefore a strong tendency to omit from consideration any specification of environments at all; and this is particularly true when we come to the distinctively social aspects of environment. Sociologists have been concerned particularly with the identification of "culture" and of "primary group" constellations[2] as determinants of behavior. They customarily use these factors to "explain" psychosis, neurosis (7), criminal tendencies, and sometimes psychosomatic disorders, and personality traits such as genius, mental defect, and the like. Freud, Charles Horton Cooley, William Graham Sumner, Ruth Benedict, A. Kardiner: these names indicate the sociological explanations referred to.[3]

To be sure, most sociologists, if pressed, would admit that "constitutional" and "genetic factors" may play a part; and presumably, if pressed, most geneticists would admit "sociological" factors may play a part. But the clinician or student who reads one group of writings will find their "explanations" of the phenomena almost unconnected with the "explanations" advanced by the other. Students in medical genetics might be taught a "hereditary" explanation of schizophrenia or mental defect, which would be pooh-poohed in another course or school where maternal overprotection or social isolation would be regarded as the etiologically significant factor.

Basically, the need is for a rigorous specification of environments. No such specification is offered here, for the task is too large for the present occasion, but some suggestions are made, which are useful in working toward such specification.

1.   Sociologists generally, I judge, tend to feel that "genetic" explanations have a racist or aristocratic taint attached. Myrdal in the book, which has probably been more influential than any other single sociological treatise of the last fifteen years says: "It is hardly possible to be a true biological determinist and yet, a political liberal,"[4] and most sociologists have read or misread writings by geneticists as implying biological determinism. Pastore (11) in a rather careful study has in fact shown that among American scholars genetic *explanations* are more apt to be correlated with conservative" or "reactionary" political views and sociological ones with "liberal" or "radical" views *(10)*. Of course if this is true, it has nothing to do with the merits of analysis, report, or experiment, provided that we content ourselves with exploration on the scientific level, and distinguish that sharply from political and social inferences. Nevertheless, advocates of genetic determination have this obstacle to overcome in being accepted—nowadays one might almost say against being heeded—by social scientists. Hitler is still working in mysterious ways to influence human affairs, and this is an example.

2.   Both geneticists and social scientists need consistently to talk and write as though they took seriously this proposition (unless of course at some time it is disproved): "We cannot predict what phenotype a given zygote will develop into unless we know something about the environment in which it is to develop."

3.   If such a statement is accepted, then we need to specify environments as carefully as we can. Now the great difficult with genetic studies as contrasted with social scientists' level of observation is that geneticists and clinicians are observing and reporting on the level of development of individuals organisms when studying such phenomena as mental

defect; whereas social scientists frequently talk about "culture" and "social environment" in gross general, average, statistical terms applying to populations. "Culture" does not as such directly affect a person; the person is brought up in a particular environment and in the present state of sociology it is difficult to find sociological literature, which carefully indicates the level of abstraction used in describing environments.

4. A good deal of writing on genetics—and much clinical genetics—is of course concerned with predicting the risk involved in certain kinds of matings. But so far as the more complex and difficult-to-observe psychological factors are concerned, when we introduce the phrase "the environments remaining constant," we really—in the present state of our knowledge—throw out much possibility of making any long-range prediction. Capable sociologists, psychiatrists, and psychologists maintain that a good many psychoses or neuroses develop because of the stress of environmental factors, as a result, for example, of the inability to reconcile conflicting role or status demands, and that these psychoses or neuroses are in a sense "adaptive," viz., they are said to be means of reconciling or evading the conflicts involved in the situation. If this be so, then the issue is to determine which human organisms, granted the presence of equally conflicting status or role demands, will find psychosis or neurosis "adaptive" and which ones will not. Now this means that we have first to develop a criterion for "measuring" role conflict, *which is independent of the psychosis or neurosis.* For, in fact, the environment of the person who is suffering from a severe role conflict is different from the environment of the person who is not. If we take a pedigree where several persons appear to have suffered from psychoses of one sort or another, we have to rule out the likelihood that all these persons suffered from such role conflicts, for instance, before we can make any reasonable prediction about the risk that their descendants will experience similar psychoses or we have to show their descendants are equally likely to experience such role conflicts; or alternatively we have to show some aspect of constitutional development, which makes persons far more prone to find psychosis or neurosis adaptive than others with equally great role conflicts.

Let us give a few examples of the difficulty of segregating the effect of environment on all the members of a kinship group from the effect of possible genetic transmission. There is nothing new in the point that it is difficult to distinguish the effect of "heredity" from that of "environment" on the individual; but less has been done than we might wish in exploring the possibility of differentiating the effect of "culture" or "social status" upon groups of related individuals from that of genetic transmission. Suppose, for example, the family in question is Jewish. There are fairly obvious reasons why recent generations of Jews—as a result of breaking away from the Ghetto, as a result of the high degree of social mobility in many Jewish families, and of what we may call "conscientiousness" instilled in many Jewish children in early familial training, and finally as a result of the covert and overt manifestations of prejudice many Jews are exposed to—might have produced more persons suffering from role-status conflicts, who find neurosis or psychosis adaptive than would recent generations of, say, French-Canadians. I have no idea whether Jews do differ statistically from French-Canadians in this respect, and because of the absence of trustworthy statistics on any of these matters, neither had anybody else. The point is merely that the social environment of Jewish professional men in, say, New England, has been different from that of a French-Canadian family in Quebec, but—and this is crucial—differences, which have existed in the past between these groups may, and probably, will, diminish in the future; discrimination against Jews in this country appears to be less destructive in its psychological consequences than it used to be, and more Canadians are breaking away in adolescence or adulthood from a group and family system of values (or so it is alleged by the French-language press of New England). So the environments are not constant and prediction rests upon very dubious ground.

Or take "mental deficiency," particularly the 80 percent of the so-called "familial" mental deficients, who show no clear constitutional differentiation from the rest of the population, except that they are mentally deficient. (Persons with visibly defective nervous systems, or those with rather rare constitutional conditions, which can be recognized fairly readily, such as phenylpyruvic amentia, fall into a different category.)

How do we identify high-grade mental defect? By determining in effect the degree of aptitude persons show for performing certain types of operations. Generally, the operations, which they are asked to perform consist of "intelligence tests" of one sort or another. We know that "culture," "social status," and "motivation" all play a considerable part in determining the seriousness with which such tests are taken, and the degree of ability shown in manipulating them. Unless we succeed in specifying that culture and social status and motivation have not entered into the grading of test results, we can not arrive at any very solid genetic conclusions.

An additional point should be made here. Frequently, we can quite usefully predict what persons will do in one situation on the basis of their skill or behavior in another; motivation in an individual personality has a tendency to remain constant in a wide range of situations and few personalities completely revise their "definitions of situations" once these are acquired, even though the external social "reality" may change considerably. Consequently, intelligence tests or other tests of intellectual aptitude may be "true," that is, have an extremely high predictive value, for an individual without necessarily having any bearing on the transmission of developmental potentialities from one generation to another.

Naturally, clinical psychologists are trying to develop better instruments for the identification of "true" mental defect[5] and the measurement of intelligence generally. But no matter how valid the instruments, which may be developed, all they can show is that persons with a certain developmental potentiality, genetically acquired, can develop into what we call "mental defectives," *under certain environmental conditions,* and that the problem is to specify the environmental conditions under which such development is (or is not) likely.

5. This means that we have to develop a series of hypotheses, which, directly or indirectly, can be tested about environment and development. The practical difficulty is, of course, that we do not have available to us the kind of controls, which laboratory conditions, for example, permit so that we can quickly and readily specify the full total of relevant environmental conditions. No doubt one reason we have failed to formulate useful principles about development is precisely the difficulty suggested; but the fact that we have not been able to resolve these is no excuse for not specifying what we don't know. For if we fail to specify what we don't know, and just take it for granted, there's a tendency to forget that we don't know it, and characteristically to formulate principles and laws, which give no indication of our underlying ignorance. Whereas if we keep on obstinately trying to formulate what we don't know, we may discover a way of getting around the difficulties.

One favorite method of present-day geneticists for exploring the problems here referred to is the study of twins. Quite likely, such study may throw light on important issues of genetics and development but in view of present-day failures to specify, it does not have great value for the study of psychogenic conditions like mental deficiency, schizophrenia, or related disturbances. First, no study *of* twins to my knowledge suggests that some of the co-twins studied were placed in quite different cultures or subcultures from the other member of the pair. The presumption in most cases is that, although in some reported instances, the twins studied were brought up at somewhat different socioeconomic levels, they were brought up within the same general culture, (12) with the same general practices in regard to weaning, toilet training, classroom frustrations, and so forth. Now the significance for our purposes of sociological theory or of psychoanalytic theory is that these practices are crucial in determining how the personality develops; *e.g.,* a person exposed to the certain deprivational practices in weaning toilet training, or schooling is likely to develop the same deficiencies in motivation or intellectual skill as another person exposed to the same deprivational practices. This is the meaning of the use of "complex" and "type" in psychoanalytic and personality theory.

If this is true, it is probably true only if the persons in question have similar constitutional predispositions to begin with for example, if their kinesthetic response resemble each others'. But twins do have such resemblances, so the fact that they are brought up apart, in the "same" culture, does not really enable us to segregate "hereditary" from "environmental" factor in the developmental processes, which may lead to states defined as "psychosis" or "mental deficiency."

On the other hand, studies of culture differences, so far as I know, fail to take into account that co-twins reared apart often *may* have a social environment more similar to each other than co-twins reared together. This arises out of the following set of circumstances: any set of like persons living or working together tend to develop some specialization of role. Observers have reported this as characteristic of twins; one becomes "the ambassador" to the outside world, the specialist in social relations, for instance, and the other does not. Such specialization is in fact an almost inevitable consequence of the latent competition for the same attention, space, etc. between twins.

Twins reared apart, however, face no alternatives of specialization and differentiation on the one hand or competition on the other if, as is more often than not the case, they are brought up in the same general socio-economic level by much the same sort of people, it can be anticipated that because of their constitutional similarities their development *may be* very much alike. One reason for such development is the role appearance and constitution play in social development; red-haired people in many environments will respond, either positively or negatively, to the social expectations about red hair. But red-haired twins may find it difficult or impossible for both of them to develop the quick temper, for instance, characteristically expected of the red-haired, if they live together; and in any case, being twins will be a dominant social experience for them. Reared apart, they may both respond similarly to the characteristic social expectations in our society about red-haired people.

Of course, if one twin is brought up as the youngest of a large family of foster-siblings and the other is brought up as an only child, one might expect differences to develop; but so far as I know observations and experiments in the field have not been focused on such factors, which constitute such "real" differences in the stock environment. And, obviously, if a red-haired twin of Anglo-American ancestry were to be brought up in rural Japan by Japanese foster-parents, social expectation about red hair would be far less significant than other visible differences between the person and other persons in his environment.

None of this is to assert firmly that mental defect or schizophrenia may not be well explained in terms of genetic transmission. It is merely to assert firmly that no one at present knows whether this is the case or not; because no specification of environments adequate for the purpose of analysis and observation has as yet been developed. For example, some of the familial "mentally defective" might in fact be so almost entirely because of certain factors in weaning, toilet training, etc. *combined* with exposure to the educational experiments and skill of our society (13). If the educational techniques and requirements to which they are subjected were modified in terms of their aptitudes, (14) (15) it could conceivably turn out that a large part of what we now call "mental deficiency" would not become developmentally manifest. In the "mental hygiene" area many practitioners preach a similar premise, and sociological rather than rational reasons explain why we regard "mental defect" as more inherent and therefore less modifiable than psychosis or neurosis.[6]

Present-day knowledge can be used to support unfamiliar and seemingly bizarre conclusions such as that just stated, just as Woodworth used present-day knowledge (for we know little more about the topic than we did twenty years ago) to report: "On the strength of some ... findings, the suggestion has been made (impliedly by qualified psychologists) that society, instead of seeking *to* minimize the fecundity of feeble-minded women, should utilize them *as* breeders of children for adoption into high-level homes.[7]

We can more freely do one thing, however, which was not possible much before Woodworth made the report *to* the Social Science Research Council just cited. We can break down the almost unanalyzed conception "social environment," which he employed into a series of suggestions for specific observation about actual behaviors.[8]

Since my concern here *is* in the social science field, I have discussed the specification of social environments, but a similar specification of physical environments may be necessary. We *know* of course that under certain conditions, the biochemical and physical environment *of* the embryo can make *an* enormous difference in the development *of* mental defect; *and* that probably seventy *of* certain diseases in infancy can also materially affect the nervous system. But *it* is not inconceivable that other, less obvious differences in climate, presence of industrial wastes, and so forth, may also modify the development of development of potentialities; and in any case simply because we do not believe that such factors will make a difference, is no reason for refusing to consider them.

Notes

*   This paper was prepared under a grant from the Estate of K. J. Anthony of Lewiston, Maine, "to be used for the benefit of those of God's Children known as the feeble-minded." It was read at the meeting of the American Society of Human Genetics, East Lansing, Michigan, September 1955.

1.   I may add that a distinguished geneticist, prominent in the American Society of Human Genetics, perfectly seriously proposed as late as 1951 that historians take census records for 1850 for a particular state and collaborate with psychologists in estimating the intelligence of those recorded in the records, whereupon geneticists would trace the pedigrees. As late as 1940, a distinguished geneticist published a book in which he indicated that the differential fertility of the mentally deficient was an importance factor in leading to deficit spending upon the Keynesian model. For this and other somewhat similar assertions see (3).

2.   I use the term "constellation" here in lieu of the more conventional "interaction" for methodological reasons indicated in (6).

3.   During the last ten years the "culture-and-personality" school has attempted to integrate the culture and primary group constellation approaches. See (8), (9).

4.   Contemporary sociologists are usually "political liberals." See (10).

5.   *A particularly promising attempt in this direction is the Family and Health Study at the University of Delaware under the direction of Joseph Jastak.*

6.   The major social reason appears to be this: Psychosis has been of considerable, and neurosis of great, interest to social scientists during the last twenty years, and they have applied their newly acquired insights to these fields. But there has been a continuous disinterest, if not resistance, by social scientists in consideration of mental defect, and this field therefore has not changed theoretically since 1935.

7.   See (12) footnote 15.

8.   The entire literature of the personality-and-culture movements, probably the most popular current field of social psychology, supports this *statement* that other, less obvious differences, in climate, presence of industrial wastes, and so forth, may also modify the development of developmental potentialities; and in any case, simply because we do not believe that such factors will make a difference, is no reason for refusing to consider them.

References

1.   Dobzhansky, T. 1950. Heredity, environment, and evolution. *Science*, 3:161-162.

2.   Cattell , R., Blewett, D. B., and Beloff, Jr. 1955. The inheritance of personality. *American Journal of Human Genetics*, 7:122-146.

3.   Burlingame , L. 1940. *Heredity and Social Problems*, McGraw-Hill, New York.

4.   Kallmann, F. J. 1954. *Heredity in Mental Disorder*, W. W. Norton, New York.

5.   Tredgold, A. 1952. *Mental Deficiency* (8th Ed.), Williams and Wilkins, Baltimore, pp. 22-40.

6. Bentley, A. 1954. *Inquiry into Inquiries*, Beacon Press, Boston.
7. Frank, L. 1948. *Society as the Patient*, Rutgers University, New Brunswick.
8. Kluckholn, C. 1949. *Mirror for Man*, Fawcett, New York, Ch. VIII.
9. Dexter, L. 1949. A dialogue on the social psychology of colonialism. *Human Relations*, 2: 49-64.
10. Myrdal, G. 1944. *An American Dilemma*, Harper's, New York, p. 83.
11. Pastore, N. 1949. *The Nature-Nurture Controversy*, King's Crown, New York.
12. Woodworth, R. 1941. Heredity and environment. *Social Science Research, Council Bulletin*, 47, 21-33.
13. Dexter, L. A. 1955. Naming as a social process and the social classification of the mentally deficient; Toward a sociology of mental deficiency. Papers read at the meeting of the American Association on Mental Deficiency.
14. Kirk, S. A., and Johnson, G. O. 1951. *Educating the Retarded Child*, Houghton Mifflin, Boston.
15. Wallin, J. 1955. *Education of Mentally Handicapped Children*, Harpers, New York.

4

Toward a Sociology of the Mentally Defective

First we need a sociology of those who study mental deficiency. Science, ideally, of course, is objective. But science unfortunately is done by scientists, who, more or less, are lacking in complete objectivity. If deviations from objectivity were random this would perhaps not matter particularly; but in any particular field of knowledge, it generally happens that the scholars in the field are biased in the same particular ways. This is a natural consequence of several circumstances. First: the attraction of a particular field will be greatest to those with particular types of personality and interests. Second: the people already in a field with standing in a field select the newcomers in it by the impression they create and by the requirements they set up. Third: in any given field people tend to go through similar experiences, which make them particularly sensitive to some types of fact (and perhaps relatively insensitive to other types of fact).

Anyone familiar with workers in the mental deficiency area can make guesses as to what biases are most significant among them—certainly many of them seem impelled to "defend" mental defectives rather than to "explain" what is going on. Could this be a consequence both of selection in the field and of the chagrin often experienced when scholars in other areas express wonderment that they had chosen to specialize in mental deficiency?

But such guesses need to be systematized and tested before they can be of great value. It is however worth starting our discussion with reference to this almost untouched area because it helps make clear that a genuine sociology of mental deficiency would be a sociology not only of the mental defectives but of those who observe and report upon them. A full sociological picture of any situation includes all the actors in the situation, even those who are studying it.

Second, we badly need a sociology of those who work in institutions, become clinicians, etc. The same set of considerations apply here. Some

43

of the reported differences between mental defectives and other people or between mental defectives in one set of circumstances and mental defectives in another may be due as much or more to the kind of people who enter the field, mental defectives themselves. It's obvious enough by way of comparison that it is naive to talk about prisons without describing the characteristics of the guards in the prisons. It's obvious, too, that guards in most prisons differ in significant ways from the average of the population. Stanton and Schwartz (1) have shown that the social and psychological factors involved in becoming nurses may materially determine the therapeutic nature of a mental hospital. So also in mental deficiency.

Third, we need to see mental defectives in terms of the general theory of social problems. Sociologists have developed a general theory of social problems, which may be stated thus: A "social problem" exists where there is deviant, irregular, disapproved, or undesired behavior; this behavior either may be described entirely in terms of a conflict or conflicts in roles, statuses, and values, or at least is accentuated by such a conflict or conflicts. Once the conflict is perceived as such, the nature of the problem may be understood (2).

Furthermore, some sociologists maintain those interested in alleviating a problem may—either through collective action or interpersonal therapy—attempt to apply the understanding thus gained so as to reduce the severity or incidence of the problem. At the very minimum, even if the conflicts, which lie near the root of the problem, arise out of conflicts in the fundamental values of a society (as we shall suggest is the case in the mental deficiency area) to learn to live with the issue, rather than to try to resolve it by cutting some Gordian knot, is a gain.

Generally speaking, social problems, according to sociological analyses, are accentuated or created by a rapid rate of social change because where such a rapid rate of change exists, it is likely that people will fail to modify their values or roles in one respect to fit into modifications they have made in another; in other words, in an unstable social situation, coherent, integrated patterns of behavior are harder to maintain. It has for example been pointed out in the literature on old age that "old age" or "the old" frequently constitute a problem at the moment in our society because of the following: (1) the longer life span provided by modern medicine for more people; (2) the increase in literacy and in scientifically induced changes in the way we live, which together with (1) means less attention is paid to the values of experience; (3) the 65-year old compulsory retirement age; (4) the postwar inflation and its effect on the value of pensions and (5) the assumption by many oldsters and by many others that there is a role for the aged of a sort, which no longer exists. Of course, aged individuals were a problem long before modern society developed; but the existence of a social problem of the old is a relatively recent development (3). Similarly, social change may have affected or be affecting the significance and role of the mentally deficient.

The increasing emphasis upon rational, efficient, measurable standards of work-performance certainly has made it tougher for mental defectives to maintain themselves economically. If automation has the predicted effects (4) this will perhaps lead even further toward the elimination of the intellectually underdeveloped worker.

In many areas, of course, an emphasis upon rationalized efficiency is an integral part of the basic economic values of our society that we can not possibly hope to do anything but recognize the situation. However, there is a correlated, somewhat dubious, assumption that literacy and verbal articulateness are necessarily related to skill at all forms of work, and that a high school diploma guarantees a better production record. There has been too little examination of this assumption in those areas where it may profitably be questioned; (and, oddly enough, the converse is true. Some employers tend to assume they need "dumb" employees; but they also do not generally check the facts of the situation).

In the last six or seven years, considerable attention has been devoted to testing the hypothesis that men over forty can not be hired for industrial work with results as satisfactory as if younger workers are employed, but less systematic attention has been given to testing the analogous hypothesis that people who are verbally skillful will do better at wide ranges of jobs.

However, this sort of approach, desirable as it is, may in some instances be a matter of locking the barn door after the horse has been stolen. Hungerford (5) and his associates and disciples in their effort to provide "occupational education" for the mentally retarded—and those who now are engaged in the sheltered workshop program for this same group—have for the most part to take the occupational system and the plants with which they deal as they are. But in a society, which is plagued by labor shortages in a good many areas, particularly in some of the low prestige or economically marginal service occupations, it would be desirable to go beyond this. Often, in planning any improvement in industrial or service technology, engineers and management men nowadays think of something which can be handled by articulate, verbally sophisticated people (this represents somewhat of a change from the 1890 situation when industrial engineering first started). If some industrial engineering in the service trades were explicitly and specifically devoted to the provision of a work technology, which could as well—or better—be performed by mental defectives this might solve some of the problems we now face.

But, under present circumstances, and perhaps even if this approach were to be adopted, we run up against another conflict in values. Many people (I myself certainly) favor a raising of the minimum wage laws; but such a raising may increase the difficulties of the mentally retarded. Of course, the same provision in these laws can be made for them as is now made for the physically handicapped, but even so the definition of "true" mental retardation has to be written into the law and to be explicable to trade union leadership—or else there will be a widespread feeling that special provision for mental defectives arises more out of a manufacturer's concern for wage scales than out of humanitarian concern for the mentally retarded.

The conflict of values involved here—between the desire, particularly supported by humanitarians for a decent minimum wage and the desire also particularly supported by humanitarians for a decent opportunity for the mentally retarded—is not unique. In fact, the aged and adolescents to some extent suffer from the same problem. Part-time work of the sort many people in their seventies would love—or work at a slower pace with correspondingly reduced wage rates—becomes difficult when unions are pressing for minimum wage laws. Also, arrangements for adolescents to enter the world of work gradually as learners or apprentices becomes difficult under such circumstances; yet such arrangements may in social-psychological terms be highly desirable for many adolescents.

If the problem of the mental defectives in this regard is seen as part of a social problem, general in nature, applying to several other groups, it has a better chance of solution than is now the case.

The foregoing discussion of minimum wage and mental defectives is of course an example. Many other similar illustrations of value conflicts and the importance of social change in creating the problems, which we regard as peculiar to the mentally defective can be cited.

Role of the "Feeble-Minded." Another of these value conflicts is indicated by our terminology in regard to mental defectives. Let's ask two naive questions. Are the adult feebleminded "children?" Yet at many, possibly most, institutions they are referred to as "children." * Are they sick? Yet clinicians in private practice talk frequently of therapy and suggest that the mental defectives with whom they are dealing are "patients."

We can dismiss the use of these terms as a verbal oddity. But, again, sociologists have suggested in many studies that characteristic terminology is rarely fortuitous.

One factor in leading to the choice of such terms may be indicated. In our society, we expect adults to assume adult responsibilities. We expect them to be self-directing, self-reliant, able to manifest some sort of mutual, civic obligation. We tend to equate such self-direction, and self-reliance, with verbal skill and literacy. We exempt certain persons from these responsibilities—those who are not fully adult. Among these, notably, are children and sick people. Parsons and Fox have pointed out that the role of the sick person is a "semi-legitimized channel of ... exemption (from) adult responsibility," legitimized by: (1) the expectation that the patient will recover or die; (2) by the belief that he or she is incapable of performing a full adult role; and (3) by sympathy or fear ("who knows? I may be sick someday myself.") "However," they continue, "the sick person is enjoined to accept the definition of his state as undesirable and the obligation to get well as expeditiously as possible" (6).

And they also say: "Childhood is (similarly) a conditionally legitimized social role involving acceptance of the obligation to grow up and to cooperate with parents in (achieving maturity)."

The use of terms like "children" or notions like "therapy" in discussing mental defectives may therefore be construed as involving an implicit plea for exemption from normal adult responsibilities on the ground that the "charges" are "growing up." It also, most certainly, involves a plea for recognizing that those "in charge of" them are engaged in an educational task. Laymen, however, by and large regard workers in the field of mental deficiency as being engaged in a strictly custodial task; and workers at institutions know that the process of education involved is somewhat different from that at a regular school.

It may well be indeed that those who choose to enter the field of institutional work for mental defectives are those who have a taste for dealing with the continuously dependent; and that one factor in preserving the orientation, which most institutions have towards the "children" is the fact that a fair proportion of their staff are self-selected persons with such a taste. This is of course a hypothesis which needs to be tested, not a statement of fact.

In actual fact, mental defectives are treated more like psychotics or prisoners than they are like children or sick people. The social role of the prisoners is, viewed from an official standpoint, to develop or manifest the ability to get along without making further trouble while in confinement. In practice, this is frequently the role of the mental defective; particularly so as those "mental defectives" who are institutionalized are most apt to be those who have got into some sort of trouble (7).

The conditionally legitimized exemption from adult responsibilities accorded psychotics is far more tenuous than that normally, in our society, given the sick or children, and depends very largely upon the degree to which the observers of particular psychotics regard their actions as (a) harmless (b) comprehensible (c) inoffensive, and also to the degree to which the psychosis in a given case interferes with the performance of a fair proportion of normal adult responsibilities. Analogously, mental defectives are more likely to be stigmatized, despised, or institutionalized if they look unusual, if they do something which other people regard as "disgusting" rather than just "silly" (which is partly a matter of environment, and partly a matter of accident) or—probably—if they have the misfortune to live in a group which places a high premium upon intellectual skill.

We know that to a considerable degree an individual's conduct is a consequence of the role and status accorded him by the society and the primary social groups in which he lives (8). The foregoing discussion suggests that different mentally defective individuals in the same society may be ascribed quite different roles and statuses. So, for purposes of diagnosis or generalization, it may be important to determine what are the variations in role-status ascriptions for mental defectives.

Formal Education and Its Effect on the Role and Behavior of Mental Defectives

My guess is that a careful study would find that those "feebleminded" persons who get along the best and who differ the most from typical mental defectives are those who have had good fortune in two related respects: (1) never to have been assigned the unique role of mental defective at least in their own primary group (2) to have been able to avoid the particular requirement for maturity, which we call "formal education." "Formal education" for large numbers is no more than an irrelevant, prolonged, and irritating initiation; but for many mental defectives (and a good many others) it is a barrier and a cross, which can not be overcome. Exposure to its requirements sets up one sort of social-psychological disability; but in a group where it is almost universally required, exemption from it, of course, may set up another. And the generally punitive nature of institutionalization may set up a third, where the child is institutionalized.

I suggest therefore that intensive case-studies of two sorts are necessary: (1) Life-histories of mentally defective persons who have gotten along in the community; (2) studies of mental deficiency in societies, which do not as completely and finally condemn "stupidity" as we do. There is not available, in published form, at least any good analysis comparing different cultures in their attitudes towards stupidity; but it is surely the case that many Oceanic, African, Asian, and American Indian cultures do not condemn stupidity as strongly as we do.

Indeed, historically, Western Europe did not look down on stupidity as much as it now does. A century ago many little girls and some little boys learned "Be good, Sweet Child, let who will be clever," but nowadays you only say that if you already know the child is not clever! Parsons has described one outstanding aspect of professional evaluation in our society as "the crushing force of such epithets as stupid and gullible" (9) and as we have developed more and more equality of opportunity ("a career open to the talents") most of us come more and more to "look down on" those who are not professionally talented. In the old predemocratic days, women, paupers, and "the lower classes" generally were not expected to manifest talent, so the "mentally defective" were not singled out as subpar.** But now almost everybody else (except the sick, the psychotic, and the criminal) are supposed to have rights, duties, and corresponding talents.

At the same time, the strong humanitarian strain in nineteenth and twentieth century society has made us labor earnestly to make everybody else like us or like our ideal picture of ourselves; and the same idealization of one set of cultural values which led us to break "the cup of life" for Ruth Benedict's Indian (10) has also led us to struggle to make "educated" men and women out of mental defectives—and where the effort did not succeed to stick them away out of sight.

In sticking them out of sight in an institution we may and probably do frequently place them in a position where those who are in charge of them are regarded as hostile much more than is the case with most people; and therefore we put them in a social situation, which is quite abnormal. (Incidentally, the absence of "due process" in commitment to an institution for mental defectives makes it quite impossible, ordinarily, for a person committed to know why he is there or what he has to do to get out.) Since much of what we "know" about mental defectives arises from observation of people who are or have been institutionalized—much of what we know may be limited in its validity or applicability; and since nearly all we know about mental defectives is based upon studies of people who were regarded as a disappointment, subpar, stupid, silly, much of what we know about "them" may apply only to our society rather than to all mental defectives in all societies.

Conclusion

If the approach here outlined is essentially valid, we may look forward to the time when the clinical sociologist diagnoses the social situation adding to what the clinical psychologist can tell us about an undivided mental defective. I am talking of course about a sort of clinical sociology, which is found but rarely; and has so far been applied chiefly by public health workers in nonindustrialized societies (11). It probably can, however, be developed and applied to the field of mental deficiency if a systematic effort is made to develop the relationship between general sociological theory and the specific life experiences of mentally defective individuals.

* A worthwhile sociological study might be made of the relationship between the terminology employed to describe the mental defectives being cared for or "treated" and the behavior and attitudes manifested towards them.

** Of course, throughout this article, I have been talking about the "high grade" "mental defectives," feebleminded," "simpleton," "moron," "garden variety mental defective" who constitutes perhaps 80 percent of all those classed as defective mentally. The other 20 percent more or less, do clearly differ in some biologically based nervous differentiation. Many, and perhaps most, of this 20 percent would not have survived early infancy in any society but one as medically capable as ours; thye probably do not have many analogues in the more technologically primitive societies today.

References

1. Stanton, A. and Schwartz, M. *The Mental Hospital*, Basic Books, New York, 1954.
2. See for instance Davis, K. *Human Society*, Macmillan, New York, 1949, passim, esp. Ch. VII.
3. These points are exemplified in J. Arthur, *How to Help Older People*, Lippincott, New York, 1954.
4. Drucker, P. "The Promise of Automation," *Harpers*, April, 1955. v. 210, 41-7.
5. See the files of the journal *Occupational Education*.
6. Parsons, T. and Fox R. an article on the social role of the ill, *Journal of Sociological Issues*, vol. 8, No. 4, 1953, pp. 31-43, esp. p. 33, p. 42.
7. See my "Naming as a Social Process and the Social Classification of 'The Mentally Deficient,'" paper given at the 1955 Convention of the A.A.M.D., to be published.
8. The literature of personality-and-culture as a whole supports this contention. For example, J. Dollard, *Criteria for the Life History*, Yale, 1935.
9. Parsons, T. "The Professions and Social Structure," reprinted in Essays in *Sociological Theory*, Free Press, New York, 1949, p. 189.
10. Benedict, R. *Patterns of Culture*, Houghton Mifflin, Boston, 1924.
11 A number of articles in the journal, *Human Organization* (formerly *Applied Anthropology*) report such application.

5

A Social Theory of Mental Deficiency*

Summary[1]

Mental deficiency may usefully be regarded as a "social problem" in the technical sense in which sociologists use the conception "social problem" (5, 6). In most, if not all, societies, mental defect tends to constitute a social problem because mental defectives fail to learn (or are supposed to be incapable of learning) the "right meanings" of events, symbols, or things; in all societies, certain "meanings" attached to events, things, or symbols, are regarded as highly significant or sacred, and those who fail to learn them therefore naturally create uneasiness or shock. In our society, mental defect is even more likely to create a serious problem than it is in most societies because we make demonstration of formal skill at coordinating meanings (reading, writing, and arithmetic) a requirement for initiation[2] into adult social status, although such formal skills are not necessarily related to the capacity for effective survival or economic contribution.

There is a distinct possibility that many mental defectives become concrete social, legal, or economic problems simply because of the direct or indirect consequences of *this* requirement for initiation into social status and for no other reason. The indirect consequences of the high valuation placed upon such skill manifest themselves in discrimination and prejudices against the "stupid," which leads them to acquire a negative or hostile self-image of themselves and therefore live according to a self-definition of themselves as worthless or contemptible. If this hypothesis is in fact valid, a substantial proportion of the cost and trouble resulting from the presence of mental defect in our society is a consequence, not of the biological or psychological characteristics of mental defectives, but of their socially prescribed or acquired roles and statutes. For clinical and diagnostic purposes, it might then become vital to differentiate those aspects of the behavior of individual mental defectives arising out of social factors from those traceable to biological and psychological bases; in concrete cases, operationally, the effects of the social factors are just as real of course.[3] But the therapy and control might well be different.

The propositions here put forward are designed to aid in the development of a social theory of mental defect; but like any other "armchair" formulation need to be refined and tested by actual field work, using systematic methods of observation and recording.

1. *Mental deficiency may usefully be regarded as a social problem in the technical sense in which sociologists use the notion* (5, 6). As contemporary sociology uses the term, a social problem exists where a significant[4] proportion of the people in a society or sub-society act (a significant proportion of the time) *as though* they regard some existent behavior[5] of others as dangerously or undesirably "abnormal"; such disapproval may be expressed in any way from frequent frowning to capital punishment.[6] The words "act as though" in the foregoing sentence are deliberately stressed; the segregation of dull children in special classes[7] or the institutionalization of the "feebleminded"[8] means, whatever the motivation, rationalization, or reasoning of those who make the decisions, that the dull and feebleminded are likely to feel that they have been treated as "abnormal" or "bad."

2. *The mental defective tends to constitute a social problem in society because he has jailed (or is supposed to be incapable of learning) the "right meaning" attached to events, symbols, or things in that society.* All societies regard it as right and proper that the young should learn the right ways to react towards symbols, things, and events—including the events of desiring food, sexual experience, attention, elimination, and "power." In a given society, the properly educated person responds to perceptions not only in terms of physical reality but in terms of social expectations and propriety (15). Shame *and* modesty for most persons in our society illustrate *the* point (16).

Certain "meanings" and responses become regarded as *absolutely* proper or normal so that any failure to learn (and act) according to them is seen as being in and of itself wicked or reprehensibly abnormal. Indeed, those who even suggest that other meanings are imaginable or conceivable or even rationally possible may be regarded with grave distrust; the suspicion, which has attached itself to Freud, Kinsey, John Maynard Keynes and certain hyper-modern musicians and artists illustrates this development.

Complex societies usually develop procedures for "Handling" carelessly unlucky, unorthodox, criminal, and alien persons who do not automatically give the "right responses." H. G. Wells in *The Country of the Blind* (17) switched the notion "in the country of the blind, the one-eyed man is king" to "in the country of the blind, the one-eyed man has to put his eye out or he will be treated as dangerously mad" to show one method of dealing with the unorthodox.

Our society has, however, found it quite difficult to handle and classify "psychotics" and "mental defectives"; we punish, or stigmatize, those who won't learn the right meanings in terms of a conception of responsibility; and we regard these two groups as lacking in responsibility, so we don't quite know what to do about them.

Forty years ago, however, the mentally defectives were regarded in the United States—in what is now universally considered an exaggerated form—as constituting a tremendous social menace (18, 19, 20). Indeed, some of the literature of that period about mental defectives sounds like fulminations against the politically unorthodox or Jews in more recent periods. It has been suggested that the most violent and unreasonable-sounding attacks on those who violate accepted social patterns or roles may be made by those who themselves fear that they do not really belong (21, 22). If this general hypothesis be correct, it may well be that the most extreme fear of the "menace" of mental defectives was expressed by those themselves uncertain or insecure of their acceptance as "intelligent."

The media of public communication have altered their emphasis on mental defect as a menace since; but the underlying attitude of uneasiness, hostility, and contempt for mental defectives appears to be still fairly widely prevalent.[9]

3. *In a society like ours, which emphasizes as an end in itself formal demonstration of skill in the technique of symbolization and coordinating meanings a far higher proportion of mental defectives are likely to be treated as cases of a social problem than would be so treated in a society emphasizing some other set of values, for instance the capacity for survival or effective economic contribution.* To some extent, inability to learn "the right meanings" and to act according to them would in any society make some mental defectives "social problem cases." But in our society learning the right meaning is of value, not only because of its consequences, but because the technique of learning has become a value in and of itself.[10] Indeed, within many American social groups, the student who in appearance or reality can demonstrate the technique of learning meanings even though in fact he disregards their implications for action, is—up to a very considerable point—less likely to be regarded as a social and educational problem than an otherwise inoffensive, socially

acceptable student who is what is called "dumb" or "stupid." That is to say, the mean, nasty, "ornery" youngster does not in such a social group create nearly as much of a "social problem" as does his tractable, well-adjusted age-mate, capable of worthwhile physical labor, if the latter "just can't learn."

We find, that is, that many mental defectives become social problem cases, even though they do in fact learn enough of the right meanings to "get by" because they do not demonstrate formal command of the technique of learning.

Of course, many mental defectives have such a low degree of skill at symbolization and communication that they would not learn the right meanings anyhow. But the maladjustment of high grade mental defectives in our society is probably not due as much to this fact as to the following circumstances: In fact modern technology and the interdependence of the modern world makes skill at coordinating symbols far more vital than it once was; the modern soldier or automobile driver ought to be able to read maps or signs exactly; whereas their fourteenth-century counterparts had no such needs. We require that young people learn complex symbols in order presumably to make themselves good citizens and in order certainly to establish their claim to social status. We live in a society, which allocates social status according to achievement *(23)*, based upon educational skill. Those who do not even make the first rung of this ladder or do so with great difficulty create a serious problem, for this reason alone.

Nevertheless, several studies show that a fair proportion of special class students or those released from institutions (24, 25, 26), once they have passed school-leaving age and the onerous requirements of formal education, get along well enough. A subject of one of these studies: (24) is quoted as saying: "I can't do much with words but give me a pile of flour and cinnamon and makings and I can turn out good bread."

Such development in adult life of those regarded as more or less mentally defective in adolescence may be explained, in several different ways. First, some type of "delayed maturation" may occur; that is they may grow intellectually more slowly but nevertheless grow (27). Second, the intelligence tests are obviously subject to error for various reasons (28), and in addition may be administered in a careless or error-producing fashion (29). A third hypothesis—and one more relevant to our effort to develop a social theory of mental defect—is that the intelligence, which the intelligence tests test is not in fact a measure of ability to make an economic contribution or to survive, but merely of the type of intelligence and clerical aptitude, which enables people to do well at school (36).

It also happens that if a person of low intellectual ability gets into some sort of trouble the difficulty is more or less automatically attributed to "mental defect" whereas if a person of "normal intelligence" gets into a similar difficulty, it is not regarded as symptomatic of anything in particular. Consequently, attention becomes focused upon the mental defectives as people who get into trouble; we have no real evidence as to whether they do (or for what reasons) in any greater proportion than do normal individuals of similar socio-economic statuses.[11] It may be that mental defect is significant as a trouble-creating factor only because of the social attitude towards it, not because of the defect itself—*in the case especially of high-grade mental defectives.* This statement is probably exaggerated; but not necessarily more exaggerated than the customary attitude towards mental defectives the other way about.

4. The self-image of the mentally defective in a society, which stresses aptitude at intellectual achievement is likely to be negative because the "looking-glass self" principle operates and they learn from their social contacts and experiences to look down upon and distrust themselves; in consequence difficulties are created, derived from the social role of the defectives rather than from anything inherent in the bio-psychological nature of defectives. Anyone's picture of himself is in large measure a consequence of his picture of other people's picture of him. That is to say, one's self is produced by the interaction of organismic structure and environment, including in environment the social environment (33). Most people do the things they do, and fail to do what they fail to do, in part, because of the socially-acquired picture they have of themselves. This social origin of self and behavior has been described as "the looking-glass self" (34, 35, 36, 37, 38). In a society where people in a given category are restricted in role, made fun of, looked down upon, and subjected to great obstacles, the people in that category are likely to learn to feel considerable self-doubt; this self-doubt may express itself in helplessness, lack of ambition, or erratic, impulsive, and highly negative behavior—"kicking out" at a world in which "the generalized other"—the typical or modal other person as they have experienced him—has frustrated, bewildered, or oppressed him. These undesirable or anti-social types of conduct are not *per se* the result of any particular abnormality, low status position, or deviation from conventional conduct; they are rather responses to the way people are treated who are regarded as abnormal, of low status, or undesirably unconventional. By way of partial analogy, members of minority groups may to some extent manifest these behaviors if subjected to enough oppression;[12] but within their own immediate social circle, they are usually regarded as normal and treated with what is regarded as fairness.

There is however a particular class of persons who are not completely members of any group, either because their ancestry is so physically mixed that in a society where "race" is important they are regarded by almost everybody as outsiders, or because their life history has been such as to make them outsiders everywhere, neither fish nor fowl. Sociologists and novelists have devoted a good deal of attention to these persons, called "marginal men" (40, 41) and it may well be that the problems of the marginal man[13] are the problems of the high-grade mentally retarded. If this hypothesis is correct, it may turn out that *the* significant therapy for the high-grade retarded is to find some place where they can be accepted completely and that the explanation of the success of those graduates of institutions and special classes who have succeeded in adult life will be discovered to be that by good fortune they found a place where they could be accepted without any sense of being left out.

But those who differ in such a way as to be regarded negatively by the people with whom they spend the greater part of their lives, their kin groups, work groups, or age mates, do not have such "moral support"; so they are likely to develop an image of themselves as incapable or of other people as being hostile, an image which extends beyond the specific areas of incompetence or hostility, which actually exist and suffuses most of their behavior.

Mental defectives are probably more likely than any other group in our society to develop such negative self-images; the nearest analogue, which comes to mind is perhaps the person afflicted by compulsive homosexual drives. In other societies, persons with certain diseases—e.g., leprosy (42, 43)—may have been likely to develop similar images of the self and of others.

Empirically, we need field studies of role development among mental defectives, designed to clarify and test the approach above suggested, by identifying the processes, by which they learn that they are not doing the things they are expected to do—initial failure at assuming the social status expected of their age, family, etc. (44)—and the accommodation they make to such failure. It is probable that a considerable proportion of the social burden and economic cost of mental defect arises, not out of lack of intellectual ability as such but out of the accommodation (45) that mental defectives learn to make to the consequences of such lack. The problem of mental defect, so envisaged, would then become *in part*, and in different amounts, a problem of learning different methods of accommodation. On such a hypothesis, one would expect to find that the less the mental defective is exposed to conventional pressure for scholastic or equivalent success, and the less he is exposed to ridicule, the greater, on the average, the adult social and economic success experienced.

An alternative hypothesis ought to be explored—and is certainly held implicitly, if not explicitly, by a number of fairly shrewd people. They believe that the mental defective is because of his defect less sensitive, or altogether insensitive, to the nuances of prestige and discrimination, which worry normal people. This hypothesis seems to me, on the basis of my own limited observation, indefensible; but it could fairly readily be tested, for instance by exposing various mental defectives to sarcasm, body styles, and gestures showing disdain, etcetera; my own guess, and it is simply a guess, is that some mental defectives would rank higher in awareness of the meanings of posture and body style than would most normal people, not because mental defect *per se* predisposes them to any special skill on these points, but much as some blind men become particularly adept at hearing and interpreting sounds, which most of us disregard, so the mental defective may develop skill at "the language of gesture and posture" to compensate for incompetence in the verbal skills (50a).

Regarding mental defect as somewhat analogous to illness—a deviant or pathological biologically-based condition—an illuminating remark by Saunders (46) in a study of social factors in disease may be cited. He states: "Illness and disease, it must be remembered, are social as well as biological phenomena. On the biological level, they consist of the adaptation of the organism to environmental influences; on the social level, they include meanings, roles, relationships, attitudes, and techniques, that enable members of a cultural group to identify various types of illness and disease (and to behave thereto in what is regarded as an appropriate manner)." It is, for instance, highly probable that in a social system in which victims of witchcraft (47) or menstruating women (48) or illegitimate mothers (49) or illegitimate children (50) or twins (9) learn to regard themselves in certain ways, there will be differences between people in these categories and other people in the same society, differences which will reflect themselves in gross skeletal movements, motoric gestures, posture, and intensity of pain (33).

5. *The foregoing propositions remain to be tested after further clarification and comparison with alternative sociologically based propositions*

about mental defect. (It should again be stressed that the present effort has been confined to a *social* theory of mental deficiency, and therefore probably has more pertinence to high grade mental defectives than to others). The propositions here put forward assume that there is a bio-psychological condition, which can properly be identified as "mental defect," just as there "is" a biological condition of having scarlet fever (51). This may not in fact be the case; it may well be that we have for sociological reasons, fallen into the error of treating members of a null class, people who lack or appear to lack some particular characteristic, as though they have positive characteristics in common. We know that there is no scientific sense in talking of "foreigners" or "anti-Communists" or "criminals" as though all the persons in any one of these groups have anything much positive in common. Similarly, it may be that all that mental defectives (or even high-grade mental defectives) have in common is that they have gone through the experience of being treated as mental defectives and are undergoing deviant role-status experiences because of the existence of mental defect.

This point simply suggests one of the ways in which further analysis might help to develop an adequate general social theory of mental defect. Such a general social theory should also take account of the possible effects of the recent sentimental and humanitarian concern for mental defectives, an omission in the present paper.

But at the same time, empirical field work using the approaches here suggested may contribute to deeper understanding of what we are talking about. We need for instance systematic life-history studies (52) of relatively successful and relatively unsuccessful mental defectives. We need studies of mental defectives in communities (Ethiopia? Yucatan? Melanesia?) relatively unaffected by Western emphasis on efficiency, rationality, and industrialization. We need studies of processes of plaint, referral, identification, and adjudication, affecting selected mental defectives, as viewed both by the responsible persons involved and by the mental defectives and their families.[14] If such work can be undertaken on the basis of flexible conceptions such as, for example, role and status, we may see an advance in the field of mental deficiency similar to that which has recently taken place in the study of psychosis and psychotics (53, 54) and in the more general area of personality development (55, 56).

Notes

*   Read at the May, 1957, meetings of the American Association on Mental Deficiency, Hartford, Connecticut. The writer is indebted to the Kate Jackson Anthony

Trust and to Miss Anthony whose interest in the problem made the preparation of this paper possible. He is also much indebted to Dr. Ithiel Pool of Massachusetts Institute of Technology for two valuable substantive suggestions and to Dr. Leonard Duhl, National Institutes of Health, for a helpful stylistic one.

1. This article is one of a series by the writer on the sociology of mental retardation; (1) and (2)(3)(4) and the reference in footnote 14.

2. "Initiation" is used by analogy with the formal anthropological use. Miller (7) says "The prestige associated with passage through the manhood ceremonies is such that the person uninitiated is invested with complete obloquy. A child is also in an ignominious position until this event. The initiation serves as the chief vehicle to link generations in the transition of the culture complex.... The common thread essentially characteristic of all types of initialies [*sic*] lies in the integrative and subordinating tendencies of a social group to draw its members into a workable unity—a unity continually threatened *by youth or* alien." In our particular *society* persons who do not pay formal respect to the formal processes of learning are more or less alien; the degree of suspicion or estrangement varies of course by social class *or* type. (Of course on the other hand, the "egghead," the person who (allegedly) places *too much* stress upon formal learning may also be regarded as alien; one of the most difficult problems of social analysts in our society is to determine for different social groups exactly how much respect for and deference to learning is "normal."

    Of course, anthropologists have ordinarily defined initiation as referring to a "climactic and abrupt" session to social maturity, rather than as encompassing the cumulative processes, chacteristic of our educational system. (However, it might well be argued that this system in fact consists for those who find it hard or able of a series of "climactic and abrupt painful experiences, associated with tests, examinations, promotions, and the like. (See (8)) and that these periods do in fact have many of the painful, scarifying, and traumatic characteristics of primitive initiation.)

3. Of course, empirically, social and biological factors will be inextricably intermixed. Our purpose here is to try to devise a set of analytic explanations, which may help in making etiological differentiations where it may be therapeutically desirable to do so.

4. "Significant" should be here defined in terms "significant influence" as well as "significant numbers."

5. "Behavior" must be here defined very widely—"existence" is a form of behavior, and "extreme racists" may regard the mere existence of another race as per se creating a social problem. See also the literature on violent social disapproval of twins and twinning (9, 10).

6. In essence a social problem may be said to exist when a considerable number of members of society say in effect through their actions, "What you do (or are) is so bad that something ought to be done about it," in such a way that the implicit threat is regarded seriously by a good many of those engaged in the disapproved behavior and/or by a good many of those doing the disapproving.

7. The rationale underlying the attack on segregated classrooms and schools, even where facilities are equal, in the United States in recent years has been, in large measure, based upon the argument that "segregation" *per se* is discriminatory and a denial of equality of opportunity (11, 12). But see (13) for demonstration that this argument is dogmatic more than experimentally based.

8. Strickland (14), p. 510, says: "In practically all cases it can be assumed that before admission (to an institution for mental defectives) the patient has been through experiences highly charged with emotion—enforced separation from parents,

appearances in court, etc., and is finally taken to an institution where people are vaguely said to be mental, there to stay for an undefined period...." If this is not punishment, what is? The vagueness will persist and the difficulty, particularly for defectives, in knowing what they have to do to get out presumably adds to the unpleasant nature of the experience and the feeling that one must have done something wrong.

9.   We badly need "depth studies" and opinion polls of attitudes toward stupidity, dullness, and the dull; I know of none; the statement in the text is therefore based purely on impressions.

10.   Rose (6) "Theory for the Study of Social Problems" is very illuminating on this point, demonstrates the technique of learning meanings even though in fact he disregards their implications for action, is—up to a very considerable point—less likely to be regarded as a social and educational problem than an otherwise, inoffensive, socially acceptable student who is what is called, "dumb" or "stupid." That is to say, the "mean, nasty ornery" youngster does not in such a social group create nearly as much of a "social problem," as does his tractable well-adjustable age-mate capable of worthwhile physical labor, if the latter just "can't learn." We find that many mental defectives become social problem cases, even though they do in fact learn enough of the right meanings to get by because they do not demonstrate formal command of the technique of learning.

11.   The literature on the criminality of mental defectives is not particularly helpful; for a penetrating discussion see (31); Myrdal's analysis of Negro criminality (32) is probably highly relevant; we do not know if mental defectives are more predisposed to crime, more likely to be caught, more likely to be convicted if indicted, or no different from the general population.

12.   Myrdal's discussion of the analogies between the position of Negroes and of women in our society (39) could profitably be extended to the social position of mental defectives.

13.   The problem of the marginal man was apparently of more interest to sociologists a generation ago than more recently. This is partly due to a shift in emphasis in sociological theory. No doubt; but it also arises out of the fact that one generation ago it was still possible or at least seemed still possible for most people "to go home again," whereas the accelerated geographical, social, and occupational instability of the 1930s and 1940s has affected such large numbers of people that the "marginal man" *per se* does not seem as different from the rest of us as he did in 1924. But, unfortunately, this instability has increased the emphasis upon formal command of the communications skills and therefore, while normalizing the lives of many who once would have been regarded as marginal, made the high-grade retarded more marginal than they were before.

14.   Harold Mendelsohn, now of McCann-Erickson, and I in 1955 prepared a research design for such a study in Delaware and selected areas of Maryland and New Jersey.

Bibliography

1.   Dexter, L. "Towards a Sociology of the Mentally Defective," *American Journal of Mental Deficiency*, 61:10-16, 1956.

2.   Dexter, L. "Heredity and Environment reexplored; Specification of Environments and Genetic Transmission," *Eugenics Quarterly*, 3:88-93, 1956.

3.   Dexter, L. "Naming as a Social Process and the Classification of the Mentally Defective." Paper read before the 1955 (Detroit) meetings AAMD, Psychology section (may be published), dittoed, available from writer.

4. Dexter, L. "Social Processes in Studying Mental Deficiency; Selective Inattention in Social Problems; Mental Deficiency Research as a Case in Point," paper read before the American Sociological Assocation, 1956 (Detroit), may be published, mimeographed, available from writer.

5. *Social Problems: Official Journal of the Society for the Study of Social Problems,* Brandeis, U., quarterly, 1953—has more exemplifications of varying uses of this term than any other one source; the description of the conception given here varies a little from some contained therein.

6. Rose, A. "Theory for Social Problems," *Social Problems,* 4:189-99, 1957—bibliographical notes list several leading references.

7. Miller, N. "Initiation," *Encyclopedia of Social Science,* 8:19-50, 1932.

8. Dexter, L. "Examinations as Instruments of, and Obstacles to General Education," *School Review,* 55:534-41, 1947.

9. Thomas, W. I. *Primitive Behavior.* New York; McGraw-Hill, 1937, pp. 9-16.

10. The novel, by Forester, C, *The Sky and the Forest,* Little, Brown, Boston, 1948, pp. 247 ff., uses this attitude toward twinning.

11. See the decision of the U. S. Supreme Court by Warren, C.J., May 7, 1954, in Brown vs. Board of Education (Topeka, Kansas, case), overruling the doctrine of the Plessy case ("separate but equal") on the ground that "segregation in the public schools deprives . . . plaintiffs of equal protection of the laws," reprinted in full in Ashmore, H., *The Negro and the Schools,* U.N.C. Press, Chapel Hill, 1954, pp. 231-7 (decision contains references).

12. Warner, W. et al. *Color and Human Nature. American Council of Education,* Washington, DC, 1941, pp. 8-18.

13. Berger, M. "Desegregation, Law, and Social Science," *Commentary,* 23:471-477, 1957.

14. Strickland, C. "The Social Competence of the Feeble-Minded," *American Journal of Mental Deficiency,* 53: 504-515, 1948-9, p. 510.

15. Sherif, M. *Psychology of Social Norms.* New York: Harper's, 1936.

16. Piers, G. and Singer, M. *Shame and Guilt,* Springfield, IL: Chas. C. Thomas, 1953.

17. Wells, H. G. *Country of the Blind.* London: Longman's, 1947.

18. Natl. Conf. Charities and Corrections, *Feeble-Mindedness and Insanity,* 1916, 205-300.

19. Dexter, R. *Social Adjustment.* New York: Knopf, 1927, pp. 151-2.

20. See the reference to "moron" as an epithet similar to "brute" or "beast" in journalistic usage, Shaw, C. et al., *Brothers in Crime.* Chicago: U. of Chicago, 1938, p. ix.

21. Shils, E. *The Torment of Secrecy.* Glencoe, IL.: Free Press, 1956, pp. 77-89 (section on xenophobia).

22. Allport, G. *Prejudice.* Boston: Beacon, 1954. pp. 382-408.

23. "Open society" here is used as referring to a society in which there is considerable competition for achieved statuses ("a career open to the talents"). See Linton, R., *The Study of Man,* New York: Appleton, Century, 1936, pp. 115-131.

24. Charles, C. "Ability and Accomplishment of Persons Earlier Judged Mentally Deficient," *Genetic Psychogenic Monograph,* 47:9-19, 1953; review of literature; citation, p. 55 and p. 58.

25. Kennedy, R. J. R, *Social Adjustment of Morons in a Connecticut City.* Hartford, CT: Mansfield-Southbury Training Schools, 1948.

26. *Matthews, M.* "One Hundred Institutionally Trained Male Defectives in the Community Under Supervision," *Mental Hygiene.,* 6:332-42, 1922.

27.   I am indebted for awareness of this idea to personal conversations with Dr. E. Doll, 1949, 1951. He puts the notion within a general framework of mental deficiency in his valuable review, "The Nature of Mental Deficiency," *Psychological Review*, 47:395-415, 1940, on pp. 408-10, reprinted in Training School Bulletin, 1950.

28.   Stoddard, G. The Meaning of Intelligence. New York: Macmillan, 1943, pp. 241-58.

29.   Goodenough, F. *Mental Testing: Its History, Principles, and Applications.* New York: Rinchart, 1949, pp. 456-8, 463, and passim.

30.   This is a *possible* but *not* a necessary inference from such works as Binham, W., *Aptitudes and Aptitude Testing.* New York: Harper's, 2nd ed., 1937, esp. p. 155.

31.   Ferentz, E. "Mental Deficiency Related to Crime," *Journal of Crime and Criminality*, 45: 299-307, 1954.

32.   Myrdal, G. *American Dilemma.* New York: Harper's, 1944, pp. 966-79.

33.   Lindzey, G., ed. *Handbook of Social Psychology.* Cambridge, MA: Addison, Wesley, 1954, Ch. 6, by Sarbin, T., "Role Theory," pp. 223-258 (bibliog., pp. 255-8). Sarbin's otherwise brilliant survey appears to be susceptible of improvement by utilizing the notion of "transaction" (instead of interaction), introduced by (33a) Dewey, J., and Bentley, A., *The Knowing and the Known.* Boston: Beacon, 1949, and (33b) Bentley, A., *An Inquiry into Inquiries.* Boston, Beacon, 1954.

34.   Cooley, C. *Human Nature and the Social Order.* New York: Scribner's, 1902.

35.   Cooley, C. *Social Process.* New York: Scribner's, 1922.

36.   Mead, G. *Mind, Self, and Society.* Chicago: U. Chicago Press, 1934.

37.   Spykman, N. *The Social Theory of Georg Simmel.* Chicago: U. Chicago Press, 1925, esp. Ch. X, "Prerequisites of Socialization," pp. 79-87.

38.   Myrdal. Op. cit., reference 32, on Negro role-playing, pp. 27-9, 761-6, 956-66.

39.   Myrdal. Op. cit., reference 32, analysis of comparative status and roles of Negroes and women, pp. 1072-8.

40.   Stonequist, E. *Marginal Man*, New York: Russell and Russell, 1937.

41.   Forster, E. *Passage to India.* New York: Harcourt, 1924.

42.   Mercier, C. *Leper Houses and Medieval Hospitals.* London: H. Lewis, 1915.

43.   Ackernecht, E. "The Role of the Medical Historian in Medical Education," *Bulletin of the History of Medicine*, 21, esp. pp. 142-3, 1947. "Even the notion of disease itself depends on the decisions of society (rather) than on the objective facts," followed by a discussion of pinto and ague.

44.   Merrill, F. "The Self and the Other: An Emerging Field of Social Problems," *Social Problems*, 4:200-7, 1957.

45.   Park, R., and Burgess, E. *Introduction to the Science of Sociology.* Chicago: U. Chicago Press, 1921, Ch. X, "Accommodation," pp. 663-733.

46.   Saunders, L. *Cultural Differences and Medical Care.* New York: Russell Sage p. 21.

47.   Kluckhohn, C. *Navajo Witchcraft.* Cambridge, MA: Peabody Museum, 1944.

48.   Webster, H. *Tabbo, A Sociological Study.* Stanford: Stanford U. Press, 1942, pp. 82-93.

49.   Lundberg, E. (prepared). *Unmarried Mothers in the Municipal Court of Philadelphia.* Philadelphia: T. S. Harrison Foundation, 1933.

50.   Brinton, C. French Revolutionary Legislation on Illegitimacy, 1789-1804. Cambridge, MA: Harvard U., 1936.

50a. Slotkin, J. Social Anthropology, Ch. 12. New York: Macmillan, 1950.

51.   Crookshank, F., Supp. II., to Ogden, C., and Richards, I. *Meaning of Meaning*, New York: Harcourt, 1938, pp. 337-355, analyzes critically the notion that a pathological condition "has" "innate" "biological properties."

52.   Dollard, J. *Criteria for the Life History*, New Haven: Yale, 1935.

53.   Exemplified in *Psychiatry: A Journal of the Biology and Pathology of Interpersonal Relations*, Washington School of Psychiatry, 1938—.

54.   Stanton, A., and Schwartz, M. *The Mental Hospital: A Study of Institutional Participation in Psychiatric Illness and Treatment.* New York: Basic Books, 1954.

55.   Kardiner, A. *The Psychological Frontiers of Society.* New York: Columbia U., 1945.

56.   Murray, H., and Kluckhohn, C. (eds.). *Personality in Nature, Culture, and Society.* 2nd ed., New York: Knopf, 1953.

6

On the Politics and Sociology of Stupidity
in Our Society*

Why are the high grade retarded—and more generally the "dull" and stupid, slow learners of all sorts—regarded as one of the great problem groups of our society? Why is a special association devoted to mental deficiency and another set up chiefly for parents of retarded children? This inquiry is part of an effort[1] to determine whether application of a prevailing point of view in the study of social problems may be useful in thinking about stupidity. Our concern here is with what Josiah Royce[2] has described as "regulative principles of research [which may] provide the larger ideas of guidance [to] empirical investigation [but which are not in themselves subject to] precise, empirical tests; which, if they happen to prove coherent and illuminating, may provide the basis for more specific hypotheses which can be empirically tested." This prevailing point of view about social problems is based on the postulate that "social problems" are not properly or adequately defined in terms of the obvious and manifest rationalizations or explanations of them by those who experience them. Thus, Myrdal,[3] for instance, demonstrated that the problem of "race," so-called, could best be understood by analysis of *conflicting* moral values; while Wirth[4] similarly was able to show that the common-sense "explanation" of the housing dilemma in the United States in the 1930s omitted the significant *social* factors; and Davis[5] that the stigma imposed upon illegitimacy in most Western societies is subtly interrelated to neglected social institutions.

Generally, problems, ideas, and institutions are taken as given and their consequences seen as self-evident facts of nature. For decades, as is well-known, many people, white *and* Negro, saw the issues of "race relations" as self-evident. Similarly, for a century or more, statesmen and thinkers alike adopted a version of laissez-faire economics, which made mass unemployment seem absolutely natural in an industrial society. Ultimately, within the last generation, Keynesian economics clarified the conception that the 1929 type of depression is a consequence of systems and institutions, rather than a necessary product of the nature of man in industrial society. This revision of economic thought forced those of us whose economic ideas were learned before 1935 to unlearn a good deal. A similar effort at rethinking the problems of mental deficiency may be worthwhile.

An Analogy: Gawkiness as a Cardinal Social Defect: An easy way to indicate how we might reinterpret mental deficiency along these lines is by means of an analogy. Let us imagine a society in which the major target group of social discrimination is composed of the clumsy people, the so-called "gawkies." Let us assume that this is because such a society stresses grace and style in movement *as* we stress intellectual skill. Let us assume that people are taught to abhor clumsiness as many people in our society are taught to abhor stupidity. Let us suppose, to put the analogy on all fours, that there has been invented a system of writing in that society, which can only be mastered by those who are graceful; and that the technology of the society is such that a high degree of grace and skill are necessary to run its machines. This will be so, *not* because of the inherent necessities of industrial processes, but because the engineers and business men of the society arrange to have things done in a way which takes grace—as a matter of course.

The schools in such a social system would stress movement, dancing, rhythmics, etc. The psychometric institutes of the society would develop an elaborate vocabulary and even more elaborate testing mechanisms for distinguishing between *manifest* grace and inherent *potentiality* for grace of movement. A considerable literature would develop about the "pseudo-clumsy"—and in many cases, parents and schools would be so embarrassed and bothered by the presence of gawky children that they would send them to special custodial institutions where they would not be a constant reminder of parental or pedagogical inadequacy.

Naturally, under such circumstances, the marginally clumsy, permitted to remain at large in the community, would always be conscious of having two strikes already called against them. They would be liable to be institutionalized if they did anything unusual. Naturally, too, clumsy children would become social rejects and isolates, and instead of the moron jokes, beloved in this country,[6] there would probably develop pantomime jokes, directed against the gawky.

Some academic iconoclast might raise considerable doubts as to his own accuracy and academic probity by reporting that, in fact, once out of school and in those economic activities where grace of movement was not really imperative, many persons with a subnormal grace quotient (G.Q.) could earn their own living and even make an economic contribution. There would be great surprise when it was reported that some superficially or evidently clumsy persons could hunt effectively, walk competently, even play games successfully; those reporting such findings would be under considerable pressure to "explain them away." And a scholar, giving a paper with such findings at the National Association on Clumsiness, would find that the news report on her paper made her the target of many scurrilous letters, much as though she had written a Kinsey-type book.[7]

Nevertheless, under the circumstances just described, clumsiness would be regarded as pathological. And these circumstances are analogous to Western European and American attitudes towards stupidity. In making such an assertion, there is no intention to deny the reality of the social problem created by mental deficiency. In the first place, mental deficiency is a problem, or creates problems, because, in fact, there are many activities in our society which *demand* a substantial degree of verbal intelligence. As our analogy suggests, it is probable that some of these activities could be reorganized so as to lessen the problems attendant upon mental deficiency. Nevertheless, mental deficiency would still remain a problem.

But even more significantly in terms of our hypothesis, and going back to the analogy for the moment, clumsiness in our imaginary society would be a real social problem with real social consequences, for as W. I. Thomas[8] has pointed out, the way situations are defined by the society as a whole is for the people in that society the realest of realities. The mother of twins in a society which regards twin-bearing as wicked and repulsive, cannot escape from that "reality"; (nor can the mother of twins in a society which regards twin-bearing as a noble act escape from that reality either!).[9] In our imaginary society, clumsiness would be a real social problem with real consequences. It is necessary to emphasize this because it sometimes happens that if we raise questions about the one factor strictly physiological explanation of a social problem, we are interpreted as denying its reality.

But Are the Stupid Really Discriminated against and Despised? Articles by Strickland[10] and by Johnson and Kirk[11] and such studies as that by Wolfenstein[12] seem to the writer to demonstrate that indeed they are. There is also the experience, which may be observed over and over again of the denial of employment, of legal rights, of a fair hearing, of an opportunity, to the stupid because they are stupid (e.g., have a low IQ or show poor academic performance), *and not because the stupidity is relevant to the task, or claim, or situation.* A comment by one student of social problems[13] suggests that because discrimination against stupidity *per se* rarely comes to the attention of middle-class people, they ordinarily are quite unaware of it.

This objectively demonstrable, gross discrimination is of great significance. Within the actual life of most readers of these pages, however, the more subtle forms of "discrimination" against stupidity are more likely to be experienced; by analogy, few U. S. sociologists are likely to observe the type of crude anti-Semitism which occurred in medieval Europe or modern Germany: but most of them have seen gestures of withdrawal, listened to anti-Semitic jokes, etc. Unfortunately, no systematic, empirical study of attitudes towards cleverness or dullness is known to exist. As hypothesis, it is suggested that many influential people in our society—including particularly classroom teachers (the carriers par excellence of public, middle-class culture)—show more repugnance (e.g., frown and scold more often) towards stupidity than towards anything else except dirtiness.

A change appears to have taken place in these attitudes towards "stupidity" in recent years. At one time, the stupid were simply objects of derision or scorn: "Simple Simon met a pie man...." Then, in the first two decades of the twentieth century, in the United States and Great Britain at least (concurrently with the growth of mass education), the stupid were regarded with genuine fear and apprehension; "moron" became a synonym for rapist. Both attitudes closely resemble feelings which people have displayed towards foreigners: foreigners are either ridiculous *or* frightening and wicked. But nowadays, in the era of foreign aid and Point IV programs, we believe in teaching foreigners "democracy," modern technology, and other aspects of "our way of life." And, just as some of us are willing to spend a good deal of money on foreign aid, we are willing to do so on teaching the stupid *not* to be stupid.

But the one thing we often find it hard to tolerate about the foreigner is his remaining *fundamentally* alien *and wishing to do so*; and so, similarly, many with a deep interest in mental defectives, are concerned only to make them less defective, less stupid. This is a truism which is so obvious as to "go without saying," but since hardly anybody says it we do not perhaps fully realize its consequences.

Clearly, the hypotheses just advanced could be better tested by study of verbal expression, of gesture, of manner, than by analyses of overt ideology. The sophisticated modern, familiar with cultural differentiation, may not *express* his distaste for foreign ways of doing things, but he will manifest in withdrawal or frown exactly the distaste he is trying to conceal, and perhaps *is* concealing from himself.[14]

The analogy with reactions to stupidity is apparent. What needs to be determined is the degree to which the stupid are aware of the slights, contempt, and scolding to which they are exposed and how far they are affected by them in developing a self image. On the basis of available knowledge, the most plausible hypothesis seems to be that intellectual skill—skill at handling abstract conceptions—is not related to ability to perceive that one is the object of contempt; stupid people are quite as likely to suffer psychologically from contempt as are the more intelligent.[15]

The School, the Democratic Dogma, and the Glorification of Intellectual Aptitudes. But, in most societies, the stupid are not victims of the same overt discrimination as in our society. For in other societies, race, clan-membership, ancestry, religion, status, physical prowess, and probably appearance, play more of a part in determining what rewards one gets and what values one is deprived of than in ours. A stupid person with the right ancestry, for instance, can "get by" better than with us. A society which increasingly focuses on "excellence," meaning thereby intellectual excellence,[16] as does ours, tends more and more to discriminate against stupidity. This is not logically defensible. Because intellectual excellence is required of atomic physicists or for students of sociology is no reason to require intellectual prowess from people in most occupations and activities. In athletics, we admire skilled performance; but we do not[17] discriminate much more against the very incompetent athlete than against the merely mediocre performer. It seems probable that the attitude and response towards stupidity, characteristic of our society, is a function of the common school and of two interrelated ideologies, which affect that school. These ideologies are: (1) the post-Renaissance emphasis upon achievement in certain lines of activity as a justification of one's righteousness, the Protestant Ethic, and (2) the radical aspect of democratic thought, identified particularly with the French Revolution and, later, with Jacksonian democracy, with its emphasis on the rights and obligations of equality.

For our present purposes, it is needless to recapitulate the extensive literature on the Protestant Ethic, and its secular variants, as expressed for instance in "Poor Richard's Almanac."[18] It is sufficient to point out that the impact of that ethic upon those affected by it was to lead them to regard stupidity as a sin, rather than as a common human failing. For, it led to failure; and failure was a manifestation of Heavenly displeasure.

The French Revolutionary notion of equality, as it spread to the American frontier and, later, to Soviet Russia, involved not only the *opportunity* to be equal, but the *obligation* to take advantage of the opportunity to be equal. Equal opportunity for education tended to result in compulsory education; and this notion of compulsory equality was embedded in the institution of the public or common school. As Sarason and Gladwin[19] make clear, the school and its demands and instruments—the intelligence test, for instance—play a substantial part in making the high-grade retarded a problem to themselves and to society. The public school has become, under the inspiration of egalitarian democracy, the central sacred institution of the community to a good many people in our society—more in the suburbs than in the slums, more among the tepidly religious than among the fundamentalists, more for some occupations and temperaments than others.

The high-grade retarded become, in such an interpretation of the school, heretics—unwilling heretics, heretics despite themselves, but heretics nevertheless. By merely being what they are, they challenge and cast doubt upon the system through which most people have gone. If, as many of them do, they succeed in earning their own living and getting along well in the community, they are even more puzzlingly unorthodox than those who accommodate to the system by cheating their way through. For the cheat, like the medieval penitent, admits the *rightness* of the system by his short-cut method of conforming to it. But the stupid who get *along* well cast doubt on the *alleged* secular justification of the system—that it helps people succeed. It is repulsive for some to believe that mental defectives can support themselves, no matter how much evidence is amassed to this effect, because, if so, how can we justify the discomforts and sacrifices and anguish of schooling? And when a scholar reported that some mental defectives have been more successful than non-defective counterparts, it is not surprising that she received *fifty* or so scurrilous attacks; she was denying the sacred.[20]

Community Re-Organization and the Social Problem Status of the Retarded and Stupid: A Wholesaler's Approach to Vocational Placement of the Retarded. It follows from what has just been said that if "society" were reorganized, the social problem and the individual problems of the retarded would be much less serious. Clearly, "society" taken as a whole, is not going to be reorganized. But it may help to clarify the sociological nature of the problem of retardation by making the following conceivable assumption.

Suppose that a community were to be planned on the assumption that approximately 25 percent of its adults would be "feeble-minded." How should it differ from the towns and cities we actually know?

First: we would underline the point that there is no evidence that such a community would have any great economic difficulty. Verbal intelligence is necessary for administrators, accountants, attorneys, and engineers, for instance; but this intelligence is not necessary for all employees in manufacturing and service occupations *as such*. (It is, of course, necessary for these individuals as citizens, and as consumers, in the *modern* world, but it is precisely these peripheral necessities we wish to reconsider.)

The widespread use of secondary symbols—for purposes of legal contract and for borrowing money, even for such mechanical activities as reading road signs—is the heart of the problem of the stupid in our world. Accordingly, we would attempt to reorganize matters so that such symbols become less significant.[21]

In such a society, we would, necessarily, abandon our present pattern of education and even compulsory literacy. We would have to change patterns of voting and limit seriously the right to borrow and to lend on credit for consumer purchases. We would probably reorganize certain activities so that they would be conducted more on a group basis and less by individuals than is currently the case; a stupid woman as one nurse-maid among several caring for children may do an excellent job, but she lacks the adaptability and initiative to care for them *by herself*. In many old-fashioned villages, mothers, aunts, and cousins, on the whole, cared for children as a joint enterprise, so one particularly stupid woman did not necessarily cause too much trouble. Day-care centers could make it possible for our imaginary community to make similar good use of stupid, good-hearted, affectionate women to care for young children.[22]

The proposal is not purely speculative. If constitutional barriers could be overcome,[23] the organization of such a town or city (ideally on some isolatable spot, such as St. Croix or Martha's Vineyard) would permit us to find out how much of a handicap mental retardation really is (and vice versa, where verbal intelligence is essential). But even if the idea remains in the realm of speculation, it would be extremely valuable if specialists on retardation and backwardness worked out in detail what it would involve if put into practice, because this would permit us to "think out" the social meaning of these conditions in a way which has never been done.

Directions of Research. Usually, when research is started on social problems, it is based upon common-sense assumptions. The history of knowledge suggests, however, that common-sense assumptions are frequently inadequate or erroneous. Until fundamental assumptions have been critically examined, and alternatives postulated and explored, much talent and ingenuity may be wasted. The entire argument of the present paper rests on the assertion that perhaps the common-sense assumptions about mental deficiency need more criticism than they have received. One way to criticize them is to suggest alternative ways of looking at the issues as in the examples of the "gawkies" above, or the proposal in the last section for setting up a community with 25 percent retarded adults. It is very likely that the last approach is unworkable; but this is not the major point. So long as effort is devoted to formulating alternative constructions[24] and alternative formulations of the issues, there is a better prospect of resolving our problems successfully than there is if we simply stick to elementary common sense.[25] In other words, the greatest current need in mental deficiency research is the search for new, unorthodox perspectives; they can help to test the value and appropriateness of the prevailing doctrines.

Notes

*   Free-lance consultant. Financial aid was provided in the preparation of this paper by the Kate Jackson Anthony Trust of Lewiston, Maine; I also am grateful to Michael Begab (U. S. Children's Bureau), Chairman of the Section of the American Association for Mental Deficiency at which the original version of the paper was read (in 1960).

1.   Other articles in the series include: Lewis A. Dexter, "Research on Problems of Mental Subnormality," *American Journal of Mental Deficiency*, 64 (1960), 835-8; Lewis A. Dexter, "A Social Theory of Mental Deficiency," *ibid.*, 62 (1958), 920-8 (bibliog.); Lewis A. Dexter, "Towards A Sociology of Mental Deficiency," *ibid.*, 61 (1956), 10-16; Lewis A. Dexter, "The Sociology of Adjudication: Who Defines Mental Deficiency?" *American Behavioral Scientist*, 4 (October, 1960), 13-15; Lewis A. Dexter, "Heredity and Environment Re-explored," *Eugenics Quarterly*, 3 (1956), 88-93; Lewis A. Dexter, "A Note on Selective Inattention in Social Science," *Social Problems*, 6 (1958), 176-82.

2.   Josiah Royce "Introduction" to Henri Poincare, *The Foundations of Science*, New York: Science Press, 1921, pp. XIV-XXI.

3.   G. Myrdal, *American Dilemma*, New York: Harper's, 1944.

4.   L. Wirth, *Contemporary Social Problems*, Second Edition, Chicago: University of Chicago Press, 1940.

5.   K. Davis, "Illegitimacy and the Social Structure," *American Journal of Sociology*, 45 (1939), 215-33.

6.   M. Wolfenstein, *Children's Humor, A Psychological Analysis* (esp. the chapter on the moron joke), Glencoe, IL: Free Press, 1954.

7.   This actually happened in the field of mental deficiency.

8.   W. I. Thomas and F. Znaniecki, *Polish Peasant in Europe and America*, New York: Knopf, 1927.

9.   W. I. Thomas, *Primitive Behavior*, New York: McGraw-Hill, 1937, pp. 9-18. (The three articles by Dexter, cited in footnote 1, which were published in American

Journal of Mental Deficiency, expand the relevance of Thomas' theory of "definition of the situation" to the social role of the retarded.)

10. C. Strickland, "The Social Competence of the Feeble-Minded," *American Journal of Mental Deficiency*, 1949, 53:504-15.

11. G. O. Johnson and S. Kirk, "Are Mentally Handicapped Children Segregated in The Regular Grades?" *Journal of Exceptional Children*, 1950, 17:65-8.

12. *Op. cit.*

13. On my article dealing with the judicial treatment of alleged mental defectives, *American Behavioral Scientist, op. cit.*

14. Edward T. Hall, *The Silent Language*, Garden City, NY: Doubleday, 1959, shows how unspoken Latin-American and Anglo-American reactions to the emhrazo, for instance, and the degree of physical distance it is appropriate to maintain, color many transcultural relationships. The type of analysis, which underlies Hall's entire argument could most profitably be applied to the sphere of disapproval.

15. A particularly perceptive social scientist who has had some contact with retardates, was much surprised at this hypothesis: he had assumed that sensitiveness to slight and intelligence go together. No doubt, the definition or recognition of slights depends upon intelligence: a stupid person may notice the praise and not the damnation in being "damned with faint praise," but this and similar facts do not in all probability permit the stupid to live according to the widely accepted stereotype of "the happy moron ... who does not give a damn."

16. Many stupid would be better off if we attached more weight to moral excellence: "Be good, sweet child, let who will be clever."

17. Some groups of young males may, in fact, make such a distinction; but it is not a norm for the society as a whole.

18. M. Weber, *Protestant Ethic and The Spirit of Capitalism*, New York: Scribner's, 1948.

19. S. Sarason and T. Gladwin, "Psychological and Biological Problems in Mental Subnormality: A Review of Research," *American Journal of Mental Deficiency*, 63 (1958), 1115-1307 (reprinted from Genetic Psychology Monographs, 1958, and in S. Sarason, *Psychological Problems of Mental Deficiency*, Third Edition, New York: Harper's, 1959).

20. Fortunately for the stupid, the eccentric, and the unorthodox, we are not consistent in our acceptance of the sacredness of schooling. There are reservations and ambiguities, which permit loopholes for escape and accommodation. This is presumably always true of attitudes towards the sacred.

21. See Lewis A. Dexter, *American Journal of Mental Deficiency*, 1958, *op. cit.*

22. Another example: in the nineteenth century, in a large house with several servants, one stupid maid might be very useful. Nowadays, most large houses have only one maid, and she is expected to write down telephone messages, cope with door-to-door salesmen, and otherwise manifest verbal intelligence.

23. Real barriers are constitutional, and for the idea to become practical, a very careful study of constitutional law as it affects proposals of this sort would have to be made. This fact is extremely ironic, because in reality, as I have pointed out in my article in *American Behavioral Scientist, op. cit.* (and as the National Council for Civil Liberties has demonstrated in great detail in Great Britain), under present circumstances, retardates do not receive the benefits of due process. Nevertheless, we can be reasonably certain that a formal proposal of the sort here made would, in the present temper of the Courts and especially of the U. S. Supreme Court, be regarded as depriving stupid citizens of essential rights (even though these citizens do not, in practice, get the opportunity to exercise many of these rights).

24.   The ideas in the present paper were in part stimulated by the theory of postulation, by the theory of naming and by the transactional approach of the late Arthur F. Bentley in his *An Inquiry into Inquiries*, Boston: Beacon Press, 1954, and also *Behavior ... Knowledge ... Fact*, Bloomington, IN: Principia Press, 1935. Mr. Bentley in correspondence with me indicated that he thought the present effort a satisfactory application of his approach.

25.   It may very well be that there is a brain damage affecting all mental defectives, not otherwise physiologically abnormal, and that this will ultimately be ascertained. Even supposing this to be so, the brain damage is not necessarily the important point. To the medieval leper, the sociology of leprosy was often more important than its pathology; to the contemporary homosexual, employed by a Federal agency, the sociology of attitudes towards homosexuality is far more significant than the physiological basis (if any) of his deviation; and so, to the "garden variety" mental defective, attitudes towards his affliction may matter more than its genesis. It might, indeed, also be literally true that the exceptionally clumsy or awkward also suffer from some form of brain damage; but, in our imaginary society, postulated above, the social psychology affecting clumsiness would be far more vital to them than the physiology of their situation.

7

The Sociology of the Exceptional Person*

I

Our concern is with "devices and instrumentalities for adjusting the (exceptional) individual to cultural situations." Since the school, teaching, etc., are the most consciously planned of such devices, a major concern will be with educational systems and learning processes.

We start out with the awareness that in many societies devices planned and designed to help individuals to adjust to cultural situations have, in fact, increased or even created difficulties of adjustment. The great value of historical and anthropological study is that it calls such dangers vividly to attention. Magic and witchcraft, we all realize, were often dysfunctional; they hurt rather than helped the individual and created new difficulties to add to old ones; so also, the history of medical practice shows many dogmas, such as indiscriminate bleeding, hostility to night air, and long-enduring attitudes towards leprosy, which made adjustment harder rather than easier.

And it is now widely recognized that the helpfulness and sacrifice of many parents in the United States a few years ago was overdone—that the sick, the blind, the crippled, the disfigured, find adjustment and a satisfactory life easier if they are not forced to adopt the role and status of the person who must always be helped.

II

Definition: An exceptional person for present purposes is any one who is an exception in substantial degree to the following expectations, which are held by most people in modern societies:

(1) We expect that exposure to the learning processes of our society will make a noticeable difference in demonstrated skill in using words, numbers, "abstract ideas," etc.

(2)   We expect that aptitude for using words and calculating, plus education, will correlate with occupational success and with the ability to manage one's own affairs in such a way as to avoid "getting into trouble with" community agencies, courts, welfare departments, credit companies, etc.

III

The first thing we need to know is: When and where does it make a difference to be educated and intelligent or to be stupid and retarded? Most of the so-called "evidence," which permits us to think that we know the answer to this question is fallacious for one or more of the following reasons:

(a) It only proves that for some kinds of activities intelligence and education are indispensable. But this hardly needs to be argued. It is clear that atomic physicists or readers of the poetry of T. S. Elliot must be intelligent and educated. The question at issue is whether most people in most activities in a society need to be particularly intelligent or particularly educated. O'Connor and Tizard (x),[1] Perry (X),[2] Dexter[3] and Sarson and Gladwin[4] have all suggested that, in fact, there is substantial evidence that retardation as such provides no particular barrier to economic and social competence.

(b) Another frequent error is simply one of logic. Someone demonstrates or asserts that "education" and "intelligence" are good things and, therefore, concludes that the inability to acquire education is a very bad one. In most fields, this fallacy of the converse would need no attention; we all agree that strength, agility, gracefulness, perfect pitch, and pleasant vocal tone are desirable. But we do not humiliate and penalize those who lack one or another of these characteristics as we humiliate and penalize those who lack intelligence.

(c) The greatest fallacy, however, of educational research and research on the experiences of exceptional children is the hardest to avoid. On the average, in our society, for most purposes, retardation does in actual fact constitute a severe handicap and intelligence confers great advantages. But that is no more—and let me emphasize, no less—meaningful than to say that in the United States in 1946 Negro ancestry and Negroid features and appearance constituted a severe handicap. And so, on the average, in almost any activity Negroes in the United States failed more often and succeeded less often than other people.

Society, that is, creates the situation of "self-fulfilling prophecy." Put in abstract terms, this means that it is at least as likely that social problems are due to the properties and characteristics of a given social structure as that they are due to the properties and characteristics of the individuals or class of individuals who are generally believed to create the problem.

IV

Sarason and Gladwin[5] show what is for reasons of time our most pressing need. In Western European Society, and in societies which have imitated our industrial patterns, one of the culture traits which go with our form of industrialization appears to be contempt for what may be roughly called "stupidity," and deference for "intelligence." But we have no evidence that in all societies such attitudes prevail. What we badly need to know, then, is: what does it mean to be intelligent or stupid, "bright" or retarded, in societies, which have not yet borrowed the Western European industrial culture patterns, and which are still fully functioning as organic societies?

Margaret Mead[6] showed in her study of adolescence in Samoa that many characteristics, which Americans tend to think arise out of the physiology of adolescence, were not present among Samoan adolescents, because in Samoa the process of growing up was so different from the American. Similarly, it would be most remarkable if intelligence and brightness have at all the same meaning in the Peruvian Amazon or New Guinea as they do in modernized groups, it is quite possible indeed that archaic groups removed from the main stream of industrial development—Canary Islanders, Laplanders, or people in the mountains of Jamaica—have not developed the same values as to intelligence and stupidity, which we "moderns" have, and that therefore their societies affect the intelligent and the stupid differently from ours.

Time is of the essence in making such studies, for there is a very real danger that the airplane, and Point Four programs, etc., will shortly destroy the unique and special life patterns of these separate groups and draw them within the modern industrial framework. So, first priority for any studies of the exceptional person and basic learning process, etc., must be given to other societies before they vanish as separate entities. Indeed, our need for acquiring information about such matters as this in these societies is so great that we ought to establish an International Cross-Cultural Biennium—a two-year period, something like the International Geophysical Year, in which all qualified and available scholars are given every opportunity to study societies which are rapidly disappearing and merging.

V

Any particular society, so far as the available evidence goes, tends to focus upon and emphasize one sort of learning process rather than another. American anthropologist, Edward T. Hall, points out: "In different cultures, people learn to learn differently. Some do so by memory and rote without reference to (what we call) logic, while some learn by demonstration....The Japanese even guide the hand of the pupil while our teachers usually are not permitted to touch the other person.

"On Truk, in the South Pacific, children are permitted to reach the age of nine...before anyone begins to get technical with them about what they are supposed to know... Americans (on the other hand) tend to correct children rather impatiently. With us, the person who learns fast is valued over the one who learns slowly. Some cultures seem to place less emphasis on speed ..."[7]

Now, it is perfectly possible that a particular set of learning processes will work fairly well with most people in a society but with others, because of such deviances as genetically derived low intelligence, work rather badly. It may be that cultural systems which stress speed are particularly bad for the retarded. Impressionistically, I would be reasonably certain that a culture which places a good deal of emphasis on learning things at five or six or measures intelligence at those or younger ages is certainly likely to harm the retarded more than a Trukese type society. By way of parallel, suppose that some society placed great emphasis on speed in running, it is quite possible that the children who were slow in physical development, might acquire such a fixed negative self-picture of themselves as "poor runners" at age six that they could never recover from it, whereas in American society a poor runner at six may run rapidly at sixteen.

Or, it may very well be that some society has developed a way of encouraging abstract thought, which would be far more helpful in turning bright but very impatient youngsters to scientific reflection than our customary methods of exposition or demonstration.

Indeed, we could find that our entire notion of talent is far too limited—that many children who are mediocre or worse, confronted with our learning processes have great possibilities if we teach them in a Hopi or Iranian fashion—just for example.

VI

We need also a codification of the fundamental impressionistic folklore of different societies about intelligence, education, schooling, brightness, and mental defect. Despite the fact that folklore is often in error, it is also often—as recent revivals of folk medicine seem to indicate—suggestive and stimulating.

VII

A reasonable approach which brings us back to our general concern with the sociology of the exceptional person and a basis for educational research is this: Genetic factors may determine the way in which people can learn, through influencing what we call "temperament," that is to say, attention span, the way in which hearing takes place, perception mechanisms, perhaps the forms of memory and the "storing" of information. In some cases, the genetic determination of such factors is so great that individuals cannot learn under the conventional assumptions and patterns to which they are likely to be exposed in a given society. But since there are other ways of learning, and other content of learning, it is quite possible—indeed likely—that individuals who are actually unfitted for learning in one society, who are retardates there, may not be unfitted for learning in another.

VIII

The paper was prepared for a workshop on the "Sociological Aspects of Mental Retardation." But much of what has been said—deliberately and consciously—has dealt with people who are not retarded at all, and my subtitle is "Ways of looking at Educational Research." For we should stress that there is no special kind of research theory or, for the most part, not even any special kind of research technology, which distinguishes research on high-grade retardation from research on other sociological and educational matters. The problems which face us—motivation, transfer of training, etc.—in the educational field are the same problems which face researchers in education elsewhere. Indeed, it is quite possible that the separation of research in retardation from other researches in education and sociology has been one of our greatest handicaps.

Our research demands an initial philosophical willingness to consider the possibility that traditional values are contradictory and dysfunctional; without a willingness to consider the possibility that the fundamental sources of the problem of high-grade retardation lies in the conflict between the insistence upon forcing everybody to be academically equal, or at least to expose themselves to the opportunity for intellectual equality, and the facts of personality difference, we are not going to get any great benefit out of sociological research on high-grade retardation. To be sure, we will get comfortable studies labeled "sociological" in the periphery of the problem, or dealing with the treatment of the severely retarded, but they will be largely irrelevant to the central issue of "adaptation" to retardation.

The point is: sociological research is often by itself of little use; to solve problems demands, also, a—willingness to reconsider deeply-felt values. The reverse may also be true. The willingness to reconsider values may be useless without implementing research. Remembering

Immanuel Kant's famous remark, "The percept without the concept is blind: the concept without the percept is empty," let us say: "Research-based knowledge without the flexible-mindedness to realize that it may imply reconsideration of basic values is blind: the flexible-mindedness which would permit the reconsideration of basic values without any supporting research data is empty."

But following what has just been said, the final point is that in the seemingly practical field of mental retardation, we need to subsidize and underwrite and encourage and listen to political and social philosophy, just as much as we need to develop field research studies. The two should go together; but in view of the greater likelihood that government will finance empirical field studies, it would perhaps be appropriate for private associations and foundations to concentrate on financing the opportunity for political and social reflection—bearing in mind in both cases that the wider the perspective, the broader the framework, the greater the likelihood of valuable results.

Notes

*   This paper was read before the Massachusetts Association for Retarded Children May 27, 1961. Dr. Dexter is Executive Director, Committee on Space Efforts & Society, American Academy of Arts and Sciences, Boston; Formerly Research Director to Governors Volpe and Furcolo of Massachusetts; Consultant, 1949— Kate Jackson Anthony Trust for benefit of "those of God's children known as the feeble-minded." Fellow, American Association on Mental Deficiency and American Sociological Association.

1.   N.O'Connor and J. Tizard, *The Social Problem of Mental Deficiency*, Pergamon Press, London, 1956, estimate (P. 130) that probably four fifths of those now called "feebleminded" can live in financial and social independence.

2.   S. Perry, "Some Theoretic Problems of Mental Deficiency and Their Action Implications," *Psychiatry*, 17 (1954) 45-73.

3.   See, "A Social Theory of Mental Deficiency" *American Journal of Mental Deficiency*, 62 (1958) 920-5, bibliog; "Towards a Sociology of the Mentally Defective." American Journal of Mental Deficiency, 1956 (61) 10-16; "Sociology of Adjudication; who decides who is mentally defective" American Behavioral Scientist, Oct. 1960, 4, 13-15.

4.   S. Sarason and T. Gladwin "Psychological and Cultural Problems in Mental Subnormality: A Review of Research," *American Journal of Mental Deficiency*, 62 (1958) 1113-1307.

5.   Ibid.

6.   "Coming of Age in Samoa," Morrow, New York, 1928.

7.   E. T. Hall, The Silent Language, Fawcett Premier (paperback), New York, 1961, pp. 53-5.

8

Toward a Sociological Analysis of Policy:[1]
Relevance ... Attention ... Perspective*

I

For several years, I have been struggling with some problems of policy analysis. It took me a while to see[2] that my notions of what policy "is" were too confused and vague[3] to enable me to handle these problems.[4] In particular, I have ultimately come to recognize that any given "policy" is in a constant state of change, or at any rate flux, but that I lacked the ability to discuss policy changes[5] in any disciplined way. This paper is a result of my efforts[6] to struggle with this awareness—justified by the consoling words of Richard Clissold, "Weak as we are, others are weaker."[7]

There is always, of course, the possibility that when we strike a widely-used term, which is not clarified, that we are simply encountering a convenient, denotative, library-classification label, which it would be absurd to try to make clear. In this instance, my efforts are doing without the word suggest to me that there are some reasonable solid meanings here if we but knew how to make them lucid.

As a tentative indication of what the term suggests: policy might be described as *expected or characteristic institutional practices, involving the allocation of significant values (positive or negative, of course) and/or the procedures by which such values may be allocated*. The word "practice" is probably the key word here. It suggests that a policy is not, in this sense, simply or merely or chiefly a rule—the first response of the analytic philosophers whom I happen to have asked about the topic has been that policy is more or less synonymous with rule. At least, practice excludes the sense of rule in the sense of formal or sanctioned law: "you must do this because it is the rule" or "you must do this because it is the law." Practice may also exclude rule in the sense of scientific law, whether contingent or absolute. "The second practice of thermodynamics" at any rate sounds somewhat awkward. Policy, in the sense of the quasi-definition just suggested, refers to the type of behavior, the pattern, which surrounds certain kinds of events in institutional life, when, as, and if these institutions perform in the way in which a reasonable man, familiar with complex institutions in complex societies, may reasonably expect them to perform. It is obvious from the preceding sentence that policy can not be determined by snapshot observations over a brief period since it refers to repeated practices—and in fact policy refers to the generalization or distillation of such practices on the basis of a historical record, or from a series of observations over time.

It will become apparent, if it is not already so, that I am not at all satisfied with my way of tackling the notion of policy; I hope that my attempt here may suggest improvements. As it is, however, the normal political science use of the term goes quite undefined—for reasons suggested below, this does in a sense permit us the feeling of having our cake and eating it, too; but, for the long-range development of our awareness, this feeling should probably be chastened, more than it is.

It would be possible to interpret what I have just said as defining policy as simply characteristic political *behavior*. The trouble with emphasizing the behavior in this context has, I think, been indicated by David Braybrooke.[8] In much social science discussion, behavior or a behavioral record refers to what can be inferred from external observation entirely.

Behavior, to oversimplify, tends to assume that we may use the same technique to *study men as to study rats*. Of course, human life can, *for some purposes*, be studied entirely externally. But Braybrooke emphasizes that it is convenient, at least, to distinguish occasions when we are studying human beings behaviorally, in this sense, from occasions in which the *meaning* of a situation to the persons being studied is significant. In the study of policy, policy formation, policy analysis, it seems to me that we are very much involved in the interpretation of meanings.

At the same time, and this will become extremely significant in the argument which follows, *policy ought not to be presented or analyzed simply from the standpoint of actors*. We want, that is, an objective (or reasonably objective) method of reporting on the development of meanings. Social scientists have, sometimes—notably in the field of anthropology, through such notions as culture—succeeded in studying meaning and meanings objectively.[9] But, the currently common vocabulary of policy analysis—with such terms as decisions, choice, and development[10]—confines us to the kinds of meanings, which the actors themselves have formulated.

As a sheer intuition, without any way, which I have yet been able to figure out, of testing the hypothesis: I would further suggest that the recent popularity of the term "policy" and the notion "policy analysis" can be interpreted in light of the tension within political scientists between an effort to be "behavioral" (in some sense, neutrally scientific) and a desire to be what is in popular academic life called "relevant," that is to engage in the meaningful interpretation of actions.

Apparently, policy and its various derivatives started to become popular about 1963[11]—in the last two or three years, I believe I have met several persons who proclaim their particular skill or concern to be "policy analysis." I have even met two or three sophisticated department chairmen who allege that skill at policy analysis is the unifying factor in their departments. Such works as those of Bauer, Drohr, Lindblom et al, and the titles of conference sessions (including this one) and papers suggest the popularity of the term. In a rather magisterial set of articles, Polsby and Greenstein have commissioned a number of papers on whatever policy is.[12]

The personal advantage of "policy" terms is that they permit us at one and the same time to *sound* "relevant" and "behavioristic." The question is whether they permit us at one and the same time to *be* both relevant and behavioristic. It is this question, among others, which seems to me to justify the present paper—and whether or not it justifies the paper, it certainly ought to justify efforts to learn what it is (if anything) we are talking about. How, if at all, does policy analysis differ from political philosophy as practiced by, e.g., Edmund Burke or journalistic commentary, as engaged in by Walter Bagehot or Walter Lippmann? What technological differences distinguish policy analysis (as the term is presently used) from other kinds of political analysis? If there is no necessary difference between what we nowadays think of as policy analysis, and Burke's *Reflections on the French Revolution* or his speech on conciliation with America, what "insight" does the policy term give us?

As in obiter dictum, I would suggest that although Burke was engaged in policy analysis, and so has Lippmann, that the final products of Locke, Aristotle, Mill, and, for the most part, Merriam and Lasswell are not in the particular sense of Burke and Lippmann, best described as policy analysis. No doubt, however, study of the underlying polemical orientations of many writers would show a basic policy analysis even though this is not manifest in the actual text as clearly as in Burke or Lippmann.

II

There are some other things which policy is not. Perhaps the most important of these is this: A policy is very rarely the optimum or ideal preferences of any of those engaged in political action. Herbert Simon has supplied us with a key notion here—that of "satisficing."[13] If a conflict, or potential conflict situation is resolved—in the sense that a generally accepted policy is agreed to by most of those who could have or did participate in the conflict—it is relatively rare that immediately the resolution will be optimum to most of those involved. Accommodation and compromise are inevitable to concomitants of the resolution of conflict—so few persons are likely to find an outcome, whatever it may be, ideally satisfactory. They get, not something they really prefer, if they had their ideal choice, but simply something they can live with—often what is in itself, intrinsically, tolerable, rather than, in itself, desirable. (Of course, because order is regarded as highly desirable and therefore, it is regarded as worth sacrificing other desirable things in order to achieve it.)

The fact that policies are tolerable rather than really desirable is reflected in the common aspersion of "policy" and "politics" as opportunistic, cunning, unadmirable; the fact that a good many people have not thought through the characerically satisficing character of policy resolutions is to be found, on the other hand in the frequency with which people term something "policy" which is in fact simply an expression of an ideal.[14] Much of the present student[15] movement (like, for instance, the early Christian movement) appears to be fundamentally opposed to policy of any sort in the sense in which the latter is here discussed.

Indeed, the different and contradictory usages of the word may be suggested by the background of the resolution adopted at the American Political Science Association annual convention in 1968, wherein the journals of the association were instructed to pay more attention to policy-oriented articles. To some supporters of the resolution, policy may have meant much what is here suggested; to others, for sure, it meant about the same thing as ideology. But the very vagueness of the term could permit the resolution to be supported for rather different reasons.

There are a number of similarly vague terms—such as opinion and attitude. For purposes of the present discussion, and without any historical warrant of which I know, I will distinguish *opinion* here from *policy preference*. That is to say, I am arbitrarily defining opinion as that which people would rather have, left to themselves—the equivalent of whatever the buyer regards as the truly fair buying price or the seller regards as the truly fair selling price in economics. Whereas *policy preference* is, also arbitrarily, defined as referring to what the individual(s) in question regard as a livable accommodative arrangement, which will permit a resolution of whatever the conflict situation is.

Much of the discussion hereafter concentrates on the somewhat more limited area of policy preferences and their formation and change, rather than upon the broader question of the nature of policy in general. However, I believe that discussion of the one will help illuminate the other; and in many instances, what is true of the one is true of the other. However, I would like to emphasize that one of the numerous sources of confusion, which I had to disentangle in beginning to get any sort of handle on the issues involved, lay here. For a couple of years, I was as I now look back, talking sometimes about actual shifts in policy, sometimes about shifts in policy preferences, and I should have distinguished the one from the other.

There are a number of reasons why it is difficult, empirically and analytically, to separate policies from policy preferences or the latter from opinions. Policies, once established and accepted, often acquire a patina of tradition or even sacredness, and are then regarded as optimal—although it is clear, historically, that to begin with they were merely satisficing agreements. The United States constitution was originally a policy preference or set of policy preferences, quite sub-optimal to most of those who in fact defended the adoption of the written document. But, as administrated[16] into practice, by national leaders of all sorts, from Hamilton and Washington on, it came to be widely regarded as very close to an ideal.

Much the same sort of thing has happened to many other policy agreements—the Emancipation Proclamation, at one time, and the Monroe Doctrine, at one time, are cases in point. And all this really means is that what was a policy preference may become a policy and the policy, established, may in turn become a tradition and sacred institution. Which is to imply that the historical context is vital in recognizing whether a given point of view is an opinion or a policy preference (or something else).

Another reason why it is difficult to distinguish opinions from policy preferences is the fact that a good many people when asked for an opinion really reply in terms of a policy preference. By analogy, and most fortunately, many people when asked who their candidate is for a given office do not reply with the name of an ideal holder, but with the name of that person, *among those given a chance of being nominated or elected*, whom they prefer. Similarly, many people, asked something about government or politics, reply, not in terms of what they want or regard as best, but with what they regard as the best *practically-acceptable* solution.[17]

On a good many issues, many respondents do not care enough to have an opinion at all in the sense in which the term is used here; they only have a policy preference. And a good many people who are politically active—whether in the politics of government or of some institution—are typically pre-occupied with the brokerage of ideals[18] so that they react to almost any issue or question in terms of this role conception. That is to say, their immediate response is in terms of policy preferences, not in terms of opinion.

Some people are so "other-directed" in this special sense that it is quite hard to find out what their opinions, as the term is defined here, are. It may even be hard for themselves to find out.[19] On many issues, indeed, they may have only policy preferences. It is also the case that a good many people talk in a kind of *bargainer's policy preference*—that is, they do not give us either an opinion or a true policy preference, but they express a preference, which could be the basis of bargaining in the direction which they favor. With most people, who express one, under most circumstances, it is reasonable to suppose that the *bargainer's policy preference* is intended to be incrementally different from their real policy preference in the direction of their opinion. But this is by no means necessarily the case; there are extremely subtle and complex definitions of bargaining situations. And, in any case, their intention may not be realized in practice, because they miscalculate bargaining practice.

It would be highly desirable and mark a real step forward in the study of politics if public opinion polls could be constructed or analyzed with such considerations as the foregoing in mind. How many so-called opinions are actually policy preferences? What calculations about policy are made by what kind of people? Roper, for instance, in 1952 asked a series of questions about taxes; it turned out that people who condemned taxes as such were much less unfavorable towards them if reminded of what would have to be given up if certain taxes were not imposed. But such efforts to distinguish opinions (absolute or idealized preferences) from policy preferences are rather unusual in theoretically organized work.

III

The distinction between policy preferences on the one hand and opinions on the other has implications for a good many political science studies. Because I failed to formulate it, there is an unnecessary weakness in an article of mine called "The Representative and His District."[20]

Although this article has been reprinted at least a dozen times and cited probably a couple of hundred, no one has to my knowledge commented on the weakness.

A major theme of the article is that members of Congress are partially free from much of what is called pressure. They can, I assert, evade or contravene or disregard many loudly-expressed demands from constituencies and supposedly powerful "pressure-groups." I failed completely to realize that, except in the particular instance discussed below, there must be a strong tendency towards such freedom in any complicated *and working* political system. The fact is that the Congressional institution as a system serves to brokerage preferences and ideals—that is to say, the Congressional institution, by the mere fact that it functions, must reach satisficing results in typical cases. Final, or relatively final legislative action is likely to be policy-oriented, satisficing, etc. Therefore, its is unlikely that it will express the optimum preferences or demands of any given group of constituents on a particular issue, or the optimum preferences of any interest group. Because the system is geared towards producing such satisficing results—must probably produce them in general if it is to remain workable in a society in which there are an indefinite and rather large number of conflicting aspirations and desires—it follows that in some way or other it must make it possible for those who finally resolve conflicts (whoever they may be) to disregard in part many of the demands made of them. That is, presumably, more or less equally true of any other workable political system; Labor back-benchers in Great Britain, still committed to the ideals of the party, may complain or grumble about the insincerity and half-heartedness of the Cabinet or the hostility and contravention of the civil service (until such time as they themselves are promoted to ministerial responsibility, when, presumptively, they learn better).

Of course, it does not follow that *all* members can exercise freedom from all constituents or all pressure groups; and it does not follow that all who could do so, in fact do so. All that is necessary is for enough members to be prepared, at key times and places, to reach satisficing agreements. In a good many cases, members of Congress profess themselves to be (and many probably actually believe themselves to be) tyrannized over by a subject-matter committee, the Appropriations Committee or the Rules Committee; when, in fact, the existence of committee power actually serves as a means of permitting the average member to release himself from responsibility for satisficing suboptimal action. Committees are simply an illustration; there are of course numerous other ways, some of them much less evasive, by which members can free themselves from pressure.

Of course, if various interest groups were to negotiate a compromise prior to Congressional action, and actually all faithfully push for this compromise, then the Congress might not be free. Such instances no doubt take place; but they are not particularly common as regards the Federal Congress.

IV

I have described elsewhere the greatest difficulty with talking about policy actions and policy preferences.[21] "For any given 'policy-maker' or set of 'policy-makers' in any central 'decision-making' body such as Congress, there is an indefinite and very large number of significant demands ..." Most of the time, most writers, analysts, and thinkers concentrate on one particular demand or set of demands—as Bauer, Pool, and I did in the initial formation of our trade study, later reported in *American Business and Public Policy*. To be sure, in the course of our study, we did learn and in our book we emphasized the number of other demands on members of Congress, and the stark impossibility, because time is short, of any given member paying much attention to most of these demands.[22] Although we do suggest that the businessmen and labor leaders who were to a substantial degree responsible for what is called "decision-making" on reciprocal trade were similarly beset by other demands for attention, the argument would have been stronger if we had made this parallel quite explicit.[23]

But, in both these books, my colleagues and I confined ourselves to those demands for attention, which were, so to speak, semi-processed—which had some kind of legitimacy, either from the operations of the institutional system, or from the individual's conceptions of his particular role obligations as a result of his position within the system. A good example of the latter kind of demand is the concern with patronage which many politicians have, often quite beyond what any rational analysis of election chances would dictate; I have, for instance, been told by some one who may very well know (and it is highly plausible) that, during the period of the Cuban missile crisis, John F. Kennedy himself actually spent the equivalent of more than a working day, on the appointment to a postmastership in a medium-sized New England city. (One assumes this was not, for him, sheer relaxation—the equivalent of golf or detective stories.)

V

1. Now, for understanding the formation and change of policy from the standpoint of individuals, it is quite adequate to know to what they pay attention, more or less consciously. But if one wants to understand the whole ball of wax, the formation of policies as a social process, more is needed. One must also have some idea of what is not paid attention to, what is overlooked, what is never realized at all. Quite aside form any other circumstances, it can very reasonably be argued:from a theoretical standpoint, that we can not very well interpret what is attended to, until we have some way of comparing it with what is not attended to.

2. From a practical standpoint that some of the great historic mistakes—perhaps most of them—have arisen because office-holders and so-called decision-makers were unaware of events, which were going on, which, in the end, made all the difference. It seems historically probable that Leox and his advisors were only vaguely attentive to the discontent of religious people in Germany and that British ministers in the 1750s were unaware of some of the most important aspects of colonial protests. And memory alone will serve for many of us: very few persons indeed, even five years ago, were attentive to the disutilities of economic growth, the costs of technology, what we now recognize, belatedly, as the ecological problem.

3. And, generally, a great deal of political debate, so-called, is actually not debate in any logical sense, on agreed-upon premises, but more exactly involves an attempt to get one's opponents to pay attention to circumstances, facts, situations, developments, which they are not attending to. For our immediate purposes here, it makes no difference whether such circumstances, events, facts, and developments are validly reported or not, or whether their relevance is correctly seen; it is just as possible to try to get one's opponents to pay attention to untrue or irrelevant "facts" as to true and relevant ones. Indeed, the problem would be quite simple if most political rhetoric involved the presentation of true and relevant assertions; but since much rhetoric is sophistic and demagogic, each particular assertion is properly regarded with skepticism. (It might also be pointed out that a very high proportion of non-political debate—between husbands and wives, for instance—involves the attempt to get one's opponent to pay attention to something he is not paying attention to.)

One way to begin to try to understand the relationship of attention to policy has been suggested, again, by Herbert Simon. Political *and business* leaders are, from one point of view, properly regarded as information-processing mechanisms.[24] But, in terms of any conceivable situation, at least in our present society,[25] the information available to any such person is far greater than he can process. Now, among the bits of information available to him, potentially at least, are demands, in the broadest sense of that term, about something to be done. These demands may also be (a) contingent (b) potential or (c) internally determined. That is to say, contingent demands are those which the leader believes will be made if certain events happen—and among the events which may happen is the granting of some demands previously made. (So, for instance, if pay raises, demanded by, e.g., policemen are granted, something which may seem right and proper to a given mayor, then pay raises, similar in percentage, may be demanded by firemen, sanitation-workers, and school teachers.) Potential demands may be those which will arise and will be a problem if they happen; certainly, had Walpole or Pelham been able to foresee in the 1740s the demands of the American colonies, in the 1760s they might have felt it worth while doing something.[26] And internal demands are those created by the personal inclinations of the individual leader—which may in a particular case exert great importance.[27] In fact, demands are ordinarily[28] so numerous, potentially, that any given leader attends only to a small fraction of the total available bits of information.

As a reasonable leading hypothesis—perhaps somewhat to exaggerate, in order to make a point which is generally overlooked in discussions of leadership, management, choice, and decision-making—*the most important determinant of people's policy preferences is what bits of information they attend to and how they attend to them.* I am not by any means sure that this approach will stand up under rigorous and careful examination; but at worst, I strongly suspect efforts to work out its consequences will modify the standard methods of analysis to be more realistic.

For instance, if the approach has any validity, the notion of decision-making is rather misleading—in the sense that many decisions are determined and predictable as soon as one knows what the so-called decision-maker has attended to. About eighteen months ago, when I first started working seriously on this paper, I was sufficiently impressed by this notion so that I put forward the idea in seemingly paradoxical form: Decisions are not decided by the deciders; they are decided for them by what they attend to, and what they attend to is, of course, a consequence of many factors of which most deciders are unaware. So, at that time, I said: *Decisions are not decided, choices are not chosen, in the active sense of the verbs, but they happen, are reached, are arrived at.*

It is probably more accurate, and certainly safer, to suggest rather that so-called decisions could in principle at least be classified along a continuum. The continuum would start with cases where all that one needs to know to "understand" the process of decision-reaching is the factors actually evaluated by the "decision-maker"—where the common-sense notion of decision-making would be adequate for understanding. But it would extend all the way to cases at the other end of the continuum where significant understanding of the development of policy preferences rests largely upon knowing what the so-called "decision-maker" attended to and knowing, also, what he neglected or refused to attend to; in such instances, the decision-maker's objective view of the process would only be of limited helpfulness for purposes of understanding. It is probable that far more cases of decision-reaching would be closer to the second pole than to the first, depending, of course, on the purposes of the analysis and the wisdom and information of the analyst.

It should, of course, be emphasized here that we are talking chiefly about policy *preferences* reached by so-called decision makers. However, in actual fact, *policies* are usually reached, not by a process of one-man action, but by an explicit or implicit process of bargaining between persons occupying different roles and having different interests, and thereby holding different policy preferences. (In the extreme case, since as Arthur F. Bentley thirty years ago pointed out "skin is philosophy's last line of defense,"[29] in other words that biological individuality is not always an adequate system divider for scientific analysis, such bargaining may take place within the individual leader, in terms of the different actual or imagined conflicting roles, which he occupies.) It seems reasonable to suppose, however, that one way of grasping the processes by which policies are reached is to try to comprehend the prior process of what is generally called deciding, that is arriving at policy preferences.

It would be extremely helpful if it were possible to present a clear notion of exactly what is meant by attention in a sociological and political context. Although the notion is, of course, one of the seemingly self-evident intuitive conceptions which we all use freely, I must confess that I have not been able to do much more with it, as yet, than assume that its meaning is clear. However, it is not quite as self-evident as it may seem—attention in the social and political sense does not seem synonymous, for instance, with attention as this is studied in psychophysiological laboratory experimentation[30] although some, at least of the latter is supposed to trace back to William James' more sociologically-oriented remarks about the nature of attention.[31] I have made several efforts to describe the phenomenon but have not succeeded.[32]

VI

It is, of course, important to see not only what bits of information are attended to, but how they are attended to. In what perspective are they seen? Are they regarded as relevant? In general, no doubt, people pay more attention to items which they regard as relevant to something than they do to bits of information which are not classifiable. But x may regard information bit y as relevant to z while q may regard the same information bit as relevant to n.

Relevance is a term, of course, extremely overused at the present time. Yet, it has no adequate substitute. Schiller in a useful discussion of the nature of relevance[33] points out that it is related to a judgment, which is to be made.

In the root meaning, relevance is problematic, because what is to be taken into account in order to make a judgment, involves an element of risk. Put another way, in terms of our emphasis upon information-processing and attention, differentiation of relevant bits of information from irrelevant ones is necessary because of the presence of far too many bits of information in the world for the actor to use; he has to gamble as to which bits of information will help him make a correct or valid judgment as to whatever he is trying to judge. Of course, normally, the process is not this conscious; the gamble and the attribution of relevance are made inarticulately. But, for purposes of understanding the process of forming policy preferences, attributions of relevance can be made either articulately or inarticulately. Either way, policy preferences may profitably be studied as a function of attributions of relevance; and either way, it is almost certain that attributions of relevance vary, depending on the social role and interests of the person being studied.

Another way of defining relevance might be as "that which ought to be taken into account, from the standpoint of a given actor" before expressing a judgment, or in order to justify having arrived at a judgment, from the standpoint of a given actor.

(The current cliché use of relevance is not, strictly speaking relevant to the problem here; but it may be worth a moment or two of discussion. If one assumes a world in which moral judgments are intuitively self-evident and unalterable, and in which any given actor knows for certain what is right in any given set of circumstances, and further if one assumes a kind of intuitive intellectual awareness that enables one to determine exactly which empirical facts one ought to take into account and which ones to discard, then it is perfectly appropriate to use relevance in the current cliché sense. Evidently, any one making such a set of assumptions would have little in common with Schiller's problematic, risk-taking logic for use.)

Perspectives are similarly, presumably, a function of interest and role. It is probable that bits of information are "put into perspective" by being placed into patterns, so that one responds to or judges in terms of the pattern, rather than in terms of the individual bit. (Patterns, of course, in a complex, information-rich world, get placed into larger patterns, and so on.) X, who is a construction laborer, hears certain news about something that has happened in Cambodia, and places it, in one pattern; Y, who is a Unitarian minister hears the same news, and, as we all realize, is inclined to place it into a different pattern.

Raymond Bauer[34] in his work on the effects of communications has placed great emphasis on the process of "triggering"—that is to say, he has argued that a major effect of communications is to trigger a preexistent tendency. The League of Women Voters, for instance, presents an argument in a given community for freer international trade, but the textile workers and executives in that community interpret this information in terms of their existent views about the threat of a foreign imports; so what the League does in such a case is to increase the likelihood that textile interests will articulate their protectionist stand. In other words, the bits of information given by the League will vivify and ordinarily be fitted into the pattern and perspective which already exists. Presumably, bits of information received by Lyndon Johnson about Thai-U.S relations might not fit into a different pattern than such bits of information when received by J. William Fulbright.

Of course, where new information merely confirms what people formerly believed, it is of no particular interest to the student of policy formation. But, quite often, new bits of information do lead people to shift their policy preferences or their foci of attention—they create a problem where none existed before. In such cases, policy preferences will change; but they will change in accord with the preexistent pattern or perspective, so although some new information about Thailand might shift the views of both Senator Fulbright and President Johnson, these views would shift somewhat differently.

VII

This article is, of course, a highly preliminary, tentative, and incomplete effort to struggle with some of the problems of policy preferences and what is often called "decision-making." It is simply a sketch, pointing generally in a direction, which may be worth exploration.

To organize the approach somewhat further, it is suggested:

1.   Attention and attributions of relevance are consequences of the roles held by those who are attending and making judgments of relevance.

2.   In part, those who occupy a given role have, through a process of socialization, learned what to attend to (as suggested by the requirements of the role) and what it is proper or rewarding to regard as relevant. Part of this learning is actually through a process of transmission; a good deal of it is, however, a consequence of perception of the expectations, which others have of one. That is, the interactionist theory in terms of which reciprocal expectations define role and personality may be used to explain what kinds of information will be processed by what political leaders show. Since it is not always obvious to those not familiar with role theory, it is probably worth underlining the point that expectations can and do sometimes create negative responses, rather than conforming ones—but they are nevertheless determinants for all that.[35]

3.   The notion of "cue" as developed by Kenneth Burke[36] is helpful here; by cues he is referring to something similar to what W.I. Thomas called the definition of the situation,[37] or in terms of the title of his own book, attitudes toward history. "Cues" may be regarded from our standpoint as the internal directive or labeling process in terms of which the individual has learned to process given complexes of information. These "cues" are, by hypothesis, in substantial measure learned through the institutional experience, formal and informal, that the individual has had. For example, an individual who has learned in a given institutional framework to regard most claims to integrative activity, interdepartmental cooperation, and the like (as of course happens in many institutions) as a threat will, confronted with some new situation, process it differently if it involves any such claims than will the individual who has not learned this particular kind of cue. (This particular example applied as much, of course, to interdepartmental efforts in universities, when I was young, as to interdepartmental cooperation in state governments.) And since he will attend to different kinds of information about such a claim and see the information he attends to in a different perspective, he will very likely develop different policy preferences than is the case with others who have learned different cues.

Obviously, there are substantial individual difference in the cues which different individuals, exposed to the same set of institutional experiences, learn. Partly, of course, these are due to differences between the total experience, biological and social, of the individual;[38] one individual may find his suspicion of interdepartmental cooperation reinforced by his social life, outside the office, another may learn to favor similar cooperative efforts outside the office; one may, for all we know, possess physiological characteristics, which make him more inclined to embrace than another. Partly, of course, such differences may and do arise from the fact that, although the institution is the same, each individual's actual experience within it is different.

Granted all these points, nevertheless, it is highly probable that *persons who have occupied similar roles in the same or similar institutions will learn to process information in similar ways and will therefore develop similar policy preferences.* Since they also learn similar methods of bargaining and accommodation, *they are likely, in those instances in which there are differences between them and in which they must bargain with each other (intra-institutional bargaining, for instance), to be able to arrive at a common policy fairly readily.*

4.   Another way of looking at the point about cues has been suggested by Durkheim[39] and his followers. Durkheim suggests that, for instance, the idea of heaven in a particular social group is a product of their particular formal conclaves. Put in more general terms, the categories in terms of which we think are products of the social processes to which we have been exposed. Political leaders who have learned about administration and politics in a given institution may, in the same manner, perceive politics in terms of the characteristics patterns of that institution. Unfortunately, we do not normally have a stark physical phenomenon like a circular tribal place of assembly to start with. We have to determine, rather, what are the "natural" ways of thinking about political processes which are learned in a given political institution.

5.   The difficulty of applying the ideas here suggested specifically lies in the last sentence. There is not, as far as I know, any available method of defining the data, which we want to tag and observe; we are in the situation of social anthropologists prior to the invention of such data-identifying notions as cultural variation. In principle, I do not see that it would necessarily be any more difficult to observe political institutions from the standpoint here presented than it was to develop the vocabulary and data-collecting tools of modern social anthropology.[40] Whether, in practice, it can be done is something which can only be tested by experience.

One way of doing it might be to try to develop tools for comparing, for instance, the organizational climates[41] of different institutions. We might, equally, try to determine what methods of recording we would need in order to observe the impact upon the individual recipient of expressed differences in policy preference and policy directives in institutions in different states, performing the same function, under similar circumstances.[42] We might try to measure whether cities or towns with formally identical governmental structures, but with different systems of selecting political leaders, do seem to differ in policies and formally expressed policy preferences in significant ways—significant, for instance, for the actual conduct of a given function,[43] as it affects those who are exposed to that function.

Notes

*   [Unpublished paper-Eds.] Prepared for delivery at the Sixty-sixth Annual Meeting of The American Political Science Association, Biltmore Hotel Los Angeles, California September 8-12, 1970. 2B, 9 a.m., Wednesday, September 9, "Policy Knowledge vs. Political Science Research."

1.   Whatever value this paper has is in large part due to the members of my seminar on The Policy Process at Ohio State University in the spring quarter of 1969.

2.   The immediate discovery or insight that, indeed, I did not know what I had for so many years been glibly talking about arose in conversation with Frederick Wirt in 1968. The awareness came to me at a given moment in the conversation quite effortlessly; I mention this merely because it serves to illustrate in another dimension the effect of a gradual shift in attention—I *discovered* that I "changed my mind" but in fact my mind had changed without any conscious effort on my part.

3.   Vague here means: When a term supposedly describes a category, its meaning may be said to be vague when its customary use is such that qualified users would probably be unable to suggest any readily comprehensible criteria by which they could judge whether or not a particular item falls within or without the category. One experience, reflection on which has stimulated my own awareness here: In 1964 I was asked to teach a course on State Public Policy, as though this were different from and analytically superior to the course on State Government which I hoped to teach. I had and have no idea of the difference. Similarly, in the literature of social work, particularly, (and increasingly in sociology) I read about social policy a good deal—which is now a field in social work. How does it differ from politics, political philosophy, and the consideration of issues? A similar "upgrading" seems to be taking place in schools of education, some of which offer and others of which are considering offering concentrations on policy. Of course, in the nature of the world, some degrees of vagueness must attach to any general term; we could not, if we would, get rid of a plurality of distinguishable conditions, attaching to each symbol.

        One source, not only of vagueness, but of confusion, should, however, be eliminated: Policy is used sometimes both as a prescriptive and in an empirically descriptive sense. "Honesty is the best policy…" is an example of what is in fact a prescriptive use. So, in fact, ordinarily, depending on context are such sentences as "My policy is to tell the truth" or "My policy is Machiavellian"—prescriptive or post-facto prescriptive (justificatory). Frequently, of course, the prescriptive and the descriptive uses are wrapped up together as in the common characteristics of a "policy manual." (The only systematic analysis of the term which I have seen, insofar as I could understand it, which was not very much, a Ph.D. thesis by Gary Iseminger (Philosophy, Yale, c. 1963) seemed to me to contribute more to clarification of the prescriptive than of the descriptive use).

        On "Vagueness" see the article by William P. Alston in the *Encyclopedia of Philosophy* on that topic.

4.   I doubt if I would have written this particular paper excerpt for support by the Social Science Research Council in an effort (largely unsuccessful so far) to make a comparative study of supposedly similar state functions (mental retardation, pollution) in several states and Canadian provinces. There were a number of reasons

(some discussed in my *Elite and Specialized Interviewing*, Northwestern U. Press, Evanston, III., 1970, pp. 15-17, 153) for my failure on this project; but probably the most important was that I did not know *what* I was trying to compare. In a general way, I ultimately realized that I was trying to compare *policy impact* upon the beneficiaries or victims, those affected by given state "policies," but since I had no meaningful way of talking about policies, I did not know how to look for "relevant" materials or how to record what I happened to see and hear. In one sense, this paper is a portion of a report on my failure in this project.

I am under considerable obligation to the Social Science Research Council and its committee on Political Behavior for the grant which led me to reflect on these problems. In a larger sense, I am indebted to a number of research sponsors, and most particularly to my colleagues, Raymond Bauer and Ithiel Pool, for many reasons—one of which was that (against my will) they named our joint book *American Business and Public Policy*; my discomfort with that title was one of the factors leading me to realize that policy really is, as generally used, a very vague conception. (*American Business and Public Policy*, Atherton, New York, 1963).

5. One of the points which I have come to realize very late in the preparation of this paper is that the term policy *change* is preferable to policy *development*, because development at least connotes an orderly progress from x to y. Such orderly progress may in many instances take place; but it should not be assumed by our vocabulary until it has been demonstrated by our observations. Changes may move to-and-fro, like a pendulum; they may be (and I suspect often are) somewhat discontinuous, Braybrooke and Lindblom to the contrary notwithstanding; etc., etc.

6. And, of course, of the influence upon me of others interested in the field—particularly Herbert Simon, and Geoffrey Vickers (Vickers through his book *The Art of Judgement: A Study of Policy-Making*, Basic Books, New York, 1965, which was a major text in the Ohio State University seminar, referred to in footnote 1.)

7. In H.G. Wells, *World of William Clissold*, Doran, N.Y.C., 1926, p. 338, quoted here to mean that I have not found much less vagueness or more *applicable* clarity in most other people's uses of the notion.

8. David Braybrooke, *Philosophical Problems of the Social Sciences*, MacMillan, New York, 1965, Introduction.

9. The most satisfactory (to me) effort to develop a system of controlling meanings is found in the later work of Arthur P. Bentley; see his *Inquiry into Inquiries*, Beacon Press, Boston, 1954 (especially the two papers, reprinted from earlier journal articles, "The Human Skin: Philosophy's Last line of Defense," pp. 195-211, and "Situational vs. Psychological Theories of Behavior," pp. 141-74) and *Behavior, Knowledge, Fact*, Principia Press, Bloomington, IN, esp. pp. 105-11. I have tried to present in my *Elite and Specialized Interviewing*, Northwestern U. Press, Evanston, IL, 1970, a technological approach to reporting meanings objectively. The best demonstration of the possibility of such an approach is to be found in the symbolic interactionist school of sociologists, such as Mead and Cooley, and (as the text suggests) in cultural anthropology.

10. Even Sir Geoffrey Vickers in his very careful *Art of Judgement; A Study of Policy-Making*, Basic Books, New York, 1965 resorts to interpreting policy formation as an appreciative assessment, thereby still confining himself, so far as the connotations go, to the viewpoint of the actor, and making it difficult to take into account the meanings not articulated, which as I suggest below are probably just as important as what has been consciously formulated.

11. I do not believe that *American Business and Public Policy* would have been called by that name had it been published as one book at the time we completed the manuscript (in 1956). But by 1963, policy had become a popular phrase; and, could we but analyze all the factors which impinged upon the judges' decision to award the book the Woodrow Wilson Award, I wonder whether the use of the by-then popular phrase might have played a part?

It should of course, be pointed out that the term policy was by no means unheard of prior to 1963; and, in fact, Harold D. Lasswell and his most immediate associates had for some years been concerning themselves with the development of what they call "policy sciences." But prior to about 1963 frequent assertion of concern with policy sciences would, among political scientists, have suggested, I believe, some sort of commitment to Lasswellian approaches; whereas since then the phrase has become far more generally employed.

12. In what is in effect a Handbook of Political Science, scheduled to be ready in manuscript form, June 30, 1970, to be published by Addison Wesley, Reading, MA.

13. See Herbert A. Simon, *Models of Man*, New York, Wiley, 1957, p. 261; See also Bauer, Pool, and Dexter, *op. cit.*, pp. 407 ff.

14. Of course, people who use the term "policy" in this sense may themselves be very well aware of the distinction, but feel themselves forced by their notion that their audience is naïve, to ignore the need for compromise or at least to use a rhetoric of perfection.

15. Of course, also a young-faculty movement:

16. Hamilton, in his correspondence, says in effect "Now, we have got a constitution, we have got to adminstrate it into viability."

17. Somewhat related is the fact that on a couple of occasions clients, engaged in preparing a proposal which ultimately demands legislation by the Congress, have approached me about analyzing the proposal in terms of guesses about how Congress might accept it (presumably with a view to weakening the more offensive aspects of the proposal). More common is the tendency of some executives to consult pollsters as to public opinion on a proposed action. In the second case, particularly, the approach is often not thought through clearly enough; in many instances, it is important only to find out what will create a good deal of trouble (if this can be foreseen), not what the public prefers—as for instance in many matters of race relations, it would be necessary only to know what would boomerang or be totally unacceptable to some group, not what they actually prefer.

18. See T. V. Smith, *The Legislative Way of Life*, University of Chicago Press, Chicago, 1940, for this very useful notion; it constitutes the major theme of his approach. I have also used it in my *Sociology and Politics of Congress*, Rand McNally, Chicago, 1970.

19. David Riesman, in *The Lonely Crowd: A Study of the Changing American Character*, Yale University Press, New Haven, 1950, makes this one of his central conceptions. It is, I think, reasonably clear that he and most of those who have quoted him regard "other directedness" as morally inferior to "inner directedness," but there is a certain kind of other-directedness, that described by T.V. Smith (footnote 18), which is essential for political stability—although it is probably aesthetically less pleasing in the Judeo-Christian tradition than inner-directedness.

20. Originally published in *Human Organization*, 1957, now Bobbs-Merrill reprints PS-63, and appears in revised form as Ch. VIII of my *Sociology and Politics of Congress*, Rand McNally, Chicago, 1970.

21. In my *Sociology and Politics of Congress*, *Op.cit.*, Part II, quotation from p. 134.

22. *Op.cit.*, pp. 409-11.
23. We should perhaps also have listed explicitly those free to give central attention to reciprocal trade—on the one hand, some small industries which, for historical actual reasons, thought foreign imports would kill them (on this point, the interview protocol with Representative Cleveland Bailey, in *Sociology and Politics of Congress, op.cit.*, pp. 223-32, is particularly pertinent); on the other, members of the League of Women Voters, most especially—yet it is to be presumed most of these members either had professional obligations or ran households (or in some cases both).
24. Herbert A. Simon, "Designing Organizations for an Information-Rich World," in Martin Greenberger (ed.) *Computers, Communications and the Public Interest*, John Hopkins U. Press, Baltimore, MD, 1970.
25. My only disagreement with Simon—really not even a disagreement but a shift in emphasis—would be this: He, naturally enough, seems to stress the "information-rich" character of the *modern* world. I am inclined to suppose that if we had an adequate report of the responses and reactions of rulers in *any* complex society, we would find that the more conscious or conscientious among them would feel themselves *potentially* overwhelmed by needed information which they could not adequately digest.
26. It is worth reflection whether such an event as Henry Dundas's manumitting of the hereditary mining serfs in Scotland (see Henry (Lord) Cockburn, *Memorials of His Time*, vol. 2 of his *Works*, A.C. Black, Edinburgh Scotland, 1872, pp. 67-69,) involved foresight of this sort? Obviously, the distinction between potential demands and those of conscience or whim becomes very fuzzy in many empirical cases.
27. Under personal inclinations, I would include not only conscience but vanity, whim, and curiosity. Caligula, according to report, was moved by (his own personal) demand to make his horse a consul.
28. Although in honesty, I must report one case where the superficial impression of a governmental office was that of a shortage of demands. When I spent several hours in the office of Premier Robichaud of New Brunswick in the fall of 1966, the phone only rang four or five times, and the Premier's administrative assistant described to me what in effect constituted a program for getting New Brunswick citizens to demand more from the government. This is the only case of the sort I myself happen to have seen (Newfoundland which I visited in the following January showed a very different pattern in the Premier's office) and I suspect that, basically, even this odd case can be fitted into the general framework.
29. In his article by that title, reprinted in his *An Inquiry into Inquiries*, Beacon Press, Boston, 1954.
30. See Paul Bakan, ed. *Attention: An Enduring Problem in Psychology*, Van Nostrand Press, Princeton, NJ, 1966.
31. Wm. James, *Principles of Psychology* (1890) Dover ed. New York, 1950, pp. 402-58.
32. See, however, David Lindsay Watson, "Selecting Mechanism as a Concept for Psychiatry," *Psychiatry*, 5 (1942) 35-47, for stimulating ideas, some of which I believe I have used in Part II, Throughout the Fog of Policy-Demands: What do Congressmen Pay Attention To? pp. 131-78, of my *Sociology and Politics of Congress*, Rand McNally, Chicago, 1970. I must admit that I have not made any extensive search of sociological, early social-psychological, or political science literature as yet.
33. Ferdinand C.S. Schiller, *Logic for Use*, New York, Harcourt, Brace, 1930, Ch. V, "Relevance," pp. 75-91.

34. See particularly his article on "The audience" in the forthcoming *Handbook of Communications*, Rand McNally, Chicago, edited by I. Pool and others. See also Bauer, Pool and Dexter, *Op.cit.*

35. I am faced here with the characteristic dilemma of someone who realizes that theories and ideas which he learned as a younger man are pertinent; several efforts to codify role theory have been made in recent years; whether these will add materially to role theory as developed by earlier sociologists and social psychologists is one of the things I must look into.

36. Kenneth Burke, *Attitudes Towards History*, (2nd rev. ed., Boston, Beacon, 1961) in his dictionary of pivotal terms defines "cue."

37. Most of W.I. Thomas' later works emphasize the notion of "definition of the situation." See, for instance, W.I. Thomas, *The Unadjusted Girl*, Boston, Little Brown, 1931, p. 42.

38. The various efforts to introduce individual psychology, such as psychoanalytic theory into political science seem to me to be weakened by the absence of institutional biographies of the individuals who are under study; many, for instance, of Woodrow Wilson's reactions, as explained by Alexander George or William Bullitt, might have been the product of institutionally-learned cues, rather than necessarily arising from that very primitive institution, the family. And, granted the tremendous practical difficulty in collecting the relevant data, an alternative set of explanations in terms of institutionally learned cues might explain much of the behavior of Lasswell's subjects in *Psychopathology and Politics*.

39. Emile Durkheim, *The Elementary Forms of the Religious Life*, (transl. J. Swain), Allen & Unwin, London, 1915, for instance pp. 9-20. The line he presented there was developed and improved by M. Granet, *La Pensee Chinoise*, La Rennaissance du Livre, Paris, 1934, and by M. Halbwachs, *La Memoire Collective*, Presses Universitaire de France, Paris, 1950. A similar but historically quite separate approach to the issues, stressing the radically metaphoric character of thought, is found in I.A. Richards, *Interpretation in Teaching*, Harcourt, Brace, New York, 1938.

40. There is one handicap which may not have been as great to social anthropologists a couple of generations ago. The bright, able, imaginative people in the political science discipline seem to be focusing, as far as I can judge, largely upon problems of data-processing, rather than upon the currently less prestigeful tasks of data-identification or even data-collection. However, I may be wrong, and fashions in such matters change.

41. See D. Katz and R. Kahn, *Social Psychology of Organizations*, Wiley, New York, 1966, pp. 65-66. In two papers (available mimeographed) read respectively at the Wayne State University Political Science Colloquium and at the Midwest Political Science Association meetings in the spring of 1967, I discussed the conception of organizational climate.

42. See James Q. Wilson, *Varieties of Police Behavior, Management of Law and Order in Eight Communities*, Harvard U. Press, Cambridge, MA, 1968.

43. Watertown and Belmont, Massachusetts, each have limited town meetings and are adjacent; I have lived in Belmont much of my life but had known little about Watertown until I made a study of some aspects of its town politics in 1957-8. I was impressed by how extremely different the towns seem to be; and further reflection suggests that Arlington and Brookline, also identical legally, differ from the other two and each other almost equally.

   But the problem is: how to describe the difference in terms which are both meaningful for the specific situation and of general value.

Part II

Political Science

1

What Do Congressmen Hear: The Mail

This article derives from an extensive report on "Congressmen and the People They Listen To" by the writer.[1] Other portions of the report deal with communications that Congressmen received by other means than mail. The report was done at the Center for International Studies, MIT, in connection with a study of business communications on foreign economic policy. (See also the Bonilla and Pool articles in this issue.) The reception on Capitol Hill of the communications from business was studied partly by interviews (more than fifty with Congressmen and a similar number with Congressional staff members, and a much larger number with businessmen) and partly by reading the incoming mail of a few members of each house. Except where otherwise indicated, the names of all Congressmen in this report have been disguised; the words and illustrations are, however, reported exactly.

The Mail's the Thing

Every congressman and senatorial assistant, when asked, "What do you hear …? or words to that effect, starts telling you about the mail. Almost every businessman when asked, "What have you done about such-and-such an issue?" tells you (if he has done anything) that he's written to his congressman or senator (or possibly telegraphed).

In the importance attached to it both by congressman and by business constituents, mail outweighs every other form of communication. Strangely, many congressmen do not raise any explicit question as to whether the mail represents the views of the district. Some Congressmen do, of course, question this. A senator, for instance, who received 100 letters from a particular city urging that he support legislation for a higher minimum wage, checked on the senders and found out that at least seventy-five of them were eligible to register but only thirty-three of these actually were registered.

Senator Service's assistant says, "If you put faith in that sort of thing (stimulated mail) you're lost. We can tell the day and hour when somebody or other starts those calls or doorbells ringing [to get people to write]; so what?" Another senatorial assistant says it is easy to identify stimulated letters by the fact that someone nearly always encloses a copy of the letter to the letter-writer asking him to write his congressman. This assistant estimates that in any batch of 1,000 letters, at least fifty will enclose the original request.

But these are the exceptions so far as formal statement goes. It is true that many congressmen and senators run counter to the mail in obedience to the dictates of conscience, party or committee. But they frequently appear to think they are controverting something very significant. This may be merely a habitual genuflection toward the right of petition and the sovereignty of the citizen; in some cases it probably is. For whatever reason, older congressmen were much less inclined to quote the volume of mail as an authority than younger ones. This may simply mean that older ones had become sufficiently familiar with the point of view expressed by the mail (since it is similar on this issue over the years) so they do not pay as much attention to the current inflow on this subject. It may also be due in part to the fact that older congressmen are busier. It is also true that older congressmen, by the very fact of being older, come from districts which seem safer and may therefore be less anxious to ascertain the views of the electorate.

For these reasons—or more likely because they have seen the same sort of thing before and know it doesn't mean much politically—many older congressmen, it seems to me, manifested a fundamental easy-goingness and willingness to disregard the mail, which was less common among younger men. But even they on the whole appear to think that the mail is important and civically significant. There are several reasons that lead them to this attitude.

In the first place, members or their staffs spend an enormous amount of time on mail. And having invested that time on it, they like to feel that it means something.

Second, a great deal of the time congressmen operate in a pretty complete vacuum so far as the voters of their district go. Most people seem to prefer to know what they are supposed to do (if even in some cases merely so that they can protest or revolt). The mail gives a sense that one is doing something that excites large numbers of people.

Third, as Paul Appleby and others have pointed out, many congressmen are irritated and annoyed because they come to Washington expecting to do and be something important; and because of the complexity of government and the seniority system they find they are hampered and shut off from effective action at every turn. Granted this rather general exasperation, handling mail is almost the only thing on which a congressman finds himself quite free; he can write any sort of letters he likes without let or hindrance from anybody. Thus letter writing becomes a disproportionately significant aspect of his job, for its represents the freedom and importance that he thought he would find when he got to Washington (but rarely does).

Fourth, most congressmen genuinely treasure the right of petition and the opportunity of the individual citizen to complain about mistreatment. This right has great importance on many issues where bureaucrats mistreat or overlook individual rights.

Fifth, whether realistically or not, some congressmen actually believe and many others like to feel that on any issue of national significance, rational communication between them and any constituent is possible. For this reason they spend a quite irrational amount of time on correspondence that is essentially academic in the sense that it is fairly clear that no political or legislative purpose is really served by the time they give it.

For these, and perhaps other, reasons congressmen come to believe that the mail bag is the secret of success. Senator Kefauver (D., TN) reports that when first elected to Congress he asked Speaker Bankhead (D., AL) how to get reelected, and that Mr. Bankhead replied, "Members get re-elected term after term without substantial opposition [because they] give close and prompt attention to mail. Votes and speeches may make you well known and give you a reputation, but it's the way you handle your mail that determines your re-election."[2]

Nearly all the businessmen we talked with also regarded writing congressmen as the basic political-legislative act. In view of the supposed popularity of public relations in a wider sense, this was a little surprising. But nearly all of them said, "I wrote," "I telegraphed," or "No, I haven't written," when asked if they had done something about the issue.

In this article we shall review some of the characteristics of the mail that seem extraordinary in so highly valued a source of information.

Little or No Mail on Many Vital Issues

A substantial number of congressmen and probably all Senators received a noticeable amount of mail about reciprocal trade legislation.

This in itself differentiates reciprocal trade from many crucial issues. For example, a senator from a major industrial state heard nothing in the 1955 session of Congress on any of the following issues, all of which were considered by the Senate during that session, and several of which were decided so closely that he could have exercised a crucial vote: Capehart Amendment on Policy Responsibility of dollar-a-year men (WOC's), Hickenlooper Amendment on permitting construction of an atomic-powered merchant ship, Home Rule for the District of Columbia, Statute of Forces Agreement (Jenner Amendment), Marine Corps increase, Mutual Aid Programs for Europe and Asia, stockpiling of minerals, confirmation of SEC and ICC Commissioners (both controversial in the extreme), Serviceman's Voting Proposal, Congressional Amendment (actually passed by the Senate) permitting governors to appoint Congressmen in event of emergency, sale of rubber plants, Housing Act of 1955, restriction of wheat and cotton acreage. Several of these are very important in fact to his state; some of them are considered by his committees. His experience is typical.

Most of the Mail Comes from Few Sources

In 1955 probably a majority of congressmen received a good deal of mail on the tariff. However, a good many rated it as 10th or 15th, relatively low in volume compared to mail received in connection with other issues. A few in 1954 heard nothing. Such figures mean relatively little, however, because a very large proportion of the mail on the tariff issue was organized and sent by a few sources. Westinghouse, Dow, Monsanto, Pittsburgh Plate Glass by themselves may easily have stimulated 40 percent or more of all mail received by all Congressmen in 1954 on reciprocal trade. These four certainly stand out as the big producers of mail on reciprocal trade. In addition to them, on the protectionist side, there were the coal, independent oil, and textile interests. Some of the textile people simply swamped their congressmen in 1955; one congressman is reported to have received well over 5,000 letters on the topic from textile workers in early 1955.

On the reciprocal trade side, there is only one big producer of mail—the League of Women Voters. Very probably three-fourths of the mail received by all congressmen in favor of reciprocal trade was directly or indirectly stimulated by the League. Even in tobacco or automobile districts, League members produced a majority of the pro-reciprocal trade mail; and in districts where there was no strong protectionist group, the congressmen may have heard mostly from League members.

In general, protectionist mail outweighed pro-reciprocal trade mail at least 10 to 1.

Inspired Mail Tends to Seem Unduly Uniform

Congressman Simpson (R., PA) received a number of letters and postcards in 1953 urging him to vote against the Simpson Bill for the imposition of a fuel oil quota. To one of his colleagues this simply represented the ineptness and political uninformedness of the much-abused "women's groups."

By and large, most protectionist mail quantitatively speaking takes the line, "Save my job." Printed cards are distributed and often collected and mailed by firms in the woolen textile industry. A manufacturer in one big port city explained why his organization had gone to the trouble of collecting and mailing the cards.

"Oh, we found most of these people just didn't know who their Congressman was, or they sent it to their State Senator or something, so we asked them just to fill in their address and we did everything else."

One congressman from that city in consequence got about 6 percent of the cards with an address but no name signed. A senatorial assistant comments, "That's doing better than par for the course."

Westinghouse and Monsanto inspired mail made a good deal also of the defense contribution of the electrical equipment and chemical industries, respectively. Monsanto inspired mail was usually neatly typed; mail from most other mass sources tended to be scrawled.

Mail from almost any given industry tends to have its own special characteristics. The cherry industry, for example, seems to promote letters, which are particularly "reasonable" sounding; "we know foreign trade is necessary but ours is a special case." It is almost impossible to organize a letter writing campaign so skillfully that an experienced mail clerk does not spot it at once as stimulated and even identify its source. Senator Philip's mail clerk said in 1954 she had heard a good deal from Westinghouse and Pittsburgh Plate Glass and the chemical industry. "We've heard from both management and labor. In the chemical people, I believe all the executives wrote in; they didn't say that's what they were, but I could tell by the paper they used. Pittsburgh Plate Glass got the bankers, the little merchants, everybody to write in."

The Mail Is Direct

Most of the mail to congressmen is quite direct; Mr. X writes to his congressman and that's that. In the letter, Mr. X may identify himself but more often is simply satisfied to say he is a constituent. Mr. X does not go through channels to write his congressman. For example, I never saw a single letter from a county chairman or other party official on trade and tariff matters with one exception—an official Republican group in Midland, Michigan had petitioned their senators against reciprocal trade. (I was told also that the Young Democrats of Newcastle County [Wilmington], Delaware, had sent their Congressman a resolution supporting reciprocal trade.)

Nor do people who write to a congressman try to get someone bigger and more important in the industry or in popular esteem to vouch for them; nor do union members write through national headquarters. This is interesting because it differs from the prevailing political pattern on patronage where endorsements are sought unless one is personally known to the congressman (and frequently when one is). It is unrealistic because in fact the attention a congressman pays to mail is in part a matter of how important the writer is—frequently the content or title make this obvious, but frequently they do not.

With letters to senators in the larger states, such endorsement or identification would seem still more appropriate since mail clerks for senators often know little about the state. I know one fairly skilled lobbyist who thinks that when he really wants something from a senator's office it is a good idea to write the senator a letter beginning "Dear so-and-so (first name)." Then the mail clerk, not to take a chance, will give the letter to one of the assistants instead of handling it himself. Ordinarily the assistant handles the subject, and the senator will never see the letter—so it will create no embarrassment.

Since many senators and congressmen simply disregard out-of-state mail altogether, it is particularly odd that people who write them from out of state do not take some steps to identify themselves. All together many thousands of dollars of postage must be spent in out-of-state mail, which is unread except for the address or first sentence.[3]

Chaff in the Mail

I have hardly ever seen a letter, which indicated any technical mastery of reciprocal trade legislation. The few people who have such mastery would probably go and see the appropriate people rather than write letters. I have never noted a letter, which contained a new or unfamiliar thought about the issue; nor have I happened ever to read one (out of several thousands I have looked at) where one could say clearly as one sometimes can with letters: Here is someone who writes with real conviction. (Letters I have seen on McCarthyism or on defense issues such as civil defense and stockpiling occasionally create such an impression.) Put another way, a detailed study of the phrases and sentences in letters on reciprocal trade and the tariff would almost certainly show an enormously high proportion of clichés and stereotyped phrases. I do not recall seeing a coherent presentation of protectionist theory; the Careys and the other mercantile political economists and nationalist theorists might as well never have lived as far as the mail goes.

Handling and Effect of Senate versus House Mail

In several cases, I read mail to a senator and also mail to one or more congressmen from the same state. I noted little difference as far as the congressmens' district was concerned. The handling of mail in senatorial offices (and its consequent likelihood of being effective) is quite different from that in the House; but the initial content and nature of this mail does not seem to differ greatly. It should of course be stressed that all this tariff mail is stimulated and on an issue of low emotional involvement; whether spontaneous mail to senators or mail to them on an issue of high emotional involvement differs from mail to House members is another matter. On stimulated mail, of course, the stimulators usually give the names of senators and congressmen to the people who write; when people write spontaneously they are more likely to know their senator's name than that of their congressman.

A good many and perhaps most representatives read all their own mail except that which is clearly routine. If they do not dictate answers themselves, they indicate who should be queried about the letter, etc. How they handle it—whether they pay attention to out-of-district mail, how much use they make of reference facilities in the Library of Congress or the Executive Departments, how far they try to use the letter as a basis for thinking of something else that will interest the constituent—depends enormously upon the representative, the subject, and how busy he or his staff are at a given time.

In general, it can be said that the overwhelming majority of representatives try to answer personally all serious letters from constituents.

In the Senate, the situation is quite different. Senators from the larger states have mail clerks who handle the mail, attend to much of it themselves, and if in doubt consult one of the senator's assistants. But most senators rarely see their mail; some of them try to keep control by signing answers.

The inability to see mail results in odd situations. Senator Philip's legislative assistant assured me that no one in the state was concerned about reciprocal trade—the senator got practically no mail on it, for instance. However, the chief mail clerk told me that it was either first or second among the issues that the senator got mail about. One of the mail clerk's favorite ways of treating such mail was to reply, "I am turning your letter over to the Chairman of the Senate Finance Committee which is now considering H.R. 1 and I am sure he will be interested in your comments." I looked at him quizzically. "No, I don't do it," he said, "but I don't think I'm being dishonest in saying that. I would if it said anything new." And this was probably true; every once in a while a letter that poses what is (at least to the senatorial or congressional office) a new question is sent to the staff of Ways and Means and Finance for comment or with the request that an answer be written for the appropriate signature.

Because at present many mail clerks have basement offices some distance away from the main senatorial offices, the mail staff is likely to develop a social life somewhat independent of the main staff. They are thus less likely to exchange comment and information with the legislative and administrative assistants or their staffs than is true in the House. Possibly this psycho-geographical factor may alter when the new Senate Office Building is completed.

Mail clerks are usually selected, I judge, on the basis of familiarity with government routine (Who should this be sent to in what agency? Who will help this fellow get his pension?) rather than on the basis of political knowledge of the senator's state, so they have less basis for evaluating the political significance of mail than might be expected. In any event, many senators and congressmen deliberately hire out-of-state residents.

No Great Difference in Mail to Committee Members

Mail to members of House Ways and Means or Senate Finance, the committees that consider reciprocal trade, did not seem to differ much in volume from mail to congressmen and senators not on these committees. This is surprising since sometimes lobbying organizations list the members of the pertinent committees. Members of the committees did not refer to any great difference in serious, personal high level communications to them as a result of belonging to the committees; one member said he probably got more "junk," e.g., press releases and the like, from outside his area. Apparently those members of the Ways and Means Committee who acquire some seniority are more likely to receive mail from their own states on Ways and Means issues as they become known in connection with them; but since junior members of the committee do not receive such letters, as far as I can tell, I judge that this is because the senior members have given speeches, been mentioned in newspaper stories, etc., on the topic, rather than because residents of the state realize the importance of the committee position. Two men with whom I talked had been shifted recently to these committees from other committees; there seemed to be no difference whatsoever in their mail except in the "junk" just referred to.

The Senate version of the Reciprocal Trade Extension Act of 1955 was quite different from the House version; so necessarily a conference committee (of five representatives and five senators) was appointed to decide on the final version. The measure was in conference for a number of weeks.

The conferees could have decided for a more "liberal" or a more "restrictive" measure. One would have thought therefore that they would have been bombarded with communications, attempts to influence them, etc. There was a real question how far Messrs. Cooper and Mills, two Democratic conferees from the House, would go in opposing the Senate version; conceivably Senator George (D., GA) who had traditionally been a strong advocate of the old Hull position and Senator Kerr (D., OK) who after all was then conceivably a potential Democratic candidate for President, might be open to some compromise on the numerous restrictive amendments written in by the Senate. Most observers felt Senator George sympathized with the House Bill rather than the Senate version.

So from the reciprocal trade standpoint, one might have expected a campaign directed at these four men at least. None took place, apparently because those people in Washington who knew of the conference committee procedure made no effort to put on a campaign. They failed to realize that the procedure had confronted them with a situation where a campaign might make a difference. The profound distaste Messrs. Cooper and Mills had for the Senate Bill made it pretty certain that there would be a delay long enough for a campaign before they signed any conference report.

On the other side, Senator Morse (D., OR), one of the most vociferous advocates of local interests in the Senate on economic matters, had succeeded in getting into the Senate Bill an amendment that was desired by Northwest fruit and nut producers and that would presumably have especially benefited them. The cherry producers in February and March had put on a fairly intensive campaign of letter writing; but as far as I heard, neither they nor the other Northwest, Michigan, and Georgia fruit-nut producers put on a campaign in May anywhere near resembling the

Morell campaign. Yet, the fact was that in May they were in a special position where a campaign would have been more helpful. In any event the only loss the protectionists suffered in conference was the deletion of the Morse Amendment.

Generally Constituents with Ideas Suggest Something That Is Procedurally Impossible

For our present purposes, it is sufficient to point out that because of the elaborate and technical nature of congressional procedure most letters to congressmen suggesting that they should do something, recommend things that they cannot, practically speaking, do. Procedural decisions or legislative custom may have allocated the responsibility to somebody else or have set the question up in such a way that what the constituent wants cannot be achieved. For instance, a large number of letters were sent to Senator Hennings (D., MO) asking that he support the Curtis Amendment.[4] But the Curtis Amendment never came to the floor of the Senate; it was not to the best of my knowledge seriously considered by the Senate Finance Committee; Senator Hennings belongs to more than a dozen subcommittees of his two major committees (Judiciary and Civil Service) and in addition serves on Rules;[5] and this is quite enough to keep the senator and his staff busy; it would be difficult for them to take on new responsibilities of the magnitude involved in an effort for the Curtis Amendment even if he should be convinced by the letters that this was important.

Of course, occasionally some senator or congressman is looking around for an issue or is much impressed by particular ideas; so there is always an outside chance that letters of this sort may have direct influence. They may certainly have a long-run "educational" effect, so that if the matter does some day come to the floor it may be received with more friendliness.

"You Don't Know What They Mean"

Several congressmen pointed out—and a number of others implied—that much of the time "When they write you, you don't know what they mean." For instance, a very large portion of the mail calls for protection for some one particular industry. Sometimes it says "but we realize the necessity of foreign trade in general"; for example, cherry industry mail usually says this. What can the average House member do with this mail? Under the closed rule procedure under which tariff bills are usually considered, the House as a whole is very unlikely to have an opportunity to vote to protect the domestic cherry processors and producers. The members will have to vote for or against the Reciprocal Trade Extension Act as reported out of committee. They can of course urge the members of the Ways and Means Committee to do something or other to help the cherry growers and producers, but precisely what? Either there has to be somebody on Ways and Means who works out the method—or somebody in the cherry growers association—or somebody in the cherry processors' association or the congressman himself has to do it.

On the cherry industry, three legislators at least have made an effort to work out a tailor-made solution—Senator Morse (D., OR), Senator McNamara (D., MI) and Congressman Holmes (R., WA). But most of the time on most of the mail they get, most congressmen and senators make no such effort. They simply receive the mail, and read and file it.

Westinghouse mail created a similar problem. It usually argued against H.R. 1. If the congressman had started to investigate he would have found that the issue that the mail usually raised—Federal purchase of foreign generating equipment—comes under the Buy American Act. Now the Buy American Act was not considered by Congress at all in 1955; there was nothing to be done about it; it was not part of the legislative calendar. What then did the Westinghouse workers really want?

Or suppose a congressman gets—as some have—letters saying "Vote for free trade." There was no free trade measure on the calendar; there is not likely to be one. Probably in January this means support the Reciprocal Trade Extension Act, as reported from committee. The measure was so riddled by amendments in the Senate that some people felt it was no longer a free trade measure; a New Deal congressman who voted for the Cooper Bill voted against acceptance of the Conference Report for the reason that the revised bill was so restrictive and protectionist.

In January 1955 a letter from a League of Women Voters or a Chamber of Commerce in favor of "more liberal" trade presumably meant "Support the Cooper Bill"; a petition from a cotton textile local to "protect our jobs" in January means "Oppose H.R. 1"; but after the Senate had adopted the committee amendments, what then? How many of those who wrote letters on either side had any idea of the significance of the changes made by the Senate? Actually, the newspapers and newsmagazines and newsletters had given only a very general and frequently a misleading picture of the drift of these amendments.

"You Always Hear from Business Too Late"

Congressman Amiable says, commenting on his wide experience in a state legislature and in Congress, "You always hear from business too late." And this is true in general because businessmen and their representatives respond to the news; they write in to protest a bill that has been reported out of Committee, for instance, because that is when they hear about it or when it really comes to seem a threat. But by the time it is reported out of committee, it is difficult to amend it; legislators have to say either "Yes" or "No." And by the time it is reported out of committee, the battle lines have formed, commitments and promises have been made, and it is harder for congressmen to change. For example, take Mr. L., a member of Ways and Means; he joins the Committee in reporting out such-and-such a piece of tariff legislation. Then he hears that the manufacturers of some product in his district would very much like a particular change in the bill; however, several members of the committee majority are opposed to this change. If Mr. L. had advocated it before the measure was reported out, he might be free to continue his advocacy or look for supporters of the position. But he is under the obligation that most decent men feel—not to throw over an implied agreement without very strong reasons.

And this obligation is backed by a very real sanction or threat. If Mr. L. wants to keep on friendly terms with his colleagues, to preserve their respect, he cannot break many such agreements; if he does he will lose his influence with them. And if he wants to serve his district not only at the moment but over the years, he must preserve his colleagues' respect.

I pressed Congressman Amiable on the "they always write too late" idea. "Oh, yes," he said, "it's just as true of trade unions." He thought of two exceptions to his generalization: the insurance industry back home in his state legislature and a particular union on Capitol Hill. And in each of these instances, there is a particularly intelligent lobbyist, apparently trusted and respected by his employers, the issues involved are both narrow and of paramount importance to the organizations, and they are largely handled by one committee instead of being spread among several.

Notes

1. The study is available in duplicated form from the Center for International Studies, MIT.
2. Kefauver, and T. Levin, *A Twentieth Century Congress*, New York: Duell, Sloan and Pearce, 1947, p. 171.
3. In other words, where the mail seems routine, repetitious, or uninspired, or where the mail clerk or the Congressional office is busy, much such out-of-state mail gets little attention. But a serious, original letter from a person who obviously knows what he is talking about or has some known claim to attention may and often does receive careful consideration.
4. Because both he and Mr. Curtis are from St. Louis and Mr. Curtis had engendered local attention to the matter.
5. A minor committee in the Senate, although a very major one in the House.

2

The Representative and His District*

I

Introduction

We talk frequently of a Representative or Senator "representing" or "failing to represent" his constituents. This is shorthand. The fact is the congressman represents his image of the district or of his constituents (or fails to represent his, or our, image of them). How does he get this image? Where does it come from?[1]

On numerous important policy matters, he hears nothing from his constituency.[2] But whether he hears anything on an issue, what he hears, whom he hears from, or how he interprets what he hears all *vary* depending upon the kind of person he is, the kind of associations he has had and has in the constituency and in Washington, the public image of his interests and concerns, and the background information or misinformation he possesses. An editorial summary of an earlier draft of this paper said, "Congressmen *make* choices about which people communicate with them.... In large part this is also a manner of speaking."[3] It would be more precise to say that the people in electing a congressman have chosen one sort of recording instrument or another, and that while one instrument may be adjusted to catch and hear one sort of communication, another will hear a different sort, and so on. Although congressmen do, to a small degree, consciously choose what they shall hear, it is probably more significant that in large measure their personalities, careers, and public images make them choose what they hear and how they interpret it.

A good many congressmen believe that their districts feel very strongly on this, that, or the other issue, and that they are constrained therefore to vote a certain way. The more sophisticated realize, of course, that legislative procedures and processes are so complex that it is more often than not possible to go through the motions of conforming to such views without helping to enact them, when they believe the public preference to be wrong.[4] On most issues, out of a desire to serve the district or from indifference, many congressmen do go along with any view which they believe "the district" holds strongly. When the chips are down, and they have to declare themselves, some will vote against their convictions and for their constituents' (presumed) preferences.

This situation has led to a series of classical utterances on the moral problem of the representative: *Should he sacrifice his judgment to his constituents' inclinations as he conceives them or not?* It would be more accurate to emphasize the ways in which representatives' beliefs about constituent preference are functions of the channels of communication and the special processes of transaction between constituents and representatives rather than of anything else.

If this is in fact so, more students of representation and representatives would concur with Congressman Veteran's[5] interpretation of the representative-constituent picture. The latter has for years been at the center of the legislative issues, which provoke the most comment by critics of "pressure," and he told me early in my study of reciprocal trade:

> You know I am sure you will find out a congressman can do pretty much what he decides to do and he doesn't have to bother too much about criticism. I've seen plenty of cases since I've been up here where a guy will hold one economic or political position and get along all right; and then he'll die or resign and a guy comes in who holds quite a different economic or political position and he gets along all right too. That's the fact of the matter.

II

The first difference between some congressmen and others is how (consciously or unconsciously) they define their responsibilities

Many of the congressmen interviewed about both tariff and defense matters referred to a personal conception of what they owe their job, of what in some circles would be called "professional obligation." A few made explicit and many apparently hold implicit theories of representation. These theories of representation were not, except for a few instances, so far as I could tell, directly derived from philosophical or academic sources. They resulted from the experiences of men facing the actual moral complexities of a job.

Some members expressed themselves in terms of their obligation to select the right course, regardless of the views of their constituents. For instance, Congressman Stubborn has for a good many years represented a district which (according to interviews with business interests in the district and from an economic analysis of its industrial situation) is inclined to favor the reciprocal trade program. Nevertheless, he says:

> Oh, knowing my stubborn characteristics, no one ever thinks he can change me, you know ... some of my people say, "You may not agree with this man, 'Stubborn', but you know where he stands."

Mr. Stubborn agreed that if fate were to select as his successor a Clarence Randall-type "free trader," such a man would be able to vote for a reciprocal trade program without much difficulty, but Stubborn interrupted an effort to probe this point further by declaring:

> That's because they (my constituents) do not really understand the matter. During the twenty-one years reciprocal trade has been in effect, it has had ... [and he named various alleged or actual consequences which he regards as evil].... There isn't any use trying to change *me!*

Congressman Emphatic on the other hand voted the same way as Mr. Stubborn on the Reciprocal Trade Extension Act of 1955 because of a quite different definition of his responsibility. He said:

> My first duty is to get reelected. I'm here to represent my district.... This is part of my actual belief as to the function of a congressman.... What is good for the majority of districts is good for the country. What snarls up the system is these so-called statesmen—congressmen who vote for what they think is the country's interest ... let the Senators do that.... They're paid to be statesmen; we [members of the House] aren't. (This was said sarcastically, but without humorous intent.)

Mr. Leader, as strong a supporter of reciprocal trade as Mr. Stubborn is an opponent of it, comes fairly close to Mr. Stubborn in his attitude towards constituent opinion. Said Leader:

> You're not identifying me on this, of course? It's strictly confidential? Always bear in mind there are those in Congress who lead their districts and those who are led by them.... It makes a lot of difference.... The "ruanga" growers of my district never opposed *me* on reciprocal trade.... The answer is government stockpiling for them.... I think I have convinced these men that a program of high tariffs would not assist them and I think my viewpoint has gained general acceptance from them.

Several times he spoke of himself as having "straightened out" people who had seen the matter "wrongly." But Mr. Leader and Mr. Stubborn do not essentially disagree. In another interview during the same session but dealing with an unrelated piece of legislation in which he had also played a prominent part, Mr. Leader showed his conception of his role on this matter to be very similar. (The reciprocal trade issue is so well-known, the origin of Mr. Leader's views so deeply-based, and his technical knowledge of the field so considerable that he is almost certainly right in his contemptuous dismissal of the possibility that any lobbying or "pressure" could change his position. However, regarding the other legislation, it is entirely probable that a skillful public relations campaign did manipulate *the facts*, which came to his attention and to the attention of some of his colleagues, much as we shall see Mr. Fourth was influenced on the reciprocal trade issue.)

Mr. Fourth represents a district in which there is vociferous anti-reciprocal trade sentiment. This district also has strong economic reasons for supporting reciprocal trade and a particularly influential number of intellectuals predisposed toward reciprocal trade. Mr. Fourth showed how a portion of the district can influence a man when he said:

> My impulses when I came down here were in favor of trade not aid, until I started to hear all sorts of things from my district... So, actually, when you stack all these things together, well you're in favor of trade not aid, but, goodness, there comes a time ...if trade means wholesale layoffs in your district.... I've got any number of letters against it ... carpets, imported rugs ... there've been around 300 layoffs in a local bicycle plant ... textiles ... chemicals ... electrical equipment ... glass salesmen. It's difficult to get figures. I assume the Randall Commission report has them.... I haven't had time to read it. I don't know ... I assume that the people I hear from exaggerate the seriousness of the situation but still that it is serious.

Mr. Fourth ultimately voted against reciprocal trade on the key votes; the decisive factor appears to have been his unwillingness to separate himself from several members from his state, also of junior status, who were definite in their opposition to reciprocal trade. Mr. Fourth, according to his colleagues. was wavering as late as two hours before the vote. Had the Chairman of his state delegation (who strongly supported reciprocal trade) personally requested his support, he might well have voted the other way. But he was obviously uncertain, *on the reciprocal trade issue*, whether to adopt the role of servant of his district (as he conceived its desires) or to think in terms of the ideology, implied by the phrase "trade not aid." How he would vote was therefore completely unpredictable. Had he stumbled into any one of three congressmen with strong pro-reciprocal trade views in the lobby or the corridors just before the vote, he might have voted the other way.

Congressman Fourth's vote was unpredictable because on this particular issue he does not have a clear conception of what his obligations are. On some issues—flood control or taxes affecting the major agricultural product of the district—one can predict that he would see his responsibility as being almost exclusively to the district. On others—particularly those under consideration by the very important subcommittee of which he is a member—he would be strongly inclined to emphasize national interest in some form as against district concern.

III

Congressmen tend to see their obligations as being either to the nation or to their constituency—other equally possible obligations are seemingly not considered

Obligation seemed to be conceived as national interest versus district interest (district interest was often, as in the case of Mr. Emphatic, related to reelection and therefore to self-interest). No congressman interviewed indicated any feeling of moral obligation to our allies or to any other country, although our allies are regarded instrumentally as means. This is contrary to a theory sometimes expressed that Americans tend to adopt some favorite foreign country as "theirs." Also, reference to representing a region (the South, the West, New England) was very slight.

The congressman's definition of national interest and responsibility on a particular issue depends in large measure upon his understanding of the facts of a particular issue

Both Congressman Leader and Congressman Stubborn are quite clear on what they believe are the facts of the reciprocal trade question, and they have no doubt about the effects of the legislation (although their facts are to a great extent contradictory, and their conclusions are opposite). Congressman Fourth, on the other hand, was susceptible to influence from either side because he lacked any clear idea of what reciprocal trade legislation means or entails. His sympathy for the phrase "trade not aid" came from a diffuse and generalized acceptance of a *slogan* rather than from an understanding of facts or consequences. He was really uncertain what, if any, difference his vote on reciprocal trade makes to the national welfare. Thus, he much more easily than Mr. Leader or Mr. Stubborn can see the matter as one of simply performing a service for discontented people in his district. It is far less likely that he will—in the absence of external stimuli—feel any strong need to learn the facts. On *service* matters—and much of a congressman's job is service[6]—most congressmen are willing to go along with those constituents who seem to know what service they want performed, and how it is to be performed (provided, of course, nothing irregular is requested). But if, for instance, Mr. Fourth were a New Deal "intellectual"—and his district is one which in my judgment might easily elect such a person—he would have interpreted the same situation quite differently. And, if he were a politically astute

New Deal "intellectual," he would have shown that the major agricultural crop of the district is exported, that several large industries in the area depend on foreign trade, and so forth.

A congressman's conception of his district confirms itself, to a considerable extent, and may constitute a sort of self-fulfilling prophecy

Early in my study of reciprocal trade, Congressman Veteran told me:

> You know I am sure you will find out a congressman can do pretty much what he decides to do and he doesn't have to bother too much about criticism.

Within the limits of the morally and sociologically conceivable (no congressman from Alabama in 1942 could have advocated integration for instance), a congressman has a very wide range of choices on any given issue, *so far as his constituency is concerned!* His relationships in the House or Senate and with party leadership, of course, limit these choices severely. It is a fact, however, that there is no district viewpoint *as such* to be represented on the overwhelming majority of issues. A few will care one way and a few the other, but the issue will be insignificant or unknown to the great majority. Indeed, in many districts, only a fraction of the voters know the name of their congressman, let alone how he voted on a particular issue.

A congressman of my acquaintance took about 100 letters which he received on a particular issue and checked the registration of the writers. He found that almost three quarters of them were not registered in his district. What difference then would their views make with respect to his prospects for reelection? Mr. Emphatic, who insisted that he was representing his district's desires, was led nevertheless, by my questions, to admit that more than likely none of the workers presumably represented by him actually knew how he had voted. "Not a single one of them," he complained, "wrote in to thank me, though hundreds had written asking me to vote their way." He attributed this in large measure to the allegation that the largest newspaper in the district is "anti-Emphatic." However, since newspapers published outside the district and which gave front page publicity to his stand have far greater circulation in the district than does the anti-Emphatic "News," this seems an unsound explanation.

Actually, most of the letters Mr. Emphatic received and most of the comments he heard originated in three large plants in the district and they represented less than *7 percent* of the voters of the district. These plants are organized by national unions which, ironically enough, in chalking up Mr. Emphatic's score in 1956, were inclined to regard his vote against reciprocal trade as an anti-labor vote. Fortunately for him, his stand on other matters and his personal contacts offset this factor. Of the groups in the district, only members of the League of Women Voters wrote to him in favor of reciprocal trade. "They aren't," he averred, "God knows, a potent political force; and all their letters are damn stilted, right out of the same handbook." Actually, however, it was likely that the League members would remember in 1956, and perhaps again in 1958, how he voted. And, because of the "racial" and academic composition of the district, League members may have some influence outside their own membership. It would have been perfectly possible for Mr. Emphatic to take the reverse position favoring reciprocal trade and still to regard himself as representing his district—particularly since the area also has a strong port interest.

A congressman has great difficulty in deciding what the viewpoint of the district is even on such an issue as reciprocal trade. Most persons with an interest or belief in the tariff will have interests or beliefs in other issues as well. Thus, the most effective representation of their overall interests may necessitate concessions on some matters, in order to get along with party leadership, colleagues, or prominent committee members in the Congress: "Joe Martin and Charlie Halleck in their heart of hearts," said a prominent Republican, "certainly go along with us, not with the White House on this; and they can swing twenty-five votes, at least, anytime they want; we lost by less than twenty-five votes, so they beat us." Martin is the Republican leader; Halleck is his likely successor as Republican leader or Speaker when he steps down. Is a congressman doing a better job of representing his district when he keeps in the good graces of such powerful men (and thereby helps to get a bridge or a new post office or a dam for his district) or when he opposes them on an issue, the details of which no one will remember six months later? The Republican who told me this is one of the most persistent enemies of reciprocal trade in the party and he is probably the most effective in a quiet way. He is opposed to reciprocal trade in part because of its "harmful" effect on his district. However, he cheerfully admitted, "It wouldn't make any difference what my congressman does on this matter," insofar as his reelection is concerned. Afterwards he qualified this by saying that perhaps the incumbent ought not stick his neck out strongly *for* reciprocal trade, but there is no call for activity of any kind.

IV

A congressman hears most often from those who agree with him

A congressman's relationships with his district tend to be maintained through a small group whom he knew before he was elected or through a group who have since then worked closely with him. Generally speaking, the views of those whom he knew prior to his election tend to be more like his than do the views of the "average" voter. It is a well-known fact that we tend to be like the people with whom we associate and vice versa. Also, most of the people who have worked closely with the congressman since his election—because he is a congressman—have a particular axe to grind. They will naturally tend therefore to stress agreement with him on issues about which they are not concerned—just as salesmen typically do not disagree with their customers on politics. For several years, I wondered about the unfavorable references congressmen frequently made to the League of Women Voters and several times to delegations from labor unions. Ultimately, it occurred to me that these two groups are probably the only ones which seriously, on a face-to-face basis, year after year, go over with a congressman the issues on which they disagree with him. Because their efforts cannot be entirely discounted as "politics," they make congressmen uncomfortable.

Congressmen may also have a few close supporters upon whom they rely who tend to become "their" men, and who shift as they shift. This is not always just a matter of holding on to a job, but may represent confidence in a man, prestige gained by association with him, or an unwillingness to sacrifice an investment in goodwill, which may be utilized for better public or personal purposes in the future. Such supporters are likely to couch any criticism in tactical terms, and ultimately, to follow the leader. Speaking as a somewhat active politician myself, the men whom I choose to follow would I am pretty sure, be *right* from my standpoint on basic issues of international agreement, national defense, civil rights, public safety and police, about which I particularly care. That is why I am for them. Consequently I can imagine no instance (with the single exception of civil defense) when I would seriously object to or criticize a stand they might take on some other and to me less important matter. This is true in spite of the fact that I am much more issue-oriented than most active supporters and campaigners.[7]

Some men automatically interpret what they hear to support their own viewpoints

Mr. First of New Hungary does not think he hears much about foreign imports. Mr. Second, coming from the same sort of district in the same city, says:

> It's either the first or second most important issue with me. Unemployment is the other. And, of course, they're really the same thing.

The last sentence is the clue to why Mr. Second hears so much more than Mr. First about foreign imports. When Mr. First hears about unemployment, he hears just about unemployment, or just about the declining industries of the area, or just about the invidious differential effect, which accelerated amortization and certain other tax provisions, have had on industry in the area. In fact, when I talked to him about the tariff, he advised me that I really ought to study accelerated amortization. Mr. Second, however, interprets almost any statement about unemployment as a plea for relief from foreign imports. Sometimes it is, but sometimes it isn't. So, seeing the same men and hearing the same things said, Mr. Second will "hear" about tariff matters, Mr. First will not. (Mr. Third, their colleague from an adjoining district, is vitally interested in wilderness preservation, hunting, and fishing. He sees many of the same men, but they are likely to talk to him about his interests, and if they do talk to him about unemployment, he is less likely to draw any special conclusions from the talk.)

The difference between Messrs. First and Second was illustrated at a dinner held by a joint labor-management committee from their area. The speaker who represented the trade association was really eloquent when he spoke for protection and against reciprocal trade. He hardly mentioned regional competition. The union executive who followed him sounded as though he were giving a courtesy speech of no importance when he attacked foreign imports. But, when he attacked the Southern states, which in his view are "robbing the North of jobs and keeping wage rates down," his manner and appearance changed to that of a deeply earnest man. Mr. First asked a searchingly critical question of the representative of the trade association, which implied that the latter really knew nothing about foreign trade and its effect on the economy. Mr. Second, however, stood up to take the bows when another colleague, Mr. Busy from an adjoining state, assured those present:

> Second and I, you can be sure, will do everything to protect our industries against foreign competition. We will be right in there fighting for you....

Almost certainly, Second actually "heard" strongly held views against reciprocal trade on this occasion, whereas First did not.

In more general terms, what congressmen hear and how they interpret what they hear depends on who they are

Conventional discussion of the relationship between congressmen and constituents assumes that the kind of man the congressman is does not influence what he hears from the district and that the question is whether he follows or contravenes district sentiment. The notion of the congressman representing "the" district at least needs restatement *in terms of a particular congressman* who represents what he hears from the district as he interprets it. And his interpretation results from his being the particular kind of person he is and is reputed to be.

Of course, congressmen will hear many of the same things. The similarity is very great since there are common factors in the careers of American politicians, and since Congress is a continuing social group where habits and attitudes are likely to persist. The old hands (staff, lobbyists, and active constituents as well as members) teach the younger ones. Furthermore, and not surprisingly, within any given district the balance of forces may continue so that several successive congressmen will belong to the same politico-social group (sometimes even when they are members of different parties). The real test of how successfully the district exerts an inescapable "pressure" upon the congressman comes when, without any sharp shift in population characteristics in the district, the congressman comes from a different social grouping.[8]

Students of comparative politics have, however, much more manageable ways of exploring this problem than by studying the activities of congressmen from the same district at different times. For instance, even in terms of our foci upon substantive issues, if I had realized the significance of knowing how a congressman's interpretation of what he hears is affected by his perception of the job, the constituency, and the facts, I could have tried to find out how senators of the same party and from the same state (but representing different factions and obviously looking at the world differently) understood the reciprocal trade question. It is almost incredible that Wiley, Republican of Wisconsin and McCarthy, Republican of Wisconsin could have heard the same messages on domestic security and international relations. It would have been interesting, therefore, to find out whether Wiley was as "convinced" as McCarthy was of the vital need for protecting Wisconsin's fur-bearing mammal growers or trappers against foreign competition. Robertson and Byrd of Virginia, Johnson and Daniel of Texas, Beall and Butler of Maryland, Martin and Duff of Pennsylvania, Cotton and Bridges of New Hampshire, Morse and Neuberger of

Oregon, would all have made interesting studies from this standpoint. As it happened, I did most of my interviewing with representatives simply because senators' schedules are so much more complex and it is harder to get to see them. (A first-term senator may serve on as many as fourteen subcommittees, something unimaginable in the House.)

For those whose focus is on the communication between a representative and his district, and who are not necessarily confined to a particular issue, there are still better cases for study. For instance, several districts in Maryland elect 7 members to its Lower House and Massachusetts has a number of three- and two-member districts (as have other states and cities). Considering the wide factional and personality differences of incumbents at the same time, an analysis of the messages they "hear" from their districts would be of considerable value.

V

Transaction rather than interaction

As long as we think of the relationship between a member and a district as in fractional—one pressing on the other in a kind of billiard-ball psychology—I suspect that we will have considerable difficulty in describing or understanding exactly what goes on. The transactional mode of analysis, as developed by John Dewey and Arthur Bentley[9] in conscious rejection of the interactional sociology of street-corner philosophy, and of the sociology textbooks—and of Bentley's own classic work on pressure—seems to me to be a more reliable picture of what really happens. And, I believe it supplies us with a leading hypothesis in terms of which political communications can be understood. Unfortunately, I came to grasp the significance of the Bentley-Dewey notion too late to utilize it satisfactorily in most of my field work.

How a congressman was "influenced" by his district: A transactional relationship

Mr. Serious-Consideration provides a very good case study of how a particular constellation of factors in the district may lead to a particular vote. The vote cannot be understood unless we recognize that both a congressman—as a personality and at a particular time—and the "district," as understood by him are variables.

During the spring of 1954, my old friend Mr. Straightforward did considerable canvassing in the district with a view to running for Congress in the primary against Mr. Serious-Consideration. Mr. Straightforward, incidentally, has held public office in the area several times before. He told me, in effect:

> There's practically no interest in trade or tariff matters in the district; if you are think-ing [as we were] of interviewing businessmen and labor leaders about it, don't bother. None of them know anything about it; it just doesn't bulk large in their sight.

Mr. Serious-Consideration, however, in the same year reported that in his view it was the most significant or certainly one of the three most significant issues to his constituents.

Why the difference? It can be explained, I think, partly by the fact that Mr. Serious-Consideration is, consciously, or unconsciously, look-ing for ways in which he can appeal to local labor without offending local business. Protection against "low-wage foreign imports" is, as trade association executives have pointed out to us, an excellent issue for *uniting* labor and management in depressed or dying industries (of which there are several in the district). Mr. Straightforward, on the other hand, has a program for economic redevelopment and reform of labor legislation, which deflects the attention of those whom he meets, whether they agree with him or not, from such issues as the tariff. He, therefore, probably rarely hears about the tariff as an issue. Then, too, in manner and bearing, Mr. Straightforward is clearly an intellectual and one of the popular conceptions of the intellectual is his belief in free trade, unless evidence to the contrary is supplied.[10] Mr. Serious-Consideration is not at all of this type. Finally, Mr. Straightforward's worst fault as a politi-cian is a rather curt dismissal of anything he regards as nonsense. Mr. Serious-Consideration, on the other hand, might justly be criticized for not being able to distinguish between more or less unmotivated grum-bling and serious pleas for effective action. (Mr. Serious-Consideration is, in other words, the kind of man who could be readily persuaded that every businessman who complains about taxes is earnestly desirous of reducing armaments.)

Mr. Serious-Consideration is (rather remarkably among congress-men) a worrier. He seems genuinely to believe that we must shore-up NATO by strengthening trade relations. Therefore, he called a meet-ing of everyone in his district who might be interested and wanted to come to discuss the problem. After this meeting, his office, which had already received a good deal of mail on the subject, was simply overwhelmed by protectionist mail. This came about because people who had attended the meeting told their friends and business acquaintances about his indecision. Mr. Serious-Consideration had called upon persons whom he thought might be interested. Naturally most of those who turned up were from protection-minded industries. It is much easier for the businessman who is, or thinks he is, in considerable economic danger from foreign imports to take a day off to attend a meeting on trade and tariffs called by the congressman (he can charge this as a business expense) than it is for the businessman who *might* benefit economically if international trade were increased in total. It is more difficult of course for non-businessmen to take such time off and it is usually quite impossible for them to charge the cost off as business expense.

So this meeting, because of the way it was called, was "stacked" in this particular district. If, on the other hand, Congressman Lankford of the Fifth Maryland had called such a meeting it might well have been stacked the other way. His district is a big tobacco-growing area, which is well aware of its dependence on sales to Switzerland, and there have been Swiss threats to cut off purchases unless the U.S. withdrew its trade barriers to Swiss watches. Congressman Serious-Consideration or even Congressman Lankford, however, by some planning could have gotten a more balanced attendance. A different picture would have developed: if national or state leaders of those unions in the district whose headquarters favor reciprocal trade had been consulted; and if the several college professors of economics in the district and representatives of the Grange and the Farm Bureau had been invited; and if an effort to get some of the nationally known supporters of reciprocal trade having some ties with the district to present their viewpoints, had been made. Or several organizations could have been asked to do what the League of Women Voters has done in some areas—study the dependence of the local industries on foreign trade.

Mr. Serious-Consideration would have had to be a different kind of man to provide wider representation at his meeting. However, three or four imaginative supporters of reciprocal trade could equally well have produced the same result. And if the agricultural commodity in which Mr. Serious-Consideration himself has had an interest were on an export basis (as it was prior to World War II), his picture of the situation might well have been altered. He would then have been hearing from his own associates in his own trade association. (The only reason that the commodity is not now exported is that the American market consumes all that is presently produced.)

Mr. Serious-Consideration finally decided to vote against the party leadership on the key votes on reciprocal trade. He justified himself by objecting to various procedural aspects of the legislation—for instance, the so-called "gag rule" under which the Bill was brought to the floor. But he had not objected to this gag rule, which is standard parliamentary practice, in other cases where it was invoked. He continues to regard himself as a strong advocate of reciprocal trade.

When a congressman was not much influenced by his district

Representative Warburton (R., DE, 1953-5) provided a particularly clear example of the way in which a congressman may select the kind of communications he hears. In answer to a question from me, he said to his secretary, "Am I right? We haven't received mail from more than five people on this tariff business." I looked somewhat astounded and she replied, "Yes, except of course for the pressure groups." The congressman had instructed her to segregate all recognized pressure-group mail. And he added, quite offhandedly, that he would discount "because of his self-interest," one out of the five people who had written him about the tariff. His attitude may, in part at least, explain why the chemical companies and other industries in the state had never given him "any particular specifications" on the tariff. It certainly clarifies his assertion that his approach to the problem of communications had "choked off" pressure-group mail.

Such an approach is relatively easy in Delaware[11] where DuPont, because of its tremendous size and consciousness of its own vulnerability, has developed a practice and to some extent a doctrine of self-restraint. In a sense, Congressman Warburton's procedure[12] was made much easier because of the effect upon DuPont of the munitions investigations of twenty years ago and its subsequent earnest effort never, never, never to get into that sort of trouble again. Thus it could happen when a prominent Delaware Democrat was asked why DuPont had not put on a campaign in regard to tariff matters (if, as it was reported, DuPont was hostile to the Reciprocal Trade Extension Act) that he said in a genuinely shocked voice, "Oh, the company would never allow that, two or three letters at the most."

A congressman's reputation among those who might want to influence him, determines in large measure what actually is said to him

Most lobbyists appear to follow the principle of going to see only those who already agree with them. "Work with your friends, but don't stir up your enemies" is a principle fairly widely believed by Capitol Hill lobbyists. (Since each congressman has his own office and can be approached separately, this is fairly easy. However, in state capitols where members of a committee even though they may disagree on a particular issue nevertheless hang around a lot together, it is reportedly more difficult. Here the lobbyists use a different technique.) There is a reason for this prudence. Most investigations of lobbying and of particular lobbyists seem to have been started by congressmen who were annoyed at being continually approached by lobbyists with whom they disagreed. There is also another possible reason—it makes the job easy for the lobbyist. Representatives of the League of Women Voters and of labor union councils, who do not follow this principle, make themselves unpopular in some quarters.

The tendency to abstain from trying to influence those whom you believe to be against you affects the districts back home as well as professional Capitol Hill lobbyists. The Farm Bureaus in Congressman Stubborn's district, like most Farm Bureaus, were definitely committed to the reciprocal trade program. Nevertheless, when a delegation went to see him, they made no effort to talk in favor of reciprocal trade (although delegations from neighboring bureaus from similar districts did reportedly do so when talking to *their* congressmen). Our correspondent in Mr. Stubborn's district inquired of Farm Bureau representatives why they made no such effort and he summarizes their attitude as follows:

> The farmers deliberately avoided mention of tariffs; when I asked one of them why he didn't beard old "Stubborn" in his high-tariff den, he replied, "Nothing in the world will change his thinking on tariffs, so why bother? He knows how we feel and can't help but feel a little nervous about the situation. So we can take that nervousness and get him to go along with us on things he isn't so dead-set against."

The probability is that they didn't *change* him on anything, but that they may have influenced him to take a more aggressive and effective part on an issue of importance to them—an issue on which he did not disagree, but which he considered less important than they did.

In another instance, the congressmen from a certain area are inclined to be rather blunt and not to rely on any indirection. Before the 1955 vote on reciprocal trade, the Farm Bureau sent representatives in to talk with these congressmen. One of them, Congressman Ridge, told me that the farmers said, "National asked us to pass the word along that we're in favor of reciprocal trade—but we shan't be mad if you vote against it." Then, according to Mr. Ridge, one of the congressmen asked the Farm Bureau men if any one of them really favored reciprocal trade. Anyone who knows the congressmen present can be sure that at least two of them would look ready to slay on the spot any farmer bold enough to say "Yes." Apparently no one did say "Yes" and the reason may have been similar to that advanced by the Farm Bureau member from Mr. Stubborn's district. So Mr. Ridge, who is not as strongly opposed to reciprocal trade as some of his colleagues, was pushed to this conclusion:

> Everybody in my state is against reciprocal trade. . . . The only ones for it would be the ultra-internationalists.

Of course, if Mr. Ridge were a devoted supporter of reciprocal trade, or if he were a really sophisticated analyst of interpersonal relations, he might well have felt that the conclusion is not that easy. But he is neither of these and so he allied himself entirely to his colleagues' opposition to the reciprocal trade program.

Several congressmen told me, in effect, that they tell their constituents:

> I want a letter of such-and-such a kind or I won't pay any attention to it.

One of the most dedicated opponents of reciprocal trade in the country is a man who has often pointed out that reciprocal trade is really an invention of Karl Marx himself, designed to "make us captives of the Kremlin," developed and implemented by Harry Dexter White. This congressman states that he tells his constituents that he is only interested in "factual, thoughtful" letters, nothing mass-produced or propagandistic. He also told me that in three months he had not received one single letter opposing his views on reciprocal trade; he had received over 2,000 supporting his position, 1,750 of which were definitely individual letters. The very extremity of his position apparently leads those who might disagree with him to feel "Oh, what's the use?" Senators who make statements of this kind, however, may simply not know what mail they get since the mail clerks handle it. Most members of the House do have a fairly good idea of what is coming in to them. Of course, protectionist mail was mass-produced in a way that reciprocal trade mail was not, and it is far more likely that a protectionist congressman would receive nothing in opposition to his stand rather than the reverse. (Oil interests on the Atlantic seaboard did mass-produce mail protesting the fuel-oil quota but few of the congressmen to whom they wrote favored a fuel-oil quota, whatever their general tariff views.)

We need more studies of what the image of a person to whom a communication is sent is in the minds of the sender. By and large, I strongly suspect that the bulk of political communications in the United States today tends to be addressed to those believed most likely to be sympathetic. Exceptions may occur when an issue becomes one of great involvement (as reciprocal trade did *not*, 1953-1955) or of interest to persons politically very unsophisticated who have no image of specific political figures. (Occasionally, too, a writer may regard his request as one for a personal service but in the recipient's view, it may involve an issue. A sympathetic response is expected, of course, to a request for a personal service.)

Some communications tend to be unclear in their meaning

A good deal of so-called "lobbying" by constituents tends to be nothing more than a social visit and a general discussion. One senator's assistant said:

> You know, many of these guys who come in here from back home never talk about issues at all. I've seen lots of them supposedly lobbying. Now, "Roughie," [the Senator] takes me to lunch with them and we go out to lunch, but they don't necessarily talk about anything. "Roughie" just knows a good guy may be going out of business because he doesn't get more trade or so. It's the spirit that influences him.

Interestingly enough, some weeks later I found that this particular assistant was completely ignorant of the quite strong feelings (verbalized in other quarters) on tariff matters of an important industry in the state. This is an industry whose representatives had visited him and the Senator, and in whose behalf he personally had spent many hours performing other chores in administrative agencies.

Mr. Busy represents a district very much like those of Messrs. First, Second and Third discussed above and he is home every weekend. He was professedly strongly opposed to reciprocal trade, but when I questioned him, he said he really did not know whether people talk about the tariff with him or not. At first, it seemed as though this might be because of his schedule, which is so heavy that most men could not stand it and he must be, as a result, always fatigued. But the real point appears to be that Mr. Busy's focus and attention in oral conversations back home are given to requests for personal services. He is the archetype of the errand-boy congressman and the only things he seems attuned to hear are requests for personal services. He shunts comments on issues to one side or regards them as preliminaries to requests for favors. When Mr. Second hears someone talk about unemployment caused by foreign imports, he regards this as a request to fight reciprocal trade. Mr. First regards it as nonsense, although possibly nonsense of which he should be cognizant. But Mr. Busy pays only vague attention to it except insofar as it leads or may lead to a request for him to perform a service. In this he may well be correct, for very few constituents talk about an issue with a congressman just to talk about the issue. I spent about twenty man-days in the winter of 1956 acting as co-manager of a candidate in a congressional primary campaign and about half of this time I was actually with the candidate. During the entire twenty days only four people raised any national or international issues whatsoever with him or me. (Others who worked for him at the same time and in the same area had similar reports to make.)

It's partly accident if anybody's listening

There is a highly unpredictable element in the kind of response a particular communication will get. As a senatorial assistant said:

> I've seen it a dozen times. One time some letter or call will come in from "Minerville" and nobody will pay any attention to it. They might say, for instance, the miners are all worried about this foreign fuel oil. Another time a call will come in in the same words almost and everybody will get worried as hell about it; it might be that the State Chairman was in the day before and says, "We're not doing so well in 'Coal County'" so we all jump to the conclusion that it's fuel oil that is hurting us there. Or it may be just accident; one time the Senator is preoccupied, another in a relaxed mood, but the third time he listens eagerly. You know how it is."

This does seem natural. I've observed it in my own political activities. One day I'm too euphoric or too busy to pay much attention or take in the significance of something that, if it came to me another day, would seem to me worth a lot of thought and activity. And it is the same with the people with whom I've worked.

Since a few people in Congress, because of the committee and leadership structure, are far more capable of exercising influence on a given issue than others, it could make a great deal of difference how they hear something or not.

VI

Important instances when congressmen were changed by their districts

The two statistically notable shifts on reciprocal trade in 1955 as compared with previous years were: 1) Southern congressmen, mostly representing textile manufacturing districts, who for the first time voted against the Hull reciprocal trade program, in spite of a traditional veneration for free trade in the South; and 2) Farm Belt congressmen, from districts where "isolationist" sentiment had been fairly strong, for the first time supported reciprocal trade on the key votes. The latter were presumably influenced by the organized efforts of national Farm Bureau leaders to get their local leaders to understand the (actual or alleged) dependence of farm prosperity upon international trade and the (actual or alleged) values of a trade not aid, program. But those who were influenced were not, so far as is known, men to whom the issue mattered much one way or another. There is no way of sorting out the relative weight of the constituency's concern from that of the influence of the leadership of the Republican party, President Eisenhower and Minority Leader Martin.

In the case of the Southern congressmen the matter is clearer. Here "pressure education"—agitation in the district—worked. They broke with the leadership of Speaker Rayburn, generally said to be the most powerful Speaker since Speaker Cannon. They broke with the Southern tradition and the tradition of Cordell Hull, the father of reciprocal trade. They challenged and to some degree pressured that highly respected Southern senator, Walter George, on his long-standing pro-reciprocal trade position. And they gave, in this case, a weapon to Hermann Talmadge, George's potential opponent in the senatorial primary of 1956, in spite of the fact that practically none of them would have preferred Talmadge to George. This breaking with precedent was chiefly the result of the communications they received from their districts, largely from textile interests. Some Southern congressmen received more mail on the reciprocal trade question in a few weeks than they normally do in months on all issues combined. That the mail was more or less synthetic and stimulated is shown by the fact that some congressmen, whose positions are known to be unchangeable, received not a single letter! For these Southern congressmen, such a flood of mail was apparently like the first engagement in a war for inexperienced troops. They had never seen anything of the sort before. The results: most of the Georgia delegation opposed reciprocal trade on the key votes. Hugh Alexander, successor to "Muley" Doughton who as leader of Ways and Means had year after year pushed reciprocal trade through committee and the House, much as Cordell Hull wanted it, voted against the program of Hull and Doughton.

This does not controvert what has been said before, except in one respect. Most of these, men, although traditionally "free-traders," care very little about the issue one way or the other. If industry and the workers in their district are convinced that reciprocal trade will hurt them, they are willing enough to go along—just as most of them would go along with their farmers if the latter wanted new soil conservation legislation. In either case, they would regard themselves simply as serving their constituents.

This, of course, shows that the leaders of pro-reciprocal trade forces in the House, the State Department, and the South had not been effective in explaining their overall viewpoint. To men like Jere Cooper and Wilbur Mills, the two ranking Democrats on Ways and Means, and to Albert Gore, Cordell Hull's protégé and successor, the issue of reciprocal trade is as significant as it was to the British who led the campaign for repeal of the "corn laws."

Mr. Southern Leader's shift

Somewhere between ten and fifteen Southern congressmen probably were influenced not only by the mail but by Congressman Southern Leader's switch of position. They might have rejected Speaker Rayburn and Chairman Cooper's leadership anyhow, but Mr. Southern Leader's change apparently made it official and respectable. How, therefore, did he happen to "bolt?"

In January, 1955, he received a large quantity of mail from workers in the textile industry saying that they wanted protection against foreign goods. Shrewd enough to realize that they must have been "put up to it" by manufacturers Mr. Southern Leader said:

> I did not appreciate it. I wrote to a friend of mine who is in business, saying, in effect, "call your fellows off." I asked my friend, "Don't peril point and escape clause protect you?" He replied, "No, they don't." That shocked me. I started making inquiries. I found out. I'd been pretty naive. Peril point and escape clause did not protect our people.

(Peril point and escape clause refer to provisions of earlier Reciprocal Trade Acts, professedly designed to protect U.S. industry against ruination through goods introduced under the Reciprocal Trade Act.)

It is significant that the congressman made his inquiries in his home state almost (if not quite) entirely among people in the textile industry. Despite the fact that at least half of the economy of his district is agricultural, producing cotton among other commodities, he made no inquiry among his farmers. A superficial analysis, however, would suggest that most of his farmers profit from foreign trade, directly or indirectly, and that many of them are affiliated with farm organizations, which have endorsed reciprocal trade. Mr. Southern Leader actually represents the town more than the countryside. The town is where his roots are, where his friends are, and he thinks in its terms. Population wise, it would be perfectly conceivable that his district and several other districts over whose congressmen he had influence, might be represented by men to whom the farmer is more important than the manufacturer. (Who happens to get elected to Congress when an incumbent dies or retires is to a considerable extent fortuitous. In the particular case of Mr. Southern Leader, if he had run four years later, it almost certainly would have been too late for him, in terms of the traditions and customs involved in the selection of candidates in that area.)

VII

Reverse English

When Mr. Southern Leader became convinced that there was real merit to the contention of the textile and allied industries, he then went to the state organization representing textiles. According to his account, he politely pointed out to them that they really hadn't been on the ball—he should have heard more about the matter and so should his colleagues, presumably, this did increase the communications on the subject, by mail and personal visits, to his colleagues.

This kind of reverse lobbying—from congressmen to interest groups— is by no means unusual. I asked another prominent congressman how much he heard from the organizations on his side of the issue:

Hell no, it's just the other way. It's me calling them up and trying to shaft them to get off their fat rears and get out and do something.

More common, probably, is the senator or representative who asks the lobbyists on his side to do something, which they then generalize. A senatorial assistant needed some figures in preparing a speech and tried to get them from the lobbying group:

I absolutely had to beat them over the head to get those things.

But not long after, the same figures were cited by the organization as "proving" their point.

VIII

Pressure is how you see it

"Pressure" and "pressure politics" are regarded by most "sophisti cated" people today as "explaining" a great deal that happens. But it was frequently impossible to find any admission of or apparently any awareness of "pressure." That was not because shrewd and worldly politicians were concealing what really goes on from this naive and innocent interviewer and his naive and innocent colleagues.

The reason is explained by Senator Service's assistant:

> There are very few people actually pressuring us, even if you count all we hear about all issues. Seriously, the sense of being pressured is a matter of reaction. Other people who get no more mail than we do in this office would say, "See how much pressure is on me." We don't feel it.... Sure, you get mail. It's just that so-and-so makes more "phone calls" than somebody else. The result is purely physical. It isn't a representation of what or how or when people are going to vote in elections... My personal opinion is that members of most organizations make up their minds on what they read in the papers without reference to organizations.

With this theory of voting behavior, Senator Service's assistant naturally will not be too much worried by a good deal of effort to get him or his boss to change policies—he simply will not regard it as pressure.

Congressman Widesight amusingly illustrated the point made by Service's assistant. Mr. Widesight has moods when he reaches way out into left field looking for things to worry about, things which might possibly defeat him. One day, discussing reciprocal trade, he said that things were very bad indeed. His reason was that he was getting "so much" mail against it, "I, whom they never used to bother at all." When I checked with his secretary later, I found he couldn't possibly have received more than fifty letters (representing Stass, electrical equipment, and two or three bicycle interests) opposing reciprocal trade. This was only a fraction of the mail Senator Service receives on the same matter. It was also a fraction of what Congressman Widesight himself has several times heard on other matters such as postal pay increases. However, Widesight is accustomed to communications on that issue and he wasn't accustomed to them on the reciprocal trade issue.

As a matter of fact, on the reciprocal trade issue, most of the congressmen interviewed reported that no one had come to see them. Several of them expressed the wish that someone would make the issue clear. (This does not mean, of course, that they were not approached; but simply that they had forgotten the approach or had not realized its purpose.) Some of them tried to question me about the matter in what I think was a serious effort to get some guidance. Generally, as good interviewing technique requires, I maintained complete neutrality. However, in two conversations (after the vote when it could make no difference), I think I convinced members that a strengthened escape clause results in the worst of both worlds. This is a position which I do hold, although I am of necessity neutral on the major substantive issue. It was perfectly clear that no one had ever really explained to the two members I talked to why there is objection to the strong escape clause procedure, in spite of the fact that one of the two key votes on the issue revolved around this. (Since the key votes were decided by seven or fewer members, every vote counted.)

Our interviews confirmed the observation of a newly appointed assistant to a senator who said, speaking generally and not talking just about reciprocal trade:

> I was very much surprised how few representatives of organizations come around to make themselves known. The Senator is, as you know, on the sub-committee dealing with "ruanga" and "minorca" manufacturing; yet nobody came around to see us either from the Ruanga Makers, AFL, or the Minorca Setters, CIO. I raised hell with them about that because I know some of their top guys through the AVC; but some, who should have been up here, haven't been.... Of course, there might have been some reason they hesitated, although, hell, they ought to know the Senator is pro-labor if anybody is; and if they were in any doubt as to how they might be received, there are a dozen ways of throwing your hat in to see if it gets tossed back.

Later he continued:

> You know we are very much interested in educational legislation. I had some representatives of ... organizations here to talk with us. I sent for them, they didn't try to see us. We thought about some changes in the educational bill which looked desirable in terms of their program and worked them out. We did get their O.K., they went along with us.

The question here is: How much lobbying or pressure was there?

Even where there is a considerable amount of what the outsider would consider pressure, the point made by Senator Service's assistant is entirely valid. What you call pressure ...or what you feel to be pressure ... depends on how thick your skin is. Mr. Second, for instance, told me that he had been subject to no "pressure—that is, no threats." To many men in politics threats alone represent the only real pressure because they know very well that few votes are actually lost on any one given issue such as reciprocal trade. But, of course, what is a threat to one man is not a threat to another. (For comparison, we should have studied some explosive issues like "McCarthyism" or *humane slaughtering* or perhaps some issues in which the profit-and-loss relationship is clearer like the question of pay increases for postal employees.)

The most strongly felt kind of "pressure" on the reciprocal trade issue came, apparently, from Speaker Rayburn and the Democratic leadership against the potentially recalcitrant Democrats. Speaker Rayburn attended a breakfast for freshmen congressmen shortly before the vote and said, in effect, that he'd discovered that those who go along, get along. One new member regarded this as pressure—a threat. Another new member (actually probably more vulnerable in terms of his factional position and his position within the delegation) did not. Both of them failed to "go along." Aside from this speech, most of the "pressure" on the doubtful members seems to have come through the grapevine or from their own apprehensions as to what might happen if they bolted the party leadership.

One reason why fairly few members seem to have felt pressure on this matter is to be explained in terms of their background and associations in local politics. In many states, "pressure" on matters like highway contracts or patronage or even for or against gubernatorial programs, must be relatively heavy—that is, threats are far more common at the state level than they are in Washington. Many congressmen come from such a background and a good many are still involved in local conflicts about patronage, contracts, etc. As a result, Washington to them seems very mild.

Nagging may also be called pressure, whether done by mail or in person. When a congressman has definitely announced his stand and does not intend to switch it, he resents being bothered by avoidable pleas (pressures) to change. The resentment point, obviously, is highly individual so one man's pressure is another man's routine.

It should never be forgotten that most congressmen respect—although in an inarticulate or almost subconscious way—the right of petition. They have a general feeling that everyone should have a right to talk or write to them about any public issue—that's what they're there for. But they aren't as worried about each communication as college professors might expect. They generally feel they have an equal right to disregard the petitioner's point, once it has been courteously received and acknowledged. Until a congressman definitely makes up his mind, it isn't pressure—it's communication or instruction. Much of what Mr. Fourth, for instance, believes about reciprocal trade he learned from his mail.

IX

Opportunism is also where you see it

Outsiders, nonpoliticians, tend to attribute many political decisions to opportunism. Also, opponents in politics sometimes attribute the decisions of the other party or faction to "opportunism." However, in the interviews, which I conducted, few congressmen attributed their friends' decisions or their own to opportunism. When friends differ on a particular issue it may be explained in terms of "the heat being on." Whether any significant number of politicians anywhere would have a self-image of themselves as opportunistic, I do not know. It is certainly true that in these interviews many men were amazingly—and often embarrassingly—frank about events, relationships, and personal opinions. But insofar as the overt picture which they have of themselves is concerned, opportunism does not play a prominent role. Even Congressman District, who related his obligation to his district directly to his chances for reelection, spoke of his "duty" to get reelected. No one used a systematically opportunistic vocabulary of motives to explain himself or his actions. Perhaps a different type of interview, some sort of "depth-interviewing," would bring out a hidden set of self-images at variance with this surface picture. However, I have no evidence to that effect and am inclined to doubt it.

This report, of course, does not cover that facet of behavior which might be described as "opportunistic." It is in contrast, as far as overt self-picturing is concerned, to the views of local politicians whom I have known.

X

Conclusion

Attention has been focused in the present study on the ways congressmen view representation and on the ways in which their pictures of the world determine what they hear, how they interpret it, whom they represent, how they influence representation by others, and how they view other representatives. It omits many equally significant facets of the representative process—for example, the formal and informal structure of the congressional system. Elsewhere[13] I have discussed the formal structure. It is obvious that there is an informal structure and that it is highly significant. That it is an exceptionally complex structure to study, because congressmen are members of several different groups simultaneously, is also apparent. I have made only random observations concerning it.

Obviously, it would be enlightening and helpful to have comparative studies of state legislatures to follow up the brilliant work of Garceau and Silverman.[14] It would also be useful to have studies of other issues before Congress and of issues coming before committees. My later study of the ways in which Armed Services, Defense Appropriations, and Military Operations Committees "hear" about the issues of military policy led me to delete and question some generalizations, which I had formulated on the basis of the reciprocal trade study. The military study also made me much more vividly aware of the degree of freedom which congressmen have on the big issues where there is no aspect of personal service involved and of the fact that effective "pressure" on those responsible for presenting an issue to Congress may forestall the need for "pressuring" congressmen themselves. For example, I suspect that the weapons makers find it easier and more satisfactory to work with (or on) the Defense Department than on Congress on such issues as the great missile controversy. The military study made me aware also of the difference between issues such as reciprocal trade, where there is a quantity of accessible information, and an issue concerning the relationship of weapons construction to national policy. In the latter, access to whatever formulations have been made is practically impossible for those who provide congressmen with much of their "information," and it is often difficult for congressmen themselves to find out the facts. Congress is, therefore, compelled by "the tyranny of information" to accept the recommendations of specialists who are often more concerned with expanding their own missions or increasing technical competence than with national policy. (I leave this suggestion open because I do not know if there is available, in fact, information on these relevant problems, in classified documents, similar to that available for the analyses of the reciprocal trade question.)

The study here reported was defective in that it lacked the precision of, for example, many of the reports on industrial plants published in this journal. One reason for this is the problem of anonymity. To describe the factional conflicts in a particular congressional district, or even more personal interrelationships within a congressional committee could hardly be done with fairness to the subjects of the study. Such details are safe enough when the study concerns a factory. But aside from this problem, the "group memberships," reference groups, etc., of politicians, are substantially more complex than those reported in many professional journals. Our reciprocal trade study devoted an unusual degree of attention to the districts from which some of the congressmen we interviewed came. However, we devised no technique for observing the relationship between a congressman and his constituency in detail over a period of time. Probably, considering the workload of congressmen, this can only be done by those who become helpers and thereby preclude themselves from reporting. Studies of state and city legislatures and of the representative process therein offer more hope for the development of a sociology of representation. It should be remembered that representation exists in many cultural frameworks. How for instance, does all that is said here apply to the British West Indies? In this connection, it is noted that the representative process exists in the church (the Dominican order of the Roman Catholic Church and the National Council of Churches for example), in trade unions, in trade associations, and in fraternal organizations. So far, the process has been studied only occasionally in such contexts.

Notes

* Lewis Anthony Dexter, conducted his portion of the Reciprocal Trade Study (upon which this article is chiefly based) under contract with the Research Program in International Communications, Center for International Studies, Massachusetts Institute of Technology (part of the time under subcontract to the Bureau for Social Research, Washington, DC). The writer is indebted to the project supervisors, Ithiel da Sola Pool and Raymond A. Bauer for help and direction. Dr. Dexter's participation in the Reciprocal Trade Study resulted in a book, *Congressmen and the People They Listen To*, dittoed, copyright, 1956, which may be borrowed from 14N207, Massachusetts Institute of Technology. This book develops procedural points, community studies, etc., not discussed in this article.

The Public Opinion Quarterly, Vol. 20 (1956), contained several articles related to the Reciprocal Trade Study, including "What Do Congressmen Hear: The Mail?" by Lewis Dexter and "When is Petition 'Pressure?'" by F. Bonilla. Both of these articles were based upon Dr. Dexter's book referred to above.

The study of the Armed Services, Military Operations, and Defense Appropriations Committees referred to was undertaken in 1956 with a Carnegie Corporation grant under a contract with the Center for International Studies, Massachusetts Institute of Technology.

Campaign studies also serving as background for the article have been made in Illinois, Puerto Rico, Philadelphia, upstate New York, Massachusetts, and Maryland. A report on the last mentioned study appeared in the *Public Opinion Quarterly*, Vol. 19 (1955-56), pp. 408-14, in an article entitled, "Candidates Make the Issues and Give Them Meaning," by Lewis Dexter.

1. The present analysis is based upon about 650 interviews, 1953-7 (420 of them by the author) with politicians, businessmen trade union leaders, and departmental officials, about the influences impinging upon the formulation of policy. More than 100 interviews were conducted with members of congress and 40 with executive assistants on Capitol Hill. Four hundred of the interviews utilized dealt with the formation of policy or the communication of preference on the Reciprocal Trade Extension Acts of 1952, 1954, and 1955, and it is around these that the analysis is chiefly organized. Considerable use has been made of the writer's own participation in politics, in, for example, the state government of Massachusetts, September 1956-August, 1957, the Stevenson primary campaign of 1956, and an effort to arouse interest in a civil defense bill.

2. ee Dexter, "Candidates Made the Issues..." for supporting data, and "What do Congressmen hear: the Mail" *op. cit.*

3. Either by consciously providing distracting stimuli or by consciously exposing themselves to countervailing viewpoints.

4. See Dexter, *Congressmen and the People They Listen To ..., op. cit*, Ch. III, *passim*.

5. Except for a few obvious instances, all names used in this paper are fictitious.

6. J. F. Kennedy, *Profiles in Courage,* New York, Harpers, 1955, esp., pp. 12-21.

7. Dexter, *Congressmen and the People They Listen To ..., op. cit.*, Chs. II-III.

8. The likelihood of a break between supporter and leader on some primary matter of personal fairness and the like is considerably greater in general.

9.   J. Dewey and A. Bentley, *The Knowing and the Known*, Boston, Beacon, 1949; and A. Bentley, *An Inquiry into Inquiries*, Boston, Beacon, 1954.

10. See Dexter, *Congressmen and the People ..., op. cit.*, Ch. XIX, "Where the Elephant Takes Care Not to Dance Among the Chickens: Delaware."

11. *Ibid.*

12. Congressman Warburton followed the same procedure on other matters. He was, it is true, rather badly beaten in his try for the Senate in 1954 by the incumbent Democrat, Frear, but there is no reason to suppose his handling of communications had anything to do with the outcome. Far more significant political factors such as the opposition to integration probably explain that.

13. Dexter, *Congressmen and the People ..., op. cit.*

14. O. Garceau and C. Silverman, "A Pressure Group and the Pressured," *American Political Science Review*, *48* (1954), pp. 672-691.

3

Where the Elephant Fears to Dance among the Chickens*

Business response to political challenge or possibility has been the subject of much speculation and some recent exhortation. "Populist" and starkly "realist" elements in American political thought have tended to assume that powerful firms directly and unequivocally influence politicians.

Here, as elsewhere, simplistic political generalizations can probably be modified or discredited by the diversity of events. Westinghouse was probably more aggressive in its response to the actual or alleged threat of foreign imports than du Pont could have dreamed of being, just as the attitude of Republic Steel or Inland Steel toward the current enthusiasm for political education differs from that, say, of Allied Paper or Wilson and Company. So, the report we are about to present on du Pont and Delaware applies unequivocally only there.[1]

Its significance, however, extends to a fairly considerable number of businessmen and business firms in contemporary American society; and, indeed, the current enthusiasm about "getting businessmen into politics," represents a (probably temporary) revolt[2] against an attitude which many firms, probably the majority, have held since 1937 and in essence hold today. Du Pont probably serves as a fairly good type of this attitude.

As a part of a study of reciprocal trade legislation,[3] and communications from and within the industrial community about it, we conducted a series of interviews in several different industries and congressional districts in 1953, 1954, and 1955, when the reciprocal trade extension acts were debated in Congress. We chose to study Delaware chiefly because of du Pont.

Du Pont is huge, du Pont is colossal, du Pont is almost legendary. Du Pont is a $2,000,000,000 corporation which has grown up in a state with only one congressional district. And du Pont is traditionally protectionist. Some State Department employees, with experience in commercial policy, regarded du Pont, in 1955, as one of their most serious enemies, just as some protectionists regard the State Department as their most serious enemy.

It happens that both senators from Delaware were on the Senate Finance Committee, the committee which handles tariff matters. This is quite unusual. Both of them leaned toward reciprocal trade; as did the Delaware congressman (when we started our study he was Herbert Warburton, R., who was succeeded in *1955* by Harris McDowell, D.). If there were a knock-down, drag-out fight on reciprocal trade extension, would not these two senators be under considerable pressure? Would not Delaware business and farming interests be stimulated to try to influence them? And would not du Pont, as unquestionably the greatest of these interests, exert the most pressure?

The answer to all these questions, as it turned out, was "No." And this answer raises some very interesting problems for the student of business and politics; problems such as this: Can a business be too big to be politically effective along some lines? That is what is meant by the title of this essay. "Every man for himself said the elephant as he danced among the chickens," may well have described the attitude and outlook of big business in the days of Rockefeller and Carnegie and the railroad "robber barons." But nowadays some really big corporations do not care to "dance among the chickens" any more—the consequences are, or may be, too unpleasant.

Du Pont, because it is located in the very small state of Delaware, is more of an elephant among chickens than most of the other great corporations; Anaconda is the only parallel that comes to mind. AT&T, for instance, although great on a nationwide basis is not locally preeminent anywhere; General Electric is in New York State; Ford and General Motors are cheek-by-jowl in Detroit; the Mellon interests are in Pennsylvania and, in any event, are scattered among a number of different companies; and Standard Oil has been cut up into different companies.

But to the average outsider, du Pont is Delaware, Delaware du Pont. Thirty-odd years ago, The Nation, in a very serious (although superficial) evaluation, described the state as "the Ward of a Feudal Family"; and the notion persists. And it persists in part because du Pont, willy-nilly, is so much more in Delaware than any other corporation in any other state.

Add to this the fact that there are probably more than 100 du Pont households scattered throughout Greater Wilmington, and that the great majority of these households originally drew their influence and their wealth from the company; that they together control an extraordinarily high proportion of the total personal wealth of the state, a much larger proportion, presumably, than any other family in any other state. Not surprisingly, therefore, many of the great charities of the state are du Pont-planned, du Pont-directed, du Pont-named.

It might follow from all this that whatever the stand du Pont takes, Delaware senators and congressmen would fall into line. But, du Pont has been through many unpleasant experiences because of its size, its uniqueness, its success. In 1912, it was required by court order in effect to set up two separate and competing companies, Atlas and Hercules (of which you will read more later); but, nevertheless, it has been under continuous supervision and attack for alleged violation of the anti-trust laws ever since.

In fact, one of the reasons, perhaps, why, during the 1953-1955 period, the central management of du Pont did not focus on such matters as the tariff was that, throughout the period, it was under assault in two very ambitious anti-trust suits. Even more important in the development of the company's public relations attitude and point of view was the great Nye committee (Munitions) Investigation of the mid-thirties. Du Pont, perhaps more than any other corporation, was pilloried as the satanic munitions-maker, which gleefully piled up profits and created wars. One du Pont, remote from the company's management said:

> I think that that investigation made them [the company] feel they should be very cautious and lean over backwards.

And there is a certain local suspicion of the du Ponts. For instance, Francis V. du Pont was for some years the leading Republican in the state[4] and he was not connected with the company. One of the most skillful local political analysts says,

> There is only one reason he is not U.S. Senator: his name *is du Pont and* that would hurt.

> The situation is not only one where a senator does not now dare be for du Pont but where du Pont does not dare have a senator (and particularly a Delaware senator) "in its pocket" and would go a long way to avoid creating this impression.[5]

Of course, du Pont is continually involved in relationships with the United States Government, but, like most big corporations, it tends to deal directly with the agency in question. In the case of most corporations, this arises as much as anything out of the fact that business bureaucrats would rather deal with government bureaucrats, without being bothered by the temperamentally different politician as an intermediary; but, in the case of du Pont, this tendency is probably added to by the fear of appearing "to pick on somebody not its own size." The executive arm of the government can stand up to it; a Delaware senator looks as though he cannot.

Du Pont may work with great quietness to get Delaware senators or congressmen to follow its lead; after all, until 1948, a Delaware senator was a conservative du Pont in-law. But if it influences them on such matters as the tariff it is by stealthy maneuver, not by any overt pressure. And we do not believe it does. In any event, on the protectionist issue it was not successful if it did make any such effort in 1955; the senators and congressman supported reciprocal trade.

Of course, while du Pont may be on the whole protectionist, tariff protection probably is not the A-Number *1* issue in its table of priorities; there are a lot of things it cares about more. But if du Pont had the unquestioned dominance in Delaware that "Ward of a Feudal Family" suggests, of course that would make no difference; du Pont could treat the political officials of the state as its agents—in the way that the New England railroads at the turn of the century, according to tradition, treated their state officials. Du Pont does not, and could not, do this; it must make choices in its access to public officials, the same as any other petitioner.

Du Pont, in some respects, is in the same position as some of the great overseas investors: Standard Oil and its subsidiaries, for example. Because everybody suspects Standard Oil of being an agent of imperialism, because, for this reason, the United States Government will be more reluctant to intervene on its behalf than on behalf of some two-by-four hat manufacturer, such a corporation, in some ways, on political issues which are minor to it has less power than any other aggregation of wealth. And yet it will be held responsible for what it cannot—or does not—take any part in. So it is also with du Pont in Delaware.

Very probably this is not the only corporate reaction to the position of great power, which du Pont and Standard Oil possess. Quite likely Anaconda in Montana or the tin companies in Bolivia behave very differently. But the point is that, within du Pont and Standard Oil and some other great companies, there has grown up a tradition of restraint, restraint based upon a calculation (or a myth?) of long-run welfare. This restraint may be compared to the doctrine of judicial restraint as developed, for instance, by Justice Jackson. It is a real social fact, having important political consequences, just as the attitude of some of the White House staff (coming incidentally from business) under President Eisenhower "we can't take part in 'propaganda'" had important political consequences for the reciprocal trade program. Obviously this attitude is not the only possible one for the White House to take; it rarely hampered similar operators in President Roosevelt's time. Of course, like the notion of judicial restraint, this corporate restraint unquestionably breaks down from time to time and is differently interpreted by different officers and divisions; nevertheless, it makes a difference, on the whole, between du Pont and Standard Oil, on the one hand, and Westinghouse or General Electric or Pittsburgh Plate Glass or Republic Steel on the other.

What has just been said does not bear on the question of whether du Pont is or is not protectionist. It may be that the issue of protection matters little to du Pont; but the best guess we can make is that du Pont would align itself considerably more actively than it has with those other chemical companies, Dow and Monsanto (two of the four firms which campaigned most energetically for protection), if it were not for the general preference for corporate restraint. Reversely, we suspect that Standard Oil and/or some of the other big international oil companies would have been more directly active than they were in fighting the Neely Amendment and similar proposals to bar Venezuelan oil if it were not for the notion of corporate restraint.

There is another aspect of the matter which has some bearing: du Pont, Standard Oil, and some big companies are far more likely to have on their staffs a number of people who have held significant governmental decision-making positions than have the cherry growers trade association or a woolen-worsted manufacturer. They will, consequently, be far more aware of the general fact that legislation is put into practice through a series of administrative steps and that, at each stage in the administrative process, an interested party may have the right to ask adaptation of the decision in such a way as to avoid injury to him. Big companies have the legal resources and administrative contacts to take advantage of such rights; small companies do not.[6] And, for big companies, this activity in the administrative sphere is far more attractive; it usually avoids the publicity, which may spotlight the attempt to participate in the legislative process and is less apt to demand the time of top management; government administrators would often prefer to deal with the specialist in the corporation who knows the most about the topic, whereas senators or legislative committees are often believed to be more accessible to prominent people.

"Restraint" may also arise from the actual experience of du Pont officials. A company such as du Pont has to pay the cost of having lent top officials to government; although some government agencies may see things a little bit more as du Pont does, plenty of du Pont officials may see things somewhat more from the government agency's standpoint; and, in particular instances, even though they may disagree with the government standpoint, du Pont officials, because of their own government background, will be more hesitant to embarrass a government man for whom they have a fellow feeling by pressing a matter unduly than will a manufacturer of toy marbles or a garlic grower who has never had any reason to acquire such a fellow feeling.[7]

And officials of big corporations come to realize that their relationships with government are continuous, and that, if they press too hard for victory on one particular problem, even if they win, it may jeopardize their chances of success in some future, and more important, problem. That is to say, the relationship of such officials with government is the same as the relationship of members of Congress with each other; a congressman who presses one particular issue too hard convince or get the better of his colleagues but the price may be a considerable loss of credit and potential support on future issues.

The acceptance of the notion that du Pont will not push too hard too far occurred in several of our Delaware interviews. Two examples will suffice:

1)   A politician, who believes du Pont to be protectionist for the excellent reason that a du Pont officer[8] waited upon him to present arguments against the Reciprocal Trade Extension Act, was later discussing with us the vast volume of mail sent to congressmen and senators against the act by Monsanto and Westinghouse. One of us inquired as to whether du Pont did anything of the sort. An expression of great surprise crossed his face.
       Oh, no; the company would not allow that sort of thing. [Bulk mail.] Two or three letters, that would be the most.
       And other politicians expressed similar views.
2)   In effect, through a holding company, du Pont owns the Wilmington papers. These papers, however, we were told by the editorial staff, have always supported reciprocal trade, and the company has never raised the issue nor had it crossed the editors' minds that it would. To be sure, Fred Singer, a du Pont officer, has written the editors several times and we believe discussed the issue with them; but the editors felt themselves under no more pressure from him than a college professor in one branch of a university would if a scholar in another branch criticized the way he organized his courses.

Du Pont is Not a Unit

Both the du Pont family and the du Pont company have a wide variety of interests and orientations; there is no one point of view to which everybody adheres. Presumably, outside Delaware, the public picture of a du Pont is of a rather conservative right-wing businessman. Actually, the founder of du Pont, E. I. du Pont, was a close friend and correspondent of Jefferson's, and, in every generation since, including the present, there have been several du Ponts whose views and attitudes have been definitely Jeffersonian, and who would, therefore, tend to oppose the protectionist viewpoint which the interests of the company might be supposed to dictate.

Aside from this, there have been several family schisms among the du Ponts, which means that some of the most prominent local du Ponts might not see eye-to-eye with the company at all. Finally, among those du Ponts who particularly built the company to its present eminence, there seems to have been a very amicable difference of opinion on the tariff. Three brothers followed each other as president in building the company; it is generally reported that Pierre, the first to be president, opposed the protectionist viewpoint, in contrast to his brothers.

It may not be accidental that Pierre, serving as president at one time, was more closely involved with General Motors than the other two. For General Motors, presumably, is the type of company which profits from export. In any case, the du Pont company owned about one fifth of all GM stock and, in the first half of 1955, for instance, 85 cents per share of du Pont's earnings of $3.98 per share came from General Motors. This certainly might offset du Pont's concern as a chemical company with protection; on the other hand, as a report on Detroit[9] will suggest, GM's interest in expanding foreign trade is fairly general and unspecific. No one can really say how close the ties between General Motors and du Pont were: we were told in both Wilmington and Detroit that these made little difference. However, in view of the fact that the bigger of the anti-trust suits against du Pont (then before the Supreme Court) was directed toward ordering it to get rid of its General Motors' interests, management would naturally tend to play down the appearance of any community of interest even if it existed.

There is very real difficulty in discovering what "du Pont's interest" is because du Pont produces so many things and has so many irons in the fire. A du Pont economist at Wilmington said:

> Don't ever talk of du Pont as being an industry; it is a lot of industries.

However, this same economist estimated that, altogether for all products, exports constitute only about 6 percent of sales, so he doubted that anybody in du Pont would get much interested in expanding foreign markets. But he added:

It might well be that a man in one division would decide that he wanted to join the Henry Ford [*sic*] group [meaning the Taft Committee to support reciprocal trade]; hypothetically [although we do not think it would happen], the sales manager for foreign finishes, [selling a fair amount of paint abroad] might want to support all this reciprocal trade, whereas the rayon yarn people who are very alarmed about foreign imports would be on the other side. This whole problem is pretty academic to the people in nylon; they just would not care. So far as we know [and he is one of the twenty men in the company who could be expected to have reason to know], there is no overall company policy on trade and tariffs; it is left up to the individual divisions.

Now, du Pont is divided into ten separate operating divisions, making different kinds of products, with different general managers who, in theory, and apparently in practice, have a great deal of autonomy. For many purposes they act as separate companies. Each division has or may have its own "tariff representative," an officer charged with analyzing the foreign economic policy situation of the division. One tariff representative said:

The tariff representatives are the working stiffs. They do the leg work. The assistant general manager makes the decisions. Sometimes for months on end, I don't do any tariff work. At the moment [January, 1954] it is quite active because of customs simplification.

Another tariff representative said:

I cannot speak for other divisions. Different departments have varying interests. For instance, the textile fibers division never opened its trap about a tariff on nylon and I would think polychemicals would have a different [less protectionist] view on such things than organic chemicals.

We went through various major products with different officials and repeatedly heard the theme:

Each division has a different focus.

One man, for instance, continued:

Explosives are primarily concerned with quick service, shipping, and timing; foreign competition would not matter. Film and cellophane—they don't get into export much and are not adversely affected by imports.

Another middle echelon official added:

On balance, I think our paint department would gain more than it would lose by a reduction of tariffs. But at the other extreme is the dyestuff business which requires a combination of labor and technological skill, dependent on plodding, ordinary Ph.D.'s—who in Germany get 25 percent less salary than here, so that alone gives the Germans a substantial advantage.

Other men from other departments or with other orientations developed fully the argument that du Pont's "bread and butter," certain kinds of chemicals, can and will be produced more cheaply abroad than in this country—so du Pont needs protection. When we raised a question about some of these points, we were told:

> Top management has been debating this whole area; they don't wish their position to be interpreted as extreme protectionist; they are trying for a middle-of-the-road position.

Singer Creates an Impression of du Pont

Mr. Fred Singer was chairman of the Tariff Committee under the Executive Committee of du Pont; this is the tariff committee for the (in essence) central staff, as distinguished from the tariff representatives who work for the operating divisions (described above). A tariff representative said:

> Oh, the tariff representatives of the different divisions may see each other occasionally but they act quite independently; when they get together it is usually just to hear Singer [express his viewpoint]. But that central committee of his cannot tell any of the ten divisional managers anything; if the manager wants to do anything, he can; he is the kingpin.

But Mr. Singer can and does devote a good deal of time and effort to the cause of protection. He has been a stalwart supporter of the American Tariff League; he also serves on the trade association policy committees of eight different trade associations; he is, or has been, chairman of several of them. In this capacity, he makes statements and writes reports; and, since few people know or recognize the trade association name, and everybody has heard of du Pont, he is usually identified as a spokesman for du Pont rather than for whichever trade association he is at the moment speaking. For example, he testified before the House Ways and Means Committee in 1955 in opposition to the Reciprocal Trade Extension Act, as chairman of the International Trade and Tariff Committee, Manufacturing Chemists Association. At no point in his testimony did he mention or refer to du Pont in any way (although the representatives of Monsanto, Allied, Dow, and American Cyanamid testified presumably for their firms along the same lines).[10]

The question as to whether he does, in fact, speak for du Pont's top management or not is an interesting one. On the one hand, it may be that this indirect approach through trade associations is a tactical matter, designed to avoid controversy within du Pont. On the other hand, Mr. Singer may hold the same position as a university professor who testifies. When Seymour Harris, Harvard economist, testified, in effect, "in opposition" to reciprocal trade at the same hearings, no one (presumably) supposed that he was speaking for Harvard and everyone recognized his right to academic freedom. Du Pont may also give Mr. Singer a similar freedom without endorsing his views.

Historic Background of the Notion du Pont is Protectionist; American Association of University Women, Wilmington

Historically, the vast development of the United States' chemical industry took place during and immediately after World War I. It appears to have taken place because of the protection against German competition and the seizure of German patents, etc., which resulted from the war. The chemical industry, therefore, has been regarded and has, on the whole, regarded itself as a beneficiary of protection.

In the interwar years, several du Pont economists, for example Edmund Lincoln, were particularly articulate spokesmen of protectionist views. It is generally believed that they played an influential part in the behind-the-scenes planning of the post-war tariff acts. These men were dead or retired at the time of our study but they were remembered in Wilmington and throughout the chemical industry.

We heard one interesting sidelight about the effect of du Pont on the community; The Wilmington chapter of the American Association of University Women is naturally composed, to a considerable degree, of wives of men in du Pont. A prominent member of the Wilmington group told us that the chapter

> . . . disagrees with the stand of national AAUW on several matters, such as the tariff.

She then told me about a visit of a national officer of the AAUW to Wilmington to present the national's legislative program. The visitor, we were told, was "simply shocked" at the way the Wilmington group "tore her platform to pieces."

The two other big Delaware chemical companies, Atlas and Hercules, were separated from du Pont as a result of anti-trust action in 1912. We were told in several interviews that the president of one of these companies has privately expressed considerable support for freer trade, and we got the impression that the other company does not care much about the issue but might lean toward reciprocal trade. But neither of them would want to take a policy stand opposite to du Pont on such an issue. Both are willing to let the trade associations to which they belong (there are several in the chemical industry) speak for them, but evidently none of the company officials most likely to know has great interest in, or a clear impression as to what the trade associations actually do say. Communications from the associations to the firms on foreign economic policy receive little circulation within the companies.

It is not, of course, only du Pont's influence which keeps such firms as these from supporting reciprocal trade; it is the cumulative weight of the numerous protectionist firms in the chemical industry. One official of one of these firms said, in effect, that the firm is neutral on reciprocal trade because:

> ... the whole chemical industry buys and sells from each other; [so] we have important customers who definitely are for protection and these things make a difference. Personally I think the customers are making a mountain out of a molehill.

Both Atlas and Hercules are often confused with du Pont despite the fact that they have been forty years separated. Both firms showed a strong desire to differentiate themselves from du Pont without differing on policy from the latter. One reason is that they believe du Pont is unpopular in down state Delaware.

Other Delaware Businesses

Two Wilmington firms which might have had some industry associations, which would lead them to be protectionist —although apparently neither of them themselves suffer from foreign competition—are managed and owned by old Quaker families. The managers possess the "concerns" which good Quakers are supposed to have, hence, in principle, both firms would support reciprocal trade.

One firm in another industry intended to oppose reciprocal trade because the trade association had asked it to do so. The export manager had not been abroad for many years; nevertheless exports run to 7 percent or so of gross; but the export manager was delighted to oppose reciprocal trade because he is so irritated at foreign restrictions on trade. Other firms in the area, on the whole, had less interest even than these in the issue.

Dover is the state capital and second city. An informed person told us he had heard

> ... no complaints [there] about and no discussion of foreign trade or imports. In 1954, the community was absorbed in tremendous expansion due to a newly established air base.

International Latex, which has since been sold, had done nothing and had been exposed to no pressures or requests on foreign economic policy.

Outside Wilmington, Delaware's population is predominantly agriculture-based. The poultry business is large; broilers and the like are processed as well as raised. The poultry processors or growers face a lot of direct political problems in the state and area—stream pollution, general nuisances, etc., and any political concerns they have go into these issues. Whether much of the poultry is ultimately exported, we have no way of telling; figures and records which would enable one to tell are not kept.

There is a good deal of processing also of sweet corn and lima beans, etc. There are apple people, who, according to a state agricultural authority, are on an export basis, and wheat people. Most of the wheat growers, as part of a diversification program, are also in dairying (and dairying is generally protectionist although wheat is export-minded). We were told that 30 percent of the wheat acreage goes abroad.

At the instigation of Farm Bureau officers, because, Secretary of Agriculture Benson said he wanted to know how farmers felt in regard to issues on foreign trade, a series of discussion meetings on the subject were held by farmers throughout the state. They took raised-hand votes afterwards, which showed a considerable margin in favor of lower tariffs. About 500 people took part in these discussions.

The senators and congressman are supposed to have heard about the results; but, in fact, remembered them only extremely vaguely or not at all.

We asked a farm leader if he knew how du Pont, etc. felt as to tariffs. He replied:

> No! I have often wondered about these matters and would like to know whether industry feels it would gain or lose by a tariff. I just don't know how they feel. No doubt agriculture would benefit more than industry would lose from more exports. ... Of course some industries like watchmaking (not a Delaware area industry at all) would lose.

This is typical!

What the Congressmen Heard and Did Not Hear

Substantially, the congressman and senators in 1954 appear to have heard very little from the state about the reciprocal trade extension act. One of them said:

> On the Randall Commission, I am sure I did get some letters or calls but I cannot even recall them. No doubt somebody did [call].

Since all three are alert, attentive men, this means that the calls were probably not too important.

No, I don't hear much at all on this issue ... there is such a vacuum in our markets and the foreign markets there is no problem. [This at the time the coal, pottery, glass, chemical, textile, and many other industries were complaining rather bitterly about foreign competition and unemployment.] Our farm commodities aren't too exportable; Farm Bureau meetings on foreign trade might not mean too much.

There aren't any real problems of voting on reciprocal trade. I have always voted for it and I just don't hear much on that; so far as any particular complaint or gripes or so forth on that, there just haven't been very many.

Another said:

> I've talked directly with the chemical companies about problems of interest, and I have received no particular specifications as to their views on the Randall Commission and the tariff; certainly they would be the most concerned; at the present time [April, 1954], therefore, we have no special reason to expect to hear much when any legislation is introduced.

The third thought the chemical industry might have a predominant interest, had heard something from farmers, and:

> ... pretty heavily from the leather industry. [He was not sure whether in or out of the state.] The greatest interest may well reflect the views of the Farm Bureau. It is rare that we have a person of unlimited means make a demand on us.

He then commented on the self-restraint of wealthy Delawareans. He had also heard from machine tools outside the state.

None of them had heard from labor on the issue, *in the state*, in 1954 or 1955. A few apparently randomly directed letters were received from outside textile or electrical workers against H.R.1 in 1955 (some of these workers may have lived in the state and worked outside).

In 1955, the three received considerably more mail. The League of Women Voters was noticeable as supporting reciprocal trade. Apparently all three received more pro- than anti-reciprocal trade mail from the state, although a good deal of anti-mail from outside. But, in the pressure of business on members of the Finance Committee, as a staff member put it:

> So many people have come in on all these things ... we just haven't been able to hear in mind which was which.

That, again, indicates that the mail and visits on H.R.1 either were not impressive or the senators and congressman were immune to noticing that sort of pressure. One person close to a senator told me:

Oh, these pressure campaigns don't happen in Delaware. Never on any issue.

There is awareness in the congressional delegations that different divisions of du Pont might have different views on H.R.1. They know du Pont employees personally. The Northern Newcastle Young Democrats Club, composed according to the congressman, "largely of du Pont chemists, young businessmen, etc.," approached Congressman McDowell in favor of reciprocal trade. This is the only instance we encountered of a local political organization taking a definite stand with the congressman or senator for reciprocal trade; in Midland, Michigan, where Dow Chemical is located, the local Republican organization passed a resolution, which it sent to the senators against reciprocal trade; but, in general, party organizations everywhere stay out of political issues such as this.

Professional Employees: A Brake on du Pont?

In interviews with some business firms, the writer has been struck by the degree to which calculation about employee reactions affects them. One firm hesitates to take part in the current business-in-politics program because it is not unionized and fears anything that would "stir" the workers up; another is unionized but fears "jeopardizing a very amicable relationship with the union," which might conceivably interpret such a program as a threat.

Du Pont has this problem in a different and exaggerated form. Wilmington is du Pont headquarters; it depends for its very existence upon skillful and educated scientists, with educated wives. These men and women may, to be sure, influence the AAUW to drop one or another plank in its platform—locally! But, more significantly, they are part of and respond to the climate of opinion, which the League of Women Voters, the AAUW, and other such internationally oriented groups express. They would object strenuously to any company program which sounded like economic nationalism; or, if not, a rational calculation by management would be that it is far more risky to chance losing their goodwill than to chance losing some sales to foreign competitors. In any company, this might be true; but du Pont depends on professionals to a singularly high degree. Wilmington to a like high degree has communities of like-minded scientists, and, with the history of the munitions investigation and FDR's attacks on "economic royalists," employees of du Pont may well be more sensitive to the possibility of being stigmatized as working for reactionaries than employees of, say, General Electric or Dow.

Conclusion

In general, Delaware congressmen and senators appeared to be free to choose for themselves, without much pressure, on foreign economic policy issues. No interest in the state is vociferously opposing reciprocal trade; and, although du Pont may lean in that direction, senators and congressmen in a state as small as Delaware know the rifts and cross-pressures within du Pont on such an issue as this, if they are at all "hep" and know du Pont will have issues on which it feels much more strongly. Nor is any interest in the state vigorously supporting reciprocal trade. The issue apparently stirred up less excitement than, say, the St. Lawrence Seaway. Although both senators are on the Finance Committee, and Delaware is economically part of the Philadelphia-Maryland area, they do not seem to have been expected by anyone to do anything for the firms in that area outside the state in this connection. Such instances as there were of possible injury due to foreign competition created no stir; Wilmington had then a situation of approximately full employment.

A Delaware senator or congressman could, if he were so minded and chose to dramatize it, probably get some following and attention by speaking up for old-fashioned protectionism; the vulcanized fiber plants, some of the textile plants, conceivably du Pont and the traditional conservatism of several areas, provide soil within which applause, votes, and some sympathy might be given to a man who tried to defend American industry against "cheap foreign labor." Particularly, if he made a good deal of the national-defense, preservation-of-skill argument, he might find financial support from some members of the du Pont family.

On the other hand, a Delaware senator or congressman who chose to dramatize the issue might also crystallize the latent freer trade concern in Atlas, Hercules, and International Latex, and among some of the farmers. Either way, protectionist or reciprocal trade, he could make an issue for himself which would attract some favorable attention and support.

As it was, none of the four men, Senators Frear or Williams, Congressmen Warburton or McDowell, focused on trade or the tariff, nor was there any particular reason why they should. So far as the record shows, all four supported reciprocal trade as requested by the Administration.[11]

Notes

*   Lewis Dexter is a freelance consultant in Belmont, Massachusetts.
        The report here presented is part of a longer study, "Congressmen and the People They Listen To," Center for International Studies, Massachusetts Institute of Technology (dittoed), Parts I and II, 19SS, available from the University Mi-

crofilms, Ann Arbor, Michigan. (This study is copyrighted by MIT and permission to use any part of it must be obtained through Lewis Dexter.) An abstract of the entire study, called "The Representative and His District," appeared in *Human Organization*, XVI, No. 1 (Spring, 1957), 11-16. Participation as consultant to the Research Professor of Government, Harvard, 1960, in a study of business-in-politics movement led the writer to develop his views in this field; as did also participation in political campaigns.

The author is grateful to his colleagues, Raymond Bauer, Harvard University Business School, and Ithiel Pool, Massachusetts Institute of Technology, for guidance and advice in this analysis but the responsibility is, of course, entirely his own. He is also grateful to his patient informants, without whom no such study could be made.

1. It is believed that the findings are still pertinent to du Pont in 1960, but that the development of the attitude here reported occurred at du Pont between 1933 and 1947, more or less, and that it was not characteristic of the company prior to 1933.

2. A revolt, which will probably win over a few firms to follow the General Electric-type emphasis on the business climate, a good many more firms to stress political education as part of a management development program far more than has been customary, but which in all likelihood, will, in essentials, be beaten back by the limited sort of "partial incorporation" of a "revolutionary" ideology which the management development approach suggests also.

3. An extensive report on this study is to be published as R. Bauer, I. Pool, and L. Dexter, *American Business and Public Policy in 1961*. A dozen or more articles arising out of the study have already been published.

4. From 1953 to 1955, Mr. du Pont was U.S. Commissioner of Roads.

5. However, Alexis du Pont Bayard, New Deal candidate for the Senate in 1953, uses his middle name.

6. For this reason, the campaign against five-percenters hurt small business as compared with big business.

7. There have been various accounts by businessmen (such as Clarence Randall) of what they have learned from government service but presumably those who spontaneously write on such topics are not typical.

8. Actually, the du Pont officer undoubtedly identified himself representing a trade association; but the politician had forgotten this.

9. To be published in Bauer, Pool, and Dexter, *op. cit.*

10. Nor did du Pont testify as such on the customs simplification act in which some people say it is especially interested.

11. The only deviation we know of is that, in committee, Senator Frear voted for a two-year instead of a three-year extension of the 1955 Reciprocal Trade Act. We do not know why.

4

Organizational and Political Climate*

I

Does "climate" affect perception? The notion that different organizations and institutions have different climates, atmospheres, tones, is familiar enough but it has not been systematically considered. One of its most important implications, particularly pertinent for those concerned with methodology and with the validity of reported observations,[1] has never been analyzed. Assuming that organizational differences of this sort exist, they will probably affect a researcher's observations, reports and interpretations. The proposition here is that an organizational climate leads members of the organization to act in ways which affect researchers' perceptions and inferences. For example, I suspect that some Washington agencies, such as the Congress, have been especially gently treated because the organizational atmosphere and the way in which congressional researchers fitted into it led these researchers to one set of selective perceptions rather than to others.[2] Some other agencies and institutions, notably Massachusetts state government, have been less favorably handled for similar reasons. The treatment of outsiders and academics in Massachusetts, at least prior to about 1968,[3] was less friendly than in many jurisdictions because of the organizational climate of the Massachusetts politico-administrative whirlpool, as contrasted with the organizational climate in other states.

At the simplest level, some organizations may create a climate of generalized suspiciousness, especially of academic investigators. So far as I could observe and infer, Massachusetts state government has had, and apparently still has, a number of members, politicians and civil servants alike, who think somebody is out to get something on them. More members have this suspicion than in the adjoining states of Rhode Island, Connecticut, and New Hampshire. There are, historically and institutionally, explanations of this, going back to the coming of the Irish (see Handlin, 1941, and Billington, 1938, and, to some extent, Elazar, 1972), and to the particular way in which ethnic/political controversy developed in Massachusetts. But it seems reasonable to suppose that the institutional climate teaches this attitude of suspicion, not necessarily everywhere in the state government, but in many agencies and departments. New recruits learn the appropriate (more or less hostile) attitude towards clients and/or outsiders—and, on the whole, those who do not have or do not acquire these attitudes are more likely to leave the system, somewhat less likely to apply to join it, and perhaps less likely to be promoted. This is not a direct function of corruption. Florida, Newfoundland under Smallwood, and the Rhode Island legislature all probably had as much or more corruption as Massachusetts, but each of these jurisdictions showed distinctly more amiability to the person who was making claims or requests (such as for an interview). But it is more subtle than that. In Massachusetts state government, requests from "the public" for service (say, a birth record or replacement of a lost registration) were handled as a favor from x to y, who sponsors z, the favor-requestor. Academics, intellectuals, and other citizens coming into contact with state government, are, in general, unaware of, or hostile to, this notion (see for example Wood's (1947) discussion of his difficulties in doing research in Massachusetts, while studying for a Ph.D. at Harvard). Academics and intellectuals tend to regard themselves as entitled to consideration on the merits, and consequently have created hostility towards themselves, as a result of the organizational climate. In Florida, in Newfoundland (at the top levels of government), in many Washington agencies and Congressional offices, there is (or was) not the same emphasis upon a request being granted as a favor. In fact there was often a desire to do favors to increase one's clientele, or simply to get ego-gratification.[4]

Looking back, I believe that I, after working on Beacon Hill for a while, developed this attitude (even to giving interviews to other researchers!) and would take a very circuitous (and administratively inefficient) route to get favors done.

The existence of such a climate of hostility towards outsiders tends to elicit distrust and negativism from those outsiders. The emphasis on favors, and the resentment towards those who come naked, as it were, without a sponsor, leads scholars, who believe themselves to be merely asking for their rightful due, to exaggerate the corrupt aspects of the situation and to notice and record more data that fits into that perspective than they otherwise would.

Of course, such exaggerated perceptions are not confined to scholars. For instance, a manufacturing executive, whose firm had plants scattered throughout the country, complained about the "expensiveness" and difficulty of doing business in "Taxachusetts." Pushed, after some reflection, he partially backtracked: "You know, actually, we complain a good deal about how difficult it is to do business in Massachusetts. Really, I don't know that it is any worse than other states. But the thing is the people from the Department of Labor or the State Fire Marshal's office come in, and raise hell, and are generally very rude and irritating. Now, in Rhode Island, we have to submit to the same regulations in effect, but, when they come in, there, they are nice and courteous about it, and don't make us mad!" The same sort of comment was so often made in the 1950s and early 1960s that it seems to indicate a real difference between Massachusetts and Rhode Island.

Clearly, propositions of this sort need to be tested. Such impressionistic statements, prove only one point: differences in tone, style, and atmosphere may be studied profitably by scholars, and others, such as journalists. These differences are not part of the "dross" of a situation, but they may affect the way in which we study our findings, and we need to take them into account. These differences in tone, style, and atmosphere may be inferred from the general sentiments expressed by clients, customers, publics, about institutions and organizations.

II

What is organizational climate? Does it differ from culture? How does it differ from organizational structure or informal politics? As Katz and Kahn (1966) say: "Every organization develops its own culture or climate with its own taboos, folkways, and mores. The climate or culture of the system reflects both the norms and values of the formal system and their reinterpretation within the informal system." It will be apparent that one does not necessarily have to start out with the formal system; some significant aspects of the organizational climate or culture may be ignored by, or opposed to, the formal system. "Just as a society has a cultural heritage, so social organizations possess distinctive patterns of collective feelings and beliefs passed along to new group members. In an industrial concern with a long history of amicable relations, there may be no feeling that talking to a company officer is an attempt to curry favor and no countenancing of sabotage or stealing of company materials." There are other companies where the reverse is true. "Educational institutions also show marked differences in climate and culture. Even a casual visitor can detect differences between the atmosphere(s) of Antioch, Swarthmore, C.C.N.Y., the University of Oklahoma, and Princeton University." One such difference is almost identical to the example cited from business firms; in some universities, conduct often stigmatized elsewhere as apple polishing is considered perfectly natural and matter-of-course. "It is not easy to specify the dimensions of such differences.... The members will not be able to verbalize in any precise fashion this frame of reference. They will be clear about the judgments they make," in specific cases, quite frequently, "but not about the basic standards or frames they employ in reaching a judgment. Research has neglected organizational climate." The last statement is still generally true, especially for those institutions of the greatest interest to political scientists.

For example, there are several suburbs of Greater Boston operating under approximately identical statutory and constitutional provisions for what is called a "limited town meeting." Yet such towns as Arlington, Belmont, Brookline, and Watertown, exhibit great differences in political style and tone. In Watertown, for instance, politics, even for such minor offices as Tree Warden, is still genuinely partisan, but not so in the other three. In Belmont, for about a hundred years, much of governance has been conducted by a small local "oligarchy." The town hall meeting place has been too small for any large attendance of citizens, should they ever have wished to attend. There is substantially more participation in the other three towns. Different issues have preoccupied the different towns at times.

It is possible to argue that demographic differences in the four towns make the political and organizational climates different; but then one notices that people who would be behaving in a different way if in one of the other three towns, are behaving in a way appropriate for the town where they actually live and vote. That is to say, there are roles learned in some way or other, defining what to pay attention to and how to perform, which distinguish one town from another in politics. These roles are learned because something about the particular town teaches citizens to act in particular ways. To be sure, there are economic differences among the four communities, but persons inclined to be members of Americans for Democratic Action, or the like, are less active in Belmont affairs, not because of the economic differences from other towns, but because of the tendency in Belmont politics to condemn anything "extreme." When Robert Welch, the John Birch Society's leading star, wanted to run for the obscure and unimportant office of town meeting member, the very conservative leader of the town oligarchy ruled him out as "too radical."

In most other limited town meetings, he could have been elected without veto; and, had he been vetoed in Watertown, it would not have been for the style, but for the content of his ideas.

In light of such examples, it seems that Katz and Kahn and others have confused themselves and their readers by suggesting that "culture" and "climate" are more or less synonymous notions. No doubt, the organizational climate and atmosphere of any town or institution is influenced and constrained by the culture of the general society; but it is hard to suppose that the differences which Wood (1947) found between the gubernatorial offices in Hartford and Boston were reflections of far-reaching cultural differences between Connecticut and Massachusetts. Nor, when one considers how Westinghouse, DuPont, and the Baltimore and Ohio railroad differed from each other in tone, climate, and atmosphere while operating within the same Mid-Atlantic area, is it easy to attribute these differences to "culture." (Of course, I am aware that one might speak of organizational *culture*, but, because it is so easy to confuse this with culture in the sociological/anthropological sense, the term is probably better avoided.)

It might, of course, be argued that Westinghouse, DuPont, and the B & 0 have different tasks to perform, and, no doubt this is true. But whether the four Boston suburbs listed above have tasks different enough to explain the magnitude of their variations in style, tone, and climate, is doubtful. Similarly, in the 1930s, any one who traveled regularly (or shipped goods regularly) on the Baltimore & Ohio and on the Pennsylvania was aware of differences in the outlook and orientation of the two railroads: the Pennsylvania was simply and generally less courteous. This could, of course, be attributed to the fact that the B & 0 had to be more competitive but, for whatever reason, there was a difference. In any case one can find other industries where the second or third firm in an oligopolistic situation is not noted for courtesy.

We are talking about something here which is not a matter of organizational structure, in any normal sense of that term. In the first place, in cases such as the four Massachusetts towns, structures are almost identical. In the second place, many changes in structure will not change the feeling/tone which is associated with one organization or another. (Many industrial organizations, eager to overcome labor-management hostility, have found that structural changes do not, by themselves, alter established patterns of relationship.) In the third place, it is probable that we could find a good many instances where there are similar organizational climates and different structures, as well as the reverse. For example, party affiliation and outlook in the Connecticut legislature is (or at least was in 1965 or so) much more comprehensible to people from Nova Scotia or New Brunswick than it is to people from Massachusetts, New Hampshire, or Maine (as I found at a New England regional conference where I was rapporteur for a round table on legislative practice). The party means something in Connecticut, as it does in the Canadian provinces (for what are in the latter case, but not in the former, apparently structural reasons). Just as the party means much more in Watertown politics than it does in Arlington, Belmont, or Brookline. No doubt, structure can, to some degree, encourage the learning of given roles or inhibit the learning of others, but the characteristic roles of an institutional system must be distinguished from the structure of that system.

Analogously, the notion of organizational climate is a bit like the notion of personality. All of us know that X has a personality, quite different from Y's, although they do the same jobs, belong to the same family, and so on. We also know that to explain personality differences in terms of cultural differentiation is fantastic *if carried to extremes*; we also are aware, that although differences in physiology, birth order, early family training, and experience affect personality, they do not explain all differences in personality. (Of course, ultimately, such differences may be "reducible" to genetic factors, but having said this, we know very little more than we knew before.)

One other use of the term "culture," aside from the standard sociological-anthropological sense, ought to be referred to here. Political culture has come, unfortunately, to refer to characteristic sets of belief-systems and values. This is true in the broadest sense: institutional climate is a function of belief systems and values. People working for the Baltimore & Ohio in 1934 were, statistically speaking, more likely to attach importance to courtesy than people working for the Pennsylvania, and there were certainly differing values at work when a prominent Maritime politician who had been visiting Western Canada said, after we had chewed the political fat about our experiences in New England and Maritime politics: "I see, you understand how these things are. You see that what people call *dirty* campaigns are important." He justified as a matter of principle the tricks, slanders, and libels in which some Maritime and New England politicians engage; they test the mettle of men in politics, they identify those who can not face difficulties, and they help the public know what is going on. In contrast, he felt the nice innocence of Western Canada is politically pernicious. I suspect this belief system reflected organizational climate. As one with some background in Massachusetts politics, I find myself uncomfortable with the post-Muñoz-Marin relative "innocence" of Puerto Rican politics, and I am surely, like the man just quoted, uncomfortable with Minnesota or Saskatchewan (see Elazar, 1972). Were I not affected by an analytic and sociological/historical background, I might seriously profess the notions which he held, but I suspect both of us learned the way of thinking about political campaigns first, and the belief system and values followed; climate came first.

Having cast doubt on the normal cultural explanations of organizational climate, it must now be admitted that there is one respect in which, if observation and analysis are carefully controlled, the concept of culture might be useful. Within any given population, of course, there are variations in expected, anticipated, rewarded, and penalized behaviors leading to typical definitions of situations (see Thomas and Znaniecki, 1927) and to particular responses. For instance, one set of people, isolated by geography or separated by occupation may vary in some of these respects from other groups. This differentiation flows in part from a process of self-selection; people with certain tendencies, predispositions, and interests enter certain fields, move to certain areas. Such a selective process is sometimes correlated with the demands of the job or the organization, but may sometimes be due to circumstances which are, from the standpoint of the task, incidental: certain activities are sex-determined, for instance, thus few engineers are women; other occupations demand considerable skill at card-playing or a head for hard drinking. Not quite seriously, but not quite humorously either, an acquaintance of mine, assigned by his firm to a good deal of lobbying in a state capitol, reported that he had discovered two major reasons why he was not qualified for the assignment. He had never learned how to play poker well enough to manage to do a little less well in an evening than legislators with whom he had to play (a good deal of business was apparently introduced and impressions certainly made at legislative poker games). Also he was unable to whistle, so he could not whistle up taxis at the legislators' requests. Of course there is no reason to suppose that in all legislative bodies, these particular skills are important. One would be startled to find poker-playing ability important in Salt Lake City (Mormons not being particularly appreciative of card-playing) or taxi-whistling-up momentous in Fredericton, New Brunswick (there simply not being that many places to go in Fredericton).

So, people with certain backgrounds, certain abilities, certain skills, enter into and are retained or promoted by certain organizations. And these backgrounds, abilities, and skills, although not necessarily characteristic of any culture or subculture, may be more common in certain cultures than in others. But it should be emphasized that those possessing skills required or rewarded by a particular organization or institution will probably not be representative of the subculture as a whole; for instance, the Yankees who do well in lobbying on Beacon Hill may well not be representative of the Yankee community of Massachusetts or of New England as a whole. Irish-American policemen may not be representative of other Irish-Americans, and I would be inclined to suspect some contrast between Italian-Americans active in the Massachusetts Democratic party, and Italian-American social scientists. And, more to the point, Italian-Americans who enter a state welfare department, and stay there, may differ in temperament, skill, and personality, quite sharply from Italian-Americans in the same state who enter, and stay in, the state highway department.

The unresolved problem, the problem of organizational climate (which can only be resolved by sketches, preferably over time, of persons in different agencies, of different backgrounds) is to what extent a selective process is at work and to what extent an adaptive one. It is helpful to think of what goes on, I suspect, as adaptive, as a form of continuing adult resocialization, continuing as the individual shifts from one agency or organization to another.

The closest approach to the notion of organizational climate which we have is probably the description of the differences among villages and towns in a fairly mobile society (Zeleny, 1937). Within a large society, such as the United States in the nineteenth century, individuals had a fair degree of freedom to move from one village to another; to a lesser extent, there was freedom to do so in much of Europe. Villages are described as having personalities and characteristics; no doubt some individuals who did not fit in moved elsewhere.

III

Some Examples of Organizational Climate. In 1960, a division of a large company sold many of its products to state highway departments. An executive of this division, who struck me as sophisticated and cautious, listed for me the states where sales could be based on merit, and those where the approach required favors (what some might call corruption). This difference may be attributed to organizational climate: the products (and, for the most part, the competitors) were the same, there were no geographical or obvious economic or budgetary differences. There may, of course, have been structural differences in purchasing procedures of which we were unaware, but it is likely that the climatic assumptions about how things should be done played a part. In Massachusetts, West Virginia, Oklahoma, and Indiana many highway construction jobs were often, as a matter of expectation, related to what is called political favoritism. Yet, I have spent some days with an Oregon highway official, a competent engineer, who did not know what I was talking about, literally did not understand, when I asked him all the questions, which would have been evident in West Virginia or Oklahoma.

Such differences do not appear to be a matter of personality or of culture—a particular governor or commissioner or chief executive may, now and then, make a difference (as, probably, Daniel Willard did for some years in influencing the Baltimore & Ohio) but, in general, the traditions and habitual expectations of the agency, the way the middle-level people and the rank-and-file have learned the job, are more important.

Another characteristic of organizational and political climate is the way in which members of an agency respond to, reject, contravene, interpret or misinterpret, disregard or accommodate to the expressed orders and desires of hierarchical superiors. In all agencies, probably, some attention is paid to such orders and desires (although it would be interesting to look for exceptions to this seemingly truistic proposition). It is also probably true that in all organizations authority is never really able to compel explicit and implicit obedience. But, between these two extremes there are many possibilities. In some agencies, any chief executive who proposes or orders common courtesy or common honesty will be shrugged aside or laughed at, in others, resented. According to Charles E. Merriam (orally) in the Chicago police, circa 1920, a "wrong guy" meant a man who might be honest, might reject graft. The phrase suggests something about the organizational climate and the probable response which a "Christer" (a "wrong guy") would have received.

In some organizations, many university departments (after all, we professors are experts, why should we heed the administration on pedagogy or even budget?), police and fire departments, mental health departments, there is a traditional, strongly entrenched resistance to accepting anything that comes from "laymen." Professors sometimes see this resistance as a kind of concomitant of "academic freedom." But the intensity of such resistance, the ease with which such notions as academic or professional freedom can be made to appear relevant, the degree of hostility towards the ignorant layman, may and almost certainly do vary from agency to agency, college to college, and so on.

Organizations also differ in the sense of who "we" are. In some universities, we may mean "we" who work at the University, in others the faculty, or perhaps the division; in most, it probably means the department. Learning who "we" are, and therefore learning who are outsiders, is often preliminary to learning how outsiders should be treated. In the cases of people who are necessarily marginal (e.g., budget examiners assigned to a particular unit of government over a period of time) such learning must be quite subtle and complex. In a good many cases, more sophisticated knowledge is required: in talking with clients and customers, how far does one appear to identify with them? How far does one assert expertise? (See Goffman, 1963.) The point here is that, among various agencies and organizations there are differences in such matters (as between one welfare department and another, for instance) and that consciously or unconsciously, recruits to the organization learn how far it is appropriate to differentiate themselves from the clientele, the customers, the public. In most contexts, nowadays, college teachers, speaking of the relationship between themselves and students, appear to speak of "we" the teachers as differentiated; but, in principle, they could speak of all of "us" as persons who share similar concerns, *including* students.

Some agencies and organizations encourage their members to attack competitors in other agencies (in Washington, in 1959, I encountered this attitude among Army people ranging from officers to the wives of Army medical people, some of whom introduced me to their husbands joyfully: "He's all right! He's against the Air Force!"). It may be, of course, that hostility and expression of hostility are perfectly correlated; but, even so, the issue of how hostility is learned is significant. No doubt, again, there is an enormous reservoir of free-floating resentment, looking for a target, so that, in any university, some people will express bitterness against the competing university, the competing department, the auxiliary agencies, library, bookstore, etc., but what is appropriate among different groups presumably varies a good deal.

A rather specialized but illuminating example of the definition of outsiders was supplied to me some years ago by a Massachusetts state legislator, who was clearly at the time (and as later events proved) capable of doing extremely well professionally outside politics. He was complaining that practically the worst thing about Governor Furcolo was that Furcolo would not give jobs to ex-members of the Massachusetts General Court (legislature). "Dever did it; Herter did it; Bradford did it; Saltonstall did it; but the s.o.b., Furcolo won't," he said. Some one commented, "But after all, Jack, you know," as he clearly did well know, "so many of them are not really qualified for anything...." The relevant reply could have been "neither were some of Furcolo's appointees." But the actual response was indicative: "That has nothing to do with it. We are politicians. Everybody hates politicians. So, when we're beaten, the Governor *should* take care of us."

This particular example raises the general question of an important difference in organizational climate: how are failures, the unfortunate and the inept and the unlucky, treated? I had always assumed, on the basis of my own experience, that every organization has unfortunates who are recognized as needing to be taken care of (see also Goode, 1967). However, while interviewing in other states and provinces, (e.g., Utah and Nova Scotia) I discovered that the principle was not generally accepted, and that it is worth exploring whether the definition of unfortunates in those jurisdictions is much more restricted than in Massachusetts.

Similarly, some legislative bodies, some bureaucracies, and some faculties may go to much greater trouble than others to protect colleagues who violate public expectations. Obviously, in some professions, such as medicine, there are important reasons for doing so; but, probably, in certain hospitals or in certain medical schools, there is more emphasis on such protection than in others. One might also explore to what extent this is a "there but for the Grace of God go I" response and to what extent there is protection for ex-colleagues who do something really horrendous. Are special roles created for those who do not measure up? In studying such matters, a number of reasonably specific issues might be addressed. What, in a given agency, is the line between impropriety and sensible self-enrichment? Police in a particular jurisdiction apparently regarded as fools those among their colleagues who refused to collect graft from parking violators, but they despised men who profited from drugs or girls. In other jurisdictions, it might be different. In a particular city it was apparently regarded as scandalous for elected officials to get any rake-off from cops' income from such graft, whereas elsewhere this practice has seemingly been standard. It is also relevant to point out that in some jurisdictions (Baltimore City, Florida) there have been times when it was taken for granted that elected officials would be entitled to act as insurance agents for the jurisdiction and receive fees accordingly; in other jurisdictions this would have been looked upon as highly reprehensible.

IV

How Do We Observe or Try to Observe Organizational Climate? How are we going to test, spell out, make more precise, or disprove guesses on these issues? We might, of course, endeavor to formulate a series of explicit general propositions about possible differences in organizational climate. For instance, it might be helpful to start out with the hypothesis that the notion of what is proper behavior is modified by and, in some considerable measure, learned in a particular organizational setting. Accordingly, if we had descriptions over time of what particular individuals regarded as proper, we might expect to see changes in such notions as those individuals changed organizational settings. We might even, as Leach (1964) so vividly suggests, find that people shifting from one role and organizational constellation to another, back and forth, might develop or hold quite different notions of propriety in each organizational situation. Such an approach should start out with the awareness that our own particular judgment of values is not necessarily generally accepted; when I say "our own" I refer especially to the political scientists' belief that politicians value power. Young (1966), Bauer et al. (1972), and others have shown that there may be politicians who *in given situations* may actually try to avoid exercising power.

We might also formulate the notion that the introduction of innovations is largely determined by differences in organizational climate (most studies of innovation tend to focus on the somewhat more amorphous conception of cultural resistance or acceptance). It might well turn out that, for instance, innovative federal programs in the United States or Canada have quite different effects in different states and provinces because of the different climate of the different agencies, which react to the federal requirements. (See, for instance, Keith-Lucas', 1957, extraordinarily interesting study of the great differences in the way in which ADC programs were handled. Because of institutional differences between states, it made a great difference to a "client" whether she was one hundred yards in one state or the other.) Similarly, there is a tendency in much educational discussion to recommend programs as such. It may be that a given program, or curriculum, will "work" fairly well in a school with a given organizational climate, but not in another one.

More generally, we might find that we can set up propositions, which help us distinguish between personality and the organizational role. By studying the way in which organizational climates create or modify psychological/personal needs, we might be led to modify Lasswell's formulation that political rationalizations are a product of psychological/personal needs. (Whether climates create any of these needs I am not at all sure, but they surely modify the way in which the needs are felt and experienced and interpreted.)

We need, further, to reinterpret various historical studies to see if they can serve to explain, at least in part, how given organizational climates may have developed. For instance, as previously suggested, the political/organizational climate in Massachusetts, as Handlin and Billington suggest, may have been in part created by the experiences of Boston's Irish immigrants at the hands of the Know-Nothing legislature of 1853. The organizational climate of the House of Representatives of the United States in 1955 was, of course, partly a product of the 1910 overthrow of the power of the Speaker, and the consequent establishment of the seniority system, but Fenno (1974) has brilliantly identified other variables which affect the seniority/committee system.

One of the most promising lines of attack on the study of organizational climate may be the analysis of novels. Sir Walter Scott's account in *Redgauntlet* (and in several other works) of the way the courts and the bar operated in Scotland in the eighteenth century is the kind of report which would repay extensive study, particularly as there are a number of other volumes, biographies and sets of anecdotes, which will help to check and amplify Scott's portrayal. We might want, similarly, to try to find why Anthony Trollope's parliamentary novels (for instance, 1893, 1874) as well as his ecclesiastical ones give a highly credible and insightful account of organizational climate, whereas the majority of studies of and stories about legislative bodies are not really credible, they do not portray the climate. (But for a recent novel about Congress which has the same credibility, see Dominic, 1974.) On the whole, novels, or even biographies, which portray organizational climate accurately tend to focus on the dramatic moments or on the modification of organization in response to crisis. Henle (1970) gives a highly convincing account of the climate of a campaign organization.

There are, similarly, many historical monographs which throw light on organizational climate; the best account I have ever read of the political climate of Massachusetts was not in a book about that state, but in a book about eighteenth-century politics in Britain (Wiggin, 1958). And the second best is a description of the French Parliament under the Fourth Republic (Leites, 1962).

It is probable that analysis of literature of this sort would help to clarify the notions involved in organizational climate. Such analysis should concentrate (as, of course, actual interviewing could also) on a "What, if . . ." kind of question: what, if individuals like these had been in a *slightly* different situation, would they have done? That is, can such individuals' behavior be better interpreted in terms of organizational variables, suggested by the term climate, than by relying upon personality on the one hand, and organizational structure on the other?[5]

Notes

*   My awareness of organizational climate as a potentially significant variable for administrative and political studies was greatly enhanced by interviews conducted in Massachusetts, Puerto Rico, Michigan, Illinois, South Carolina, North Carolina, Ontario, New Brunswick, Nova Scotia, and Newfoundland, 1964-68, largely under a grant from the Committee on Political Behavior of the Social Science Research Council. Earlier concern with the problem arose out of work in Massachusetts and Maryland for the late Morton Grodzins on his Federalism study, and from interviews with a number of business firms about business-in-politics (for Oliver Garceau, Research Professor, Harvard) and about the politics of reciprocal trade, 1953-55 (in connection with the Bauer, Pool, and Dexter (1972), study).

I am grateful to Professor Charles Press, Michigan State University, for aid in preparing an earlier draft of this paper, presented in 1967 to the Wayne State University Political Science Colloquium, and to the Midwest Political Science Association.

1.   In Dexter (1970a), I have indicated the ways in which the relationship between the investigator and the group investigated may affect what is reported and how it is interpreted. This topic has had rather low priority in political science methodology. It goes beyond the general "sociology of knowledge" political bias interpretation of statements and reports. The sociology of knowledge approach (or its Freudian corollaries) focuses on the investigator and his interests as the source of bias or distortion. But it is more appropriate to regard reporting in general as *influenced* (whether biased or distorted is another, separate, matter) by the transactional relationship between the observer and the observed. That is to say, observers will note, record, and remember certain aspects of certain groups and institutions, not only because of their own characteristics as investigators and persons, but also because of the way in which the group or institution under study affects them.

Anthropologists have been more self-conscious about these issues than other social scientists. See, for instance, the classic treatment by Bateson (1958) and the practically-oriented set of reports on fieldwork, edited by Spindler (1970). See also Beattie (1965) for an explicit description of the problems of political study by an anthropologist. Also, valuable are the descriptions by Powdermaker (1966) and Dollard (1957) of the situation confronting scholars desirous of reporting on aspects of white-Negro relationships in the South in the 1930s; these are useful in part because neither author sees the difficulties in consciously political terms. Significant also are Powdermaker's discussions later in the same book of her relative failure in studying Hollywood and her relative success in studying the Zambian copperbelt. Some of the accounts in Hammond (1964) may also be profitably studied.

2.   A number of people have commented on White's (1957) book on the Senate as the product of a love affair with an institution. I suggest that to a lesser degree, the majority of political science students of that body have had a similar "crush." This was certainly true of my first report in 1955, and to some extent in the summary thereof in Bauer, Pool, and Dexter (1972). Even in 1970(b) many of my observations reflected the way in which Congressmen and staff assistants had directed my attention. Since I was the first political scientist with considerable anthropological

interest and training to undertake "field study" of Congress, and since many of the older men I interviewed and consulted (and some of the younger ones) were totally naive about the nature of academic study, I had an advantage over my successors, whose studies were from eight to twenty years later. A higher proportion of those they interviewed and consulted were aware of the academic approach to empirical problems in politics. More significant, I had only sporadic relationships with anyone else who was both a member of the Congressional institution (as an intern, recent ex-intern, or Senatorial staff assistant, or House employee) and a student of the institution and its procedures. I had no need to disentangle myself from the complexity of contacts and interests, which the existence of such a social group involved, whereas by 1967-70, most students of Congress were, inevitably, heavily involved in such an interactional relationship.

3.   I should point out that, while studying Congress, *I* was an employee of Massachusetts state government (two governors), a citizen of Massachusetts, and to a limited degree a student of Massachusetts politics. I came, by family background and suburban residence, from a social background shared with many on Capitol Hill, but in 1955-61, with few on Beacon Hill.

4.   But, it is highly significant that many more Massachusetts governmental figures (than, say, Newfoundland or Florida ones) would have been apprehensive or resentful, and thus received no ego-gratification. The apprehension may result from the feeling that if there is no favor-guarantor, no one who is asking you to see X as a favor to him, then you have no guarantee X will not make you look like a fool—and at any rate you are being foolish by wasting time on him.

5.   One possibility would be for people who have had experience in a variety of organizations to try to describe as clearly as they can from memory the differences in climate in these organizations. Having had experience in some twenty-five colleges and universities, and in a number of political organizations, I have thought of doing this; but the obstacles would be far less if this were a collective enterprise.

References

Bateson, Gregory. 1958. *Naven: A Survey of the Problems Suggested by a Composite Picture of the Culture of a New Guinea Tribe Drawn from Three Points of View*. Stanford, California: Stanford Press.

Bauer, Raymond, I. Pool and L. A. Dexter. 1972. *American Business and Public Policy*. Chicago: Aldine-Atherton.

Beattie, John. 1965. *Understanding an African Kingdom: Bunyoro*. New York City: Holt, Rinehart, & Winston.

Billington, Ray A. 1938. *The Protestant Crusade, 1800-1860*. New York: Macmillan.

Dexter, Lewis A. 1955. *Congressmen and the People They Listen To*. Cambridge, Massachusetts: Center for International Studies, Massachusetts Institute of Technology 1970a *Elite and Specialized Interviewing*. Evanston, Illinois: Northwestern University Press.

1970b *Sociology and Politics of Congress*. Chicago: Rand McNally.

Dollard, John. 1957. *Caste and Class in a Southern Town*. New York City: Doubleday

Dominic, R. B. 1974. *Epitaph for a Lobbyist*. New York City: Doubleday.

Elazar, Daniel B. 1972. *American Federalism: A View from the States*. New York City: Crowell & Company.

Fenno, Richard. 1974. *Congressmen in Committees*. Boston: Little, Brown.

Goffman, Erving. 1963. *Behavior in Public Places*. New York City: Free Press.

Goode, William. 1967 "The Protection of the Inept," *American Sociological Review* 32:5-19.

Hammond, Phillip. 1964. *Sociologists at Work*. New York City: Basic Books.

Handlin, Oscar. 1941. *Boston's Immigrants, 1790-1865*. Cambridge, Massachusetts: Harvard University Press.

Henle, Theda. 1970. *Death Files for Congress*. New York City: Vanguard.

Katz, Daniel and Robert Kahn. 1966. *Social Psychology of Organizations*. New York City: Wiley.

Keith-Lucas, Alan. 1957. *Decisions about People in Need*. Chapel Hill, North Carolina: University of North Carolina Press.

Leach, Edmund. 1964. *Political Systems of Highland Burma*. Boston: Beacon Press.

Leites, Nathan. 1962. *Images of Power in French Politics*. Santa Monica, CA: Rand Corporation: RM2954-RC.

Powdermaker, Hortense. 1966. *Stranger and Friend: The Way of the Anthropologist*. New York City: Norton.

Scott, (Sir) Walter. 1908. *Redgauntlet*. Everyman edition, New York City: Dutton.

Spindler, George. 1970. *Being an Anthropologist: Field Work in Eleven Cultures*. New York City: Holt, Rinehart, & Winston.

Thomas, William Isaac and F. Znanlecki. 1927. *Polish Peasant in Europe and America*. New York City: Knopf.

Thomas, William Isaac. 1937. *Primitive Behavior*. New York City: McGraw-Hill.

Trollope, Anthony. 1893. *Phineas Redux*. New York City: Dodd Mead.

White, William S. 1957. *Citadel: The Story of the U.S. Senate*. New York City: Harper,

Wiggin, Lewis A. 1958. *A Faction of Cousins*. New Haven: Yale University Press.

Wood, Robert C. 1947. *The Metropolitan Governor*. Cambridge, Massachusetts: Ph.D. Dissertation, Harvard University.

Young, James S. 1966. *The Washington Community, 1800-1824*. New York City: Columbia University Press.

Zeleny, Leslie. 1933. *Practical Sociology*. New York City: Prentice Hall.

5

Court Politics: Presidential Staff Relations as a Special Case of a General Phenomenon*

I

The conception of court politics provides a counterpoint or modification of Weber's classic discussion of bureaucracy. In any large-scale organization, there is, at least, a strong tendency (possibly an inevitable one) for the top officer(s) to be surrounded by a set of advisors, surrogates, agents, official, and personal servants, flunkies, handymen, technical aides, and so forth, who together constitute what in bureaucratic language is often called a "staff." But the personal staff (and we shall come back to the distinction between the personal and official staff later) of a top executive, a king, a president, a company chairman, and so on, often operates and is expected to operate in direct opposition to what are generally regarded as bureaucratic norms. Merit, formal professional achievement, standard patterns of career, selection, and promotion are the indispensable requirements of a true bureaucracy. But courtiers operate (with many empirical exceptions, some referred to below) ideally to carry out the purposes and wishes of the top man—they are responsible to the man, not to their own careers or the professionally-defined task. (For our purposes, a court exists when there are a collection of such persons, fairly continuously related to each other, dependent on the top man.)

It should be pointed out that in many organizations and polities, there may be more than one court. The chairman of a corporation and its president may have separate, perhaps competing, courts; apparently, there was antagonism between the courtiers of the Emperor Justinian and his consort Theodosia. (For all one can foresee, this could be the case between some future U.S. President and his wife.) Quite frequently, the heir to the throne, Prince of Wales or Dauphin, has had a court in opposition—Frederick, Prince of Wales, for instance, and the Dauphin, later Louis XI. The great proconsuls, men like Douglas MacArthur or Clive of India, tend to develop their own courts, whatever their formal responsibility to higher authority.

I have been able to talk in these terms, so far, because you have some idea of what a court and a palace is. But why are courts probable or inevitable? Essentially, because the man or men at the top are all, rightly or wrongly (I suspect rightly but that is beyond my current brief) able to convince themselves and others that they must have a personal team, which carries out their wishes. Admiral Lord Fisher rebuilt and strengthened the British Navy (while First Sea Lord) by promoting his men, proclaiming that "the secret of effectiveness is favoritism." To get one's policies seriously implemented is difficult enough under any circumstances—but easier if there are one's own men out there seeing to it that others know what one's wishes are and that there will be rewards for adhering to them, penalties for neglecting them.

Empirically, a court is reasonably likely to develop in any large organization, because as a practical matter, kings, presidents, governors, and the like, must necessarily have surplus resources available to handle emergencies, crises, threats—contingency funds, the ability to make appointments outside normal bureaucratic requirements—plus, of course, the capacity to give prestige to those whom they single out for positions of trust or confidence. And in most societies (certainly in ours) it would be surprising in the extreme to find men with such surplus resources at their disposal unwilling to use them for their own purposes and advantages.

The role of courtier is defined in terms of what the top man wants. This is frequently called "personal loyalty" but, throughout, we shall see that the term "personal" is tricky and equivocal. Many a fallen potentate has discovered that his former courtiers, or many of them, are no longer bound to him—their loyalty was to the man in the office, not to the man per se.[1] But, granted that the man holds the office, the courtier is far less concerned with formally assigned tasks and duties than the bureaucrat (again with exceptions noted below).

II

To be sure, members of a court are oriented toward the top man or men; but they are also oriented toward other courtiers. In general, a court—that is, several courtiers working in awareness of each other—is likely to reinforce each other's conception of their job being to serve the top man, even if they are also rivals.

It is important, however, for understanding the phenomenon to indicate how a true court may be "corrupted," how what looks like a court may fail to be such. The first corruption or deviation may be rationalized on the grounds of good service and citizenship. Members of a court may be operationally responsible for a job, or may be individually highly task-oriented, and so come to think of the specific operating tasks of the polity or corporation as their major responsibility. For this reason, it is probably dangerous to select as courtiers men with a highly professional orientation toward work. In this connection, it is important to point out that, throughout much of recorded history, there was no sharp distinction between court and cabinet. Rulers like Justinian I clearly intermingled the two, and so many of their "courtiers" became of necessity administratively oriented. In many small and medium sized organizations—university presidencies for instance—such a commingling still persists. But the mixture of courtier and cabinet officer is likely to be frustrating and tension-ridden. And in modern societies where the normative rule is to be an administrator, rather than a courtier, the mingling of the two is likely to lead to a good deal of disappointment for the top man. Individual members of "kitchen cabinets"—a Harry Hopkins, for instance—may be able to surmount the role ambiguity involved, but it is extremely improbable that most persons could satisfactorily mix the two. My own historical knowledge is too slight for me to say how such mixtures operate in absolute dictatorships or genuinely absolute monarchies (like some of those in the Middle East or under the Mongols), but I assume in such circumstances the normative rule is to be a courtier, and let the administrative role go hang, if there is a conflict.

A court may also become, as some of them have (that of Hapsburg Spain, for instance) a particular sort of bureaucracy, one organized around a ritual of ceremonial and honoring the monarch. Indeed, the great weakness of the Sun King, Louis XIV's system was that it elaborated the ritual of ceremonial and veneration as an end in itself. There are many stories of monarchs unable to get hot meals, unable to get adequate medical attention, and unable to get orders adequately implemented, because the ceremonial became an end in itself. One reason why "kings have (ever) been lovers of low company," as the old saying goes, is that frequently the nobility, conscious of the ceremonial demands of being a courtier, insist on acting by ceremonial rather than fulfilling the monarch's desires. The Mikado of Japan in the late eighteenth century caricatured this situation. Many of us, individually, have probably encountered secretaries, file clerks, and so on, in the offices of top people to whom form became so all-engrossing that implementing his (apparent) purposes gets buried in the ceremony.

Of course, also, a court like any other organization may become corrupted when the individual purposes of individual courtiers diverge very sharply from the demands of the boss. Courtiers, like bureaucrats and everybody else, are not merely role-players or functionaries; they are also self-interested entrepreneurs with purposes of their own. So a president, a King, a corporation executive, may alienate his court and lead it into contravening or counterproductive activities, because the situation does not meet their expectations, whatever these are. Obviously, human life being what it is, a good many courtiers will be disappointed; but the realistic and effective monarch or dictator will recognize that since ingratitude (from the top man's standpoint) and disloyalty (from his standpoint) are common, he had better operate in terms of some kind of exchange theory and recognize that the definition of gratitude as "the lively expectation of favors to come," has a real point. Monarchs who have themselves been through the rough and tumble of conflict and disappointment and struggle—an Alfred the Great, an Elizabeth I, a Charles II—are probably better equipped to do this than a Charles I or Louis XVI. Referring specifically to the presidency, it is probable that a candidate who has had to make deals, negotiate, and so on will be better equipped to handle a court than one who is largely a media product. (An old-fashioned president, making the kind of deals which often used to be necessary, might be better equipped to handle a court than a Nixon, relying so heavily on publicity.)

III

A true court is not a staff as such. It is a personal team, if you like, a personal staff, with the primary responsibility of carrying out the top man's purposes. Staff is also used, of course, to refer to budget and planning and intelligence and personnel records and disaster relief; but these are not functions where carrying out the top man's purposes is central. In nineteenth-century land warfare, a commanding general had a personal staff, his own aides-de-camp and officers who acted as his representatives, his eyes and ears, his trouble-shooters perhaps—they were or often acted like a court. But he also might have mapmakers, intelligence analysts, budget officers, and the like—and they were not, generally, members of his personal team. Most of them could (barring idiosyncrasies) serve one general as well as another, whereas the personal team, the personal staff, often changed with a new commanding general. So, the personal team would be loyal to the commanding general, in such key regards as covering up his mistakes, if need be, in a way which he could not expect from the professional staff. Naturally, adequate rewards had to be available to keep members of a personal team sweet, if, as often happened, they sacrificed chances of promotion (more often given to those who had held junior field commands) to stay on the staff.

Such teams are, of course, well enough known in business and government. A fair number of top executives, when they move from one job to another, carry with them, or quickly reconstitute, their personal team, because the members of that team know their ways, their preferences, and are oriented towards the top man. Since such teams appear to be a fact of life, one criterion for evaluating an aspirant for top position might be: Can he build a personal team? How well can he get rid of those on it who make trouble or don't measure up? Can he use his team without becoming its prisoner?

Indeed, were I recruiting people for top executive posts, I would focus on this sort of information, as a complement of course to information about achievement and psychological characteristics. Particularly important, I suspect, would be two questions: (1) has the aspirant faced a situation where his personal team has "let him down"? How did he handle it?; and (2) how did he make the transition from a predominantly professional job or low-level one to one where he had his own team? I would also want to know how far a particular team has worked because of idiosyncratic, nontransferable circumstances (I know a man who, in business, had been able to rely upon close relatives, whose abilities and skills were quite highly specialized in any case, and who could not be transferred to the public sector. In fact, it took him several years of fumbling to get a team in the public jobs to which he went; and I don't think he ever quite managed it).

IV

The rest of the paper is largely taken up with questions and/or guesses (what the cognoscenti call hypotheses) about the court, courtiers, personal team, top man relationships, but before getting on to them, it may be worthwhile making a further preliminary report.

In any given situation, the relationship of personal team to president, chief executive, monarch, or other similar persons, depends upon several factors:

1.   The actual (or reputed) personal character of the top man. An executive of a large organization, whom I knew well, had the reputation of

demanding "yea-sayers" in his court. In fact, I do not think this was so; what he did demand was elegance of expressions and wit, beyond any reasonable expectation. So, in his later years, even men courtiers who could have met his standard of lucidity and wit did not challenge him, because they thought he would not stand it.

2.   Previous rulers or head men may have created in any given situation an expectation about what staff can or should do. Although Elizabeth I never, as far as I know, seriously punished people for policy differences, she was, after all, "King Harry's daughter,"—the King Harry who had abandoned Wolsey and executed Cromwell. Presumably, her early courtiers must have reacted to the fear that she would be such another rather than to the reality that she did accept a good deal of critical thinking.

3.   General cultural notions about loyalty and obedience. The Highland chiefs and swordsmen who, to some degree, held the notions about loyalty depicted in Walter Scott's Fair Maid of Perth (granted that it was exaggerated in the novel), would see the duties of a courtier rather differently from the stiff-backed independent middle-class American type, who regards any kind of dependence as shameful.

4.   The way in which courtiers are selected, the professions from which they are selected, and so on, affects the kind of people recruited and the orientations they have to being courtiers. In this country, presidential or gubernatorial courts may well be recruited from the campaign teams. Campaign teams, inevitably, place a good deal of emphasis on rhetoric. In 1957, and again in 1961, I was a member of a winning campaign team in Massachusetts, from which governors selected their personal staffs. Looking back, it seems to me that we overemphasized the combat/rhetoric approach, after we got into office. (Indeed, the 1957 experience has given me some sense of identification with the Watergate conspirators; I can so easily see some of my colleagues drifting into this sort of situation, and the Governor and the rest of us trying to cover it up.)

In a way, this reference to campaign teams becoming personal staffs is to raise the wise old Mongol's question to the Great Khan: "You have conquered this realm on horseback; but can you govern it from horseback?" Which is to say that the military team which had won the victory did not necessarily provide the best team or administrators for enjoying and preserving the victory. In a media-oriented kind of campaign, at least, does the political speechwriter (such as myself of twenty years ago), as such, easily transfer to being the best kind of person to handle governmental issues or to engage in the accommodation which government demands? Can a new president or governor readily select or create another kind of court, personal team, of whose efficacy for his purposes he can be sure? If so, how?

V

1. One problem about courts and palaces is that it is probably dangerous to let them get quite large. A court or personal team which becomes a social entity in itself is hard to use as an arm of the executive; managing it becomes a task in itself. I am reminded of a U.S. housewife, accustomed to one maidservant, who went to Haiti in 1941 or thereabouts, where her husband's position and income demanded she have a staff of sixteen or so. "It's much tougher than with one," she said. "I have to spend all day, assigning duties to them, settling disputes about jurisdictional lines, and so on."

    Possibly, an unusually able man like Louis XIV—unusually able at this particular task—can dominate his entourage, but could the less extraordinary monarchs who followed him, or the German princelings who tried to emulate him, do so? Perhaps a Franklin D. Roosevelt or a Dwight Eisenhower in their different ways, Roosevelt because of an unusual sort of ability, Eisenhower because he had an unusual temperament and had years of relevant experience, could control their staffs, but that does not show that later presidents can do equally well in managing a large one. Probably the span of control issues is important here: only as many subordinates as the chief can control plus as many as the top subordinates themselves can control. Individuals will vary in temperament and capacity here, but the number involved will always be finite.

    There is of course a strong tendency toward inflation in courts and palaces; one gives prestige to somebody who is liked or was helpful by putting him in the court. Or, probably still more common, there is a problem—something does not go well—so the top man or his top subordinates think, "if only we had more hands ..." or, "if only we had people with a particular capacity," this problem could be solved. Generally, the problem is more intractable than they think it is—one new person or a dozen on the top man's personal team won't make it go away, but the new people added tend to swell the size of the court, and make it more difficult to control the members of the court, and make sure they really grasp the top man's wishes. Beyond a manageable size, for every courtier added one should be subtracted, which means there must be rewarding slots available for those who are removed from the court itself.

2. A considerable and substantial responsibility of the court and the personal team is to act as a filter against communications, including visitors and appointments. Obviously the president can not even afford the time to hear most requests made of him. Such filtering and selectivity is at least in modern society absolutely essential. Furthermore, a high proportion of communications to political executives are likely to be complaints about his program, his subordinates, and so on, and there will be little he can do about most of these complaints. But, unless he is a man of very thick skin, constantly hearing such complaints is not pleasant and often is depressing.

Yet, the chief executive does need to hear a good deal of bad news. So, the problem is: How should it be presented to him? This will vary with the man's individual psychology and perhaps with the kinds of subordinates and the nature of the bad news. But the important thing to bear in mind is that only an executive who is borrowing trouble will let his courtiers act as adjuncts to his own tendency to avoid bad news. And he should realize that unless he is quite careful, courtiers will keep bad news from him. One inference from the White House tapes was that the constant stream of complaints in which Nixon engaged would lead many subordinates to keep bad news away from him. A man with the temperamental tendency to such outbursts should strive to offset their effect; Mayor Fiorello LaGuardia, for instance, although apparently given to outbursts of rage at bad news or mistakes compensated by complaining that, for instance, a man whom he had fired the previous day, in such a fit of rage, did not turn up for work, and called the man to say in effect, "Don't take me seriously on such matters."

In different situations, of course, different ways of getting bad news to be heeded may be desirable. One executive may prefer to hear a lot of bad news all at once—another bit by bit. One may prefer to hear it tout court as is, another with suggestions for offsetting its implications (with the corresponding opportunity to vent his anger by tearing the suggestions to pieces).

Studies of failing or almost failing corporations (Penn Central, Rolls-Royce, W. T. Grant) to see how bad news got suppressed or reacted to might be valuable here. We might learn from them how unwary executives could have been alerted despite their tendencies.

But any such approach must take account of the fact that in one way or another, personal teams, staff, courtiers, will act as filters. The question is: What kind of filters? How do they filter?

3.   Both as agents and as filters, members of a court often place more weight upon the "impulses" of an executive than he himself intended or wished. Repeatedly, when I was in Governor Furcolo's office, an idle question by the governor would lead us to ask an agency to make a time-consuming report, which nobody looked at by the time it got to us, and the governor had forgotten all about. But we didn't want to be caught short, if the governor asked again; and we liked to appear important by giving orders. Both courtiers and top executives need a set of signals to distinguish between impulses and seriously intended purposes. One reason for this emphasis is that if a lot of time is spent in responding to fairly trivial impulses of the top man and his staff, it becomes easier to disregard seriously intended orders or purposes. But if only orders are given which are seriously intended, it becomes a bit harder for the operating agencies to disregard them.

There are several classic examples of trouble created for monarchs or their courtiers because impulses and orders got confused. Henry II of England was clearly a shrewd judge of possible political effects; he almost certainly did not intend his words "Will not somebody rid me of this insolent priest?" to be taken as instructions to assassinate Thomas à Becket. But four knights, hangers-on of the court if not members, scurried forth and slew the Archbishop, to Henry's grave embarrassment. A court in which promotion is obtained by catering to the top man's every whim may turn those whims into chains of iron, which hamper effective executive action. Fortunate the leader like William I of Orange who can be described as William the Silent—but since few leaders are so taciturn the best compromise is to have courtiers who understand one's sense of priorities, members of one's own team, intellectually and morally (which means a small team). Awareness of this sort means that an executive may, however reluctantly, have to rid himself of the over loyal who take every expression of his wishes at face value.

4.   As with all organizations, courts develop their own internal, factional conflicts. This can not be avoided; so it has to be lived with. But it should be made clear to courtiers that carrying such conflicts out-of-doors may have dangers for the regime, and that the conflicts may only be carried on by techniques sanctioned by the chief. A top executive, furthermore, needs to take account of every important report and piece of advice tendered him by the question: is this a way by which subordinate courtier X can get the better of courtier Y? How much do I discount for that possibility?

Franklin D. Roosevelt, according to all accounts, liked his courtiers to be at loggerheads with each other; Dwight Eisenhower, however, wanted an agreed consensus from them. Is there a general argument for the one method rather than the other? Study of business corporations, governorships, army commands, and so on, where one or the other prevails, might help answer this question.

5.   In most courts, at least those of a political sort, there is a strong tendency for some courtier or other to be regarded as identified with a particular group, more than others at the court. Hopeful groups, especially those somewhat excluded from the main concerns of the administration or regime, will seize on any clue to discover a "friend at court." Frequently, such a belief is to some extent self-fulfilling; they then approach their "friend," he may present their case or understand it a little better, and so on. Conversely, though, he may be embarrassed by being regarded as a spokesman for an out-group. However, as a matter of developing willingness to work within the system, such hopes may be productive.

But, on the other hand, in some cases a courtier who establishes such a relationship may also have, consciously or unconsciously, created a client group of his own, and be therefore harder to keep within the system of the top man.

6.   Somewhat the obverse of this is the often pathetic faith "if the top man, king, president, or whomever, only knew," he'd be "on our side." But he is misled by "unsympathetic" or "wicked" advisors. Often, to encourage national unity and hopes for accommodation, an executive has to use advisors as lightning rods in this sense. The king or president can then continue to appear the father of all his people. A few monarchs

have gone so far as to execute disgraced subordinates to make clear just how badly they were advised; but this technique does not help preserve enthusiasm and trust among their successors.

7.   One other point, characteristic of many courts, and especially that of Isabela Peron, is the importance of the confidante, whether confessor, soothsayer, astrologer, magician, valet, doctor, mistress, or paramour—the person to whom the insecure monarch or president or executive can explain his worries and concerns—by whom he can be reassured. In business firms, I suspect economic advisors or advertising consultants sometimes play a similar role. A comparative study of the confidante and the chief executive might be rewarding.

VI

Forty years or so ago, my former teacher, Charles E. Merriam, was working with Louis Brownlow and others on a program for improving the administration of the White House staff, a program now probably best remembered because of the phrase "passion for anonymity" (a characteristic desired of White House assistants). Since Mr. Merriam is one of the two modern political scientists who especially influenced me, and since in all ways he was unequivocally and indeed unjustifiably encouraging and supportive of me, there is no animus in the criticism which follows. I am indeed merely exemplifying his influence on me by the interdisciplinary effort I have made here.

Merriam and Brownlow did not distinguish the White House personal team from other bureaucratic staffs. They thought the same criteria of efficiency and effectiveness applied in all cases. It is interesting to recollect that Merriam as raconteur and gossip knew, I think, the difference; I wish I had thought to record various stories he told me, e.g., Forrestal as a White House assistant, which bore on the point. But as a formal consultant, Merriam was inclined to the rationalistic mode of analysis. Since his day, through the work of social anthropologists and others, we have reintroduced awareness of the personal, the informal, the network, and social situation, and so on into our analyses. Mr. Merriam's own enthusiasm for anthropological treatment of politics helped lead in this direction.

Merriam was, as Barry Karl shows, optimistically American in his point of view—planning and so forth as he conceived them were high forms of rational Americanism—and this point of view to some extent prevented his looking at the White House staff as a parallel with the monarchical and imperial courts of the past. Of course, in any case, the Merriam-Brownlow suggestions could not publicly have hinted at any such parallel; they after all had taken FDR's salt and could not embarrass him. But the report does not suggest any underlying awareness of this kind of point. A British observer, quoted by J.D.B. Miller, who advised a diplomat coming to Washington in the 1930s to read the memoirs of the Duc de Saint-Simon was much closer to the nub of the matter (Saint-Simon reports on the Court of Versailles under the Regent Orleans and also under Louis XIV).

Merriam was greatly concerned with stimulating political invention; in his frequent admonitions to me to carry on his work as political inventor, I think he had things like this report in mind. But he had not really come to terms with the difference in practical circumstances between political prescription and innovations which take account of existent social factors. Nor did he recognize that it is probable that any master invention consists of a whole set of subinventions—witness the automobile.

In another generation or two, we may be ready for such political invent-ing; in the meantime, the best we can do is to make tentative suggestions to President Carter. We can make better suggestions and move, perhaps, somewhat more wisely toward effective inventions by familiarizing ourselves comparatively with court and personal team politics under numerous different circumstances. Some such studies and observations would, practically speaking, be likely to be more immediately usable by business corporations (where the resistances to innovation are prob-ably less) than by the White House.[2] In conclusion, I may refer to what seems to me an appropriate attitude in making comparative observations, looking for practical hunches, an attitude which in general is useful in developing social inventions (whatever may help in preparing mono-graphs). Unamuno said, "In scholarship, one must be either a pedant or a dilettante." For creative work he preferred to choose unequivocally to be a dilettante and avoid the pedantry of specialists. With which, I turn the discussion over to my dilettantish fellows or my pedantic colleagues, as they may turn out.

Notes

* I am chiefly indebted for the idea here to Miller (1962:119-121 and 191-192). He reports his obligation to Snow and Smith (1976), which discusses a case pertinently. This paper was prepared under repeated urging from Professor J. David Barber; credit, if any, should be his, although not blame.

1. Of course, some ex-potentates may continue to command loyalty because, even out of office, association with them still confers prestige—and a good many ex-potentates are regarded as likely to return to power, so can still command a fol-lowing. (In some cases, a new regime is such a threat to close followers of the old

one that as a sheer matter of safety the latter have to hang together—although in such instances the nature of the court will change.) Incidentally, studies of courts in exile (e.g., of the Old Pretender, James III of England and VIII of Scotland) might be rewarding and illuminating in showing the difference between a true court and what is in fact a pseudomorphism of a court.

2.   Although I did not discover the connection until after I had completed the above paper, it seems to me that my article on "Organizational and Political Climate" (1976) is closely related; some organizations and political units may be described as having a highly court or courtier-like climate, others not, and we might be able to develop ways of specifying the differences rather carefully. Helpful in any such effort would be the work of recent British political anthropologists, as developed, for instance, in Boissevain (1975). Boissevain describes the kind of political and social system in which individuals operate as "self-interested political entrepreneurs" with little or no role performance restricted by, for example, bureaucratic specifications as to orientation and behavior. Since most of Boissevain's fieldwork has been in Mediterranean cultures, and because of other factors, it is arguable that, on the whole, modern Mediterranean cultures are more inclined in this direction, less likely to develop modern bureaucracies than some other societies, and possibly therefore that court politics, as here discussed, would be more dominant and pervasive there than in some other social systems.

References

Boissevain, J. (1975) *Friends of Friends*. New York: St. Martin's. Dexter, L. A. (1976) "Organizational and Political Climate." *Political Methodology*, 3: 141-158.

Miller, J.B.D. (1962) *The Nature of Politics*. London: Duckworth. Snow, C. P. and R.F.I. Smith (1976)"Ministerial advisors," in *Royal Commission on Australian Government Administration*, Appendix I-J to Volume 1 (August).

6

Undesigned Consequences of Purposive Legislative Action: Alternatives to Implementation*

This essay addresses and begins to develop the formulation of more systematic notions about the results of legislation and other legislative action. As the title is intended to suggest, the major focus is on the more or less unanticipated, unforeseen, unintended, undesigned consequences of such legislative action. As sketched below this is, of course, derived from the well-known article by Merton (1936), "The unanticipated consequences of purposive social action." The qualifying words, more or less, are, however, vital for the effort; no sharp line can be drawn between such polar opposites as designed and undesigned, intended and unintended.

Similarly, the article is on the one hand greatly indebted to another important piece of work—that of Wildavsky and associates on implementation—and, on the other hand, calls attention to an insufficiently developed aspect of that work. Majone and Wildavsky (1977) maintain that it is rare "when policy outcomes bear no recognizable relationship to the original idea." But either they are asserting an insignificant tautology, defensible, if at all, because of the ambiguities of the term "idea"—the tautology resting merely upon the claim that they will not call anything a "policy outcome" unless they perceive such a recognizable relationship—or, as the text below, I believe, shows, they are mistaken.

Probably, they shifted time frames without being quite aware of what they were doing—in a way which many of us are prone to do, so the point has general importance. After something has happened, or at any rate developed to a marked extent, there is a strong temptation to show how the consequences followed upon the antecedents. So, when, as shown below, the civil rights program, originally incorporated into a design by the U.S. Civil Rights Act, leads to or is followed by a greater emphasis in universities upon quantitative measures of publication as a basis for employment and promotion, we can, many of us, "see" how it happened. But to call such an outcome—a preferable term here would be outgrowth or offshoot—a "recognizable" derivative of the Civil Rights Act is to take the standpoint of observers after the consequences have ensued. It is highly improbable that senators or congressmen, or most lobbyists or enthusiasts for the Civil Rights program, foresaw and anticipated any such development; and clear that few, if any, thought that any such outgrowth was part of the legislative design. Or, although, after the fact, many could regard it as obvious that Prohibition legislation in the United States strengthened rackets and racketeers in big American cities, it is patently absurd to suppose that, in general, members of the Congress who supported such legislation or the "temperance" organizations, which stimulated them, had any such intention or conceived of any such design. There may, of course, have been a few individual congressmen, tied up with potential bootleggers, etc., who saw an opportunity to make some money; clearly, they were not a predominant group in the congressional membership or leadership at the time of the Volstead Act. It should also be pointed out, especially in view of the ambiguities inherent in Merton's term "unanticipated," that opponents of legislation are more apt to see undesired outgrowths or outcomes as possible or likely than are supporters thereof. See the quotation from Representative Jenkins of Ohio, below.

2. The Nature of Side Effects: Why They Are Ignored

Most persons engaged in advocating, supporting, and formulating legislative action tend to focus on what it is intended or hoped or expected to achieve. When they concern themselves with side effects, it is only with those side effects, which clearly will create obstacles to the realization of the design or with currently foreseeable *gross* perversions of the underlying purpose. Among men of affairs and practical bent, there is a strong tendency to be oriented towards what can be done, or it seems can be done, in terms of currently important and perceived purposes. Orientation on the other hand towards what might happen or may happen, not obviously connected with the initial purposes or design(s), tends to be regarded by such men—and most legislators, of course, are men of affairs and of practical common sense—as impractical, frustrating, and, correctly enough, hypothetical and therefore, incorrectly, in the invidious sense of the word, "theoretical." Now, of course, there is nothing inevitable about being dominated by such an orientation; it is, merely, natural. When, as, and if such men, in some particular case, see that side effects, or what were formerly regarded as side effects, can be of a considerable moment, they are often willing to take them into account provided these side-effects are relevant to some other purpose. The effects of government budgets and spending upon inflation are, nowadays, almost routinely taken into account, in the advanced industrial nations, at least. Nevertheless, since their concerns are practical, and, since, like everyone else, their capacity for attention is limited (see Dexter, 1970, part II; Simon, 1971), they do not tend to take into account side-effects which are, simply, unrelated to their purposes and aspirations.

For example, tax legislation may, cumulatively, have or have had the effect of substantially increasing the importance of accountants in corporate structures and among the managers of considerable pools of capital; this development, in turn, may have significant effects upon corporate values and typical corporate decisions. But, as long as taxes, are, in fact, collected reasonably satisfactorily, and as long as other purposes of the tax laws are or appear to be realized, and as long as the public insistence upon some degree of equity in the tax system is, more or less, satisfied, legislators are unlikely to be concerned with such outgrowths of their actions. These outgrowths—if of the sort just mentioned—are clearly undesigned. To consider them implementations of the tax laws is to pervert the common-sense meaning of implementation upon which Pressman and Wildavsky (1973) at least built their analysis. Post facto, no doubt, to some they may be reasonably recognizable outcomes of the legislation, but it is unlikely that they are such, looked at from the standpoint of the initiating and designing legislators, lobbyists, etc., *at the time of initiation.* Any given case, perhaps, one can interpret in some complex way to be an "implementation"; but to do this with the several cases discussed in the present article would be difficult.

Analogically, for instance, many Nazi leaders were unconcerned till after the fact that the expulsion of Jews from Germany stimulated the development of atomic weapons in the United States—this was an outgrowth or offshoot of policy, not a reasonably recognizable outcome. Almost certainly, the Nazi leaders never cared at all that the expulsion of Jews, liberals, and Social Democrats from Germany also stimulated interest in classic nineteenth century sociology in Canada and the United States or that concurrently this expulsion and the reception of the intellectual refugees in North America made it extremely difficult for those of us who were graduate students in sociology, 1936-9, of indigenous parentage, to get employment of the sort for which we were preparing ourselves.

Vice versa, although some opponents of legislation to aid refugees in the United States may have been concerned with such offshoots, its supporters looked at aiding refugees to settle in the USA as an extension of the traditional American theme of welcoming victims of tyranny.

Similarly, it is, probably, on the one hand, a matter of the completest indifference to Fidel Castro and associates that pressure upon middle-class Cubans to immigrate to the USA in the 1960s has played a substantial part in the economic development of Puerto Rico and Greater Miami. And, vice versa, although not a matter of indifference to United States legislators and policy-makers concerned with Cuban refugees, there was practically no recognition by these people that immigration of Cubans into Puerto Rico would enormously enhance the indigenous anti-Cuban feeling in that Commonwealth (bumper stickers reading "Love Puerto Rico or leave it" in the Commonwealth in the 1960s meant "You blasted Cubans get out!")—nor that the immigration of Cubans to Greater Miami would make the situation of blacks in that metropolis more difficult and demeaning (a factor, in all probability, in the riots of blacks in Miami in the 1970s and early 1980s).

A medical analogy may be helpful here. It is well-known that many physicians prescribe treatments, operations, and drugs, which have side effects. It is well-known, too, that until recently a high proportion of such practitioners were unwilling, perhaps psychologically unable, to attend to the frustrating problem of side effects.[1] Nowadays, there has been some change in the perspectives of many, though by no means all, physicians. But, in general, physicians are not, at least as yet, aware of the degree to which side effects may affect patients only decades later—perhaps in the nature of the case they cannot be expected to focus on such matters. Nor are they as vividly aware as would be hoped of the side effects of their recommendations on the occupational and social lives of patients.

The analogy probably breaks down at one point. In general, physicians, presumably ought to concern themselves chiefly with undesirable or pathological side effects—in consonance with the Hippocratic ethic of "above all, do no harm." But, in the political arena, it may be as valuable to forecast undesigned or unintended side effects of a neutral or favorable character.

In any event, even in the medical situation, physiologists—as distinguished from physicians—should be as much interested in the neutral or desirable as in the pathological side effect. And this aspect of the analogy has special meaning for students of policy and of legislative affairs who should surely be attentive to whatever happens, including outgrowths and offshoots, instead of merely accepting the definition of important reality offered by the initiators or proponents of given legislation.

Nevertheless, my experience in writing this essay confirmed the strong tendency to think of negative side-effects first. For several weeks, negative ones occurred chiefly to me; then, when I asked professional associates for examples, most of those supplied related to the failure of a policy or its nullification or at the least made it look silly.

Now, further study may show that most side effects of legislation are indeed negative and/or counterproductive in terms or original intent or underlying purpose. There may, however, be other reasons why most of us think of negative side effects first. In the first place, they are more dramatic. In the second place, they conform to the generalized sense of frustration about politics, which is to be found commonly in the United States, France, and probably generally throughout the world. In the third place, political and practical attention is frequently captured by the necessity of introducing new legislative projects in order to correct for the actual or seeming ill-effects of preceding legislation—whereas neutral or desirable consequences of preceding legislation less commonly evoke such a response. And, in the fourth place, so far as social scientists are concerned, the general lesson from some of the classic sociologists who have directed our attention towards undesigned consequences, particularly Pareto and Sumner, is that purposive social action is pretty likely to be frustrating, silly, and unproductive. (This is not true, however, of Weber or Durkheim.)

3. Theoretic Bases of a Concern with Undesigned Consequences

As the preceding paragraph indicates, the basic source of the notion of unanticipated, undesigned consequences of purposive social action comes from the nineteenth-century scholars just referred to. The most influential single study in the field is doubtless that by Max Weber, showing how Calvinism encouraged the growth of capitalism, etc. Carried one step further, it is a reasonable hypothesis that those polities, which were most strictly Calvinist were (though the chain of causation can not here be analyzed) most likely to enact Calvinist values into legislative form. And these communities would be according to the thesis, those in which the spirit and practice of capitalism would be most likely.

A second source of the emphasis on the unanticipated consequences of purposive social actions may be found in the theory of diffusion—the spread of culture traits and patterns from one society to another. For, in the first place, a considerable amount of legislation is, more or less clearly, an effort to introduce a culture trait, borrowed elsewhere, into a society and a polity. The Ombudsman notion has been, for instance, borrowed from Scandinavia and introduced into New Zealand and into American states and Canadian provinces. When Sweden adopted the requirement that traffic drive on the right-hand side of the road, or when the Canadian and United States governments try to get their populations to use a metric system, there is a similar borrowing and effort to impose or get received a foreign culture trait. Or at present there is a good deal of discussion in Nova Scotia and New Brunswick as to borrowing the Swedish requirement that hosts and bartenders are responsible for letting their guests drive, if intoxicated. A more dramatic example, now under discussion, although it has indigenous aspects, is the drive by Prime Minister Trudeau to add a Bill of Rights to the Canadian constitution. In fact, a good prediction is that it will not result in Canada's imitating the worst excesses of due process, etc., in the United States.

Thirdly, it is a commonplace of diffusion theory that any culture trait is received according to the nature of the receiving society and polity. In dealing with the borrowing of culture traits and patterns of a political sort, it should also be added that they are received—or rejected or adapted—according to the prevailing pattern of interests at the relevant times. For example, Theodore Roosevelt, presumptively influenced by the successful German and Dutch efforts along the same line, ordered the U.S. Government Printing Office to accept a reformed pattern of spelling. Among the important opposing interests were teachers of English, winners of spelling bees, and printers: the Government printers simply refused to obey, waiting for objections from "cultured people" and appeals to Congress; Congress thereupon made clear its intent that no such order from the President was to be obeyed.

Richard Crossman, as a leading member of the Labour Party, strongly supported the development of the postwar system of British health care, "socialized medicine." But he maintained (in private conversation with me in 1948) that American "liberals" should have grave doubts about proposals by government to introduce similar changes in medical delivery in the USA, because, he argued, in the United States, as distinguished from Britain, there would be so much corruption. Although the differences are by no means absolute, it does appear (the best clear summary of the situation is found in a documentary-type novel, Dominic, 1980) that as the American government has taken a larger part in medicine through

Medicare, etc., his prediction has come true. Whereas, in Britain, the major development (not unanticipated but rather undesigned!) has been "unplanned rationing … in the form of congestion, and, in the opinion of many observers, a decrease in the quality of services" (Majone and Wildavsky, 1977, 110).

Finally, awareness of the undesigned and unintended consequences of social change has developed from the study of innovation and inventions. Such writers as Ogburn (1922) and Vierkandt (1908) have shown how technological and social inventions lead to outgrowths quite different from any intended or designed, either by the inventors or by those who financed and disseminated the invention. It is improbable in the extreme that Henry Ford and contemporaries were largely hopeful of adding to the ease and indeed possibility of fornication and adultery for respectable people. Or that the inventors of movies hoped to some degree to loosen family ties, or the founders of TV chains were concerned to strengthen them. Legislation played no great part in the initial inventions in these areas; but the automobile culture of today is part of a complex of which the highway is another important element. Many consequences of highway legislation—rapid transportation, for instance—were designed and implemented. But others, such as urban sprawl, were clearly not part of any design and would have been regarded with distaste by many who supported highway legislation. Nor was the breakdown of a sense of neighborhood and community as a result of the highway designed or desired in the USA or Canada. (In some undeveloped nations, of course, a highway system might be introduced to help reduce tribalism and localism.)

So, too, when what is called in the United States the public school, the state-supported school, became widespread, it was of course a significant innovation. But few in its earliest period designed it as the major focus of community and neighborhood sentiment in the United States and Canada. To a degree, it offset the effects of the highway and the automobile and of increased mobility in general. But note: as a result of busing to larger schools from small communities since World War II, the contribution of the public school to community spirit has been reduced—but in this case the consequence was not unanticipated; there was so much locality protest oriented to just this problem. But it was undesired, and was not an implementation at all. What happened here, in general, was that on a cost-benefit analysis basis, the advantages of larger schools, which permit specialized facilities and teaching, were considered, rightly or wrongly, to outweigh the disadvantages of destroying the neighborhood center, the school, in many places.

4. Studies of Congress versus Studies of Legislation?

Concern with these matters occurred to me because in early 1980 I started planning the revision of my own book on Congress (Dexter, 1970). As I reviewed my own work on Congress and that of my colleagues, not only in congressional but other legislative studies, I was struck by the following: we have shifted perspectives about how the legislative process occurs, and now see it explicitly as a matter of accommodation, bargaining, definition of situations, and communications. In oversimplified language, we now treat legislatures as a sociological phenomenon and the process of enacting legislation as a sociological process (Bauer, Pool, and Dexter, 1963; Hayes, 1981; Fenno, 1973; Gross, 1953; the various articles reprinted in Peabody and Polsby, 1963, 1969, 1977). But we, students of legislation, in general have stopped there.

A disjunction seems to exist. Although there are a number of administrative studies which use interactional approaches (it is altogether proper here to cite Pressman and Wildavsky, 1973), and the classic text on public administration is very sociological (Simon, Smithburg, and Thompson, 1951), there is little traced out about the effects, if any, of the legislative process on the administrative one. Bauer, Pool, and Dexter (1963) for instance conclude that one agreed value of participants on both sides of legislative struggles of the sort we studied is to leave things so that both sides can come back to fight again another day—or at least to convince both sides that this is a possibility. (We did not deal with multisided issues but presumably the same thing would apply there.) Fitting ourselves into the accommodating philosophy and sociology of T.V. Smith (1940) on the legislative way of life, we suggest that such an attitude towards legislative struggles is admirably compatible with the achievement of consensus and the tolerations of parliamentary democracy.

Considering the heft of our study, it is natural enough that in that book we stopped there. But neither we, subsequently, nor any one else has carried forward the contention to see if the next step is struggle in the same way about the same issues in the administrative structures, which presumably are supposed to "implement" the legislative design. It would seem entirely natural that this should be so—that, for example, the controversies within such agencies as the Tariff Commission or the State Department about foreign trade should continue the struggles, which we reported about legislation on that issue—but, presumably, coming measurably nearer to having direct effects on the beneficiaries, victims, clients, and targets of the legislation. My emphasis on lobbying administrative agencies in a book of practical advice to organizations, which wish to influence or affect government (Dexter, 1969) simply takes for granted that this hypothesis is true. (Of course, students of the courts do undertake and have undertaken reporting on what happens to legislation in the courts; but, in general, for them "implementation" has not really meant what it means to Wildavsky *et al.* but the implementation by lower courts of whatever the higher courts pronounce. This comes closer but hardly close enough to noting the actual effects of legislation systematically, partly because so much does not filter through the courts.)

In a way, we are facing here the old problem posed by William James—"A difference to be a difference must make a difference"—and we have not a very clear notion under what circumstances with what antecedents and what kinds of legislative pronouncements, legislative action, and legislative processes make what kind of difference.

Specifically, following upon the Bauer, Pool, and Dexter study of reciprocal trade extension in 1953, 1954, and 1955, years after the study was completed, in 1973, I realized that we had devoted little attention to investigating the effects of the changes in the program. We were, practically speaking, entirely concerned with process. Partly, and probably in large measure, this was due to an occupational bias of students of politics at that time and now in favor of studying processes and in favor of studying representation. Indeed, if political scientists had been more concerned with legislation and its effects, and less concerned with representation and process, they might have contributed far more to the study of policy than they have. Vice versa, there is a strong tendency for those who have been exposed to this emphasis on process and representation to take effects as self-evident or given.

One aspect, chiefly of a later Reciprocal Trade Extension Act, suggests the naiveté (which I myself showed) of assuming we knew what consequences would ensue from legislation. During the entire period of our study and for some years thereafter many persons who believed both in foreign trade and in avoiding the traumatic or supposedly traumatic effect which foreign imports have on workers and on small business when they pass a critical point and begin to come in large quantities (thereby driving workers out of work, small businesses out of business, in competitive industries) supported what were then called the Kennedy-Williams-Humphrey-Eberharter proposals. After President Kennedy came into office, these were essentially added to the Reciprocal Trade program, under the name of Trade Adjustment Assistance Act. They in effect were supposed to provide that small businesses, so injured by foreign imports, could receive aid, basically of the sort small businesses received in other areas where it was desired to encourage them—financing, special tax considerations, or the like. They provided, essentially as an extension of social security, that workers injured by foreign imports (that is who lost their jobs) could receive special financial benefits and be entitled to retraining or counseling about work in other fields or elsewhere. So far, so good. But in the first several years that these provisions were on the book, very few cases occurred of anybody receiving assistance because of them. The conditions for proving injury due to foreign imports were simply too difficult to meet or at least, as the Tariff Commission interpreted them, they were too difficult. Presumably, some persons engaged in enacting and "implementing" (that is, in effect, here failing to implement) this program had foreseen such results; the criteria were not easy to meet. Presumably, others were simply careless about the form in which the legislation was phrased. And, presumably, still others either deceived themselves or deceived others—or hoped against hope—that the program would amount to something. An important factor, at that time, was that the industries and unions most geared towards protection, shoes and textiles, for example, had a rather deep feeling that government was always going to pretend to help them, but was not really going to offer any significant help. In some measure, these industries were beaten before they started; "faint heart never won" (or but rarely wins) unfamiliar Federal benefits.

But a change took place, partly because the Nixon administration in the early 1970s saw a chance of making a Republican breakthrough to labor, partly because by that time some of the unions, where people had the expectation, based on experience, of receiving genuine help from Washington, were suffering from unemployment, attributed to foreign imports. So, there was arranged a relaxation in the stringencies of proof about whether foreign imports were predominantly responsible for unemployment. And the Nixon administration also designated a senior official who spent his time explaining the program to labor, chiefly, and urging those who might benefit from it to seek help.

But out of this grew a very large side effect indeed. By the time President Reagan came into office, entitlements under this program mounted up into the billions annually. It is one of the "money machines" now (1981), which, if the theory that government expenditure has to be controlled to curb inflation is true, must be checked.

On the other hand, the program has had, so far as the media and leadership of unions are concerned, the reverse effect from what was expected by its supporters, 1953-61. It was supposed and expected by those (like me) who favored it that its effect would be this: if workers (and small businessmen) were less frightened of being thrown out of work by foreign imports, then they would be less likely in bad times to oppose them and to clamor against them. But, in fact, what seems to have happened is that the possibility that benefits and aid may be obtained for citizens or members of a union by demonstrating that foreign imports are responsible for their unemployment or underemployment has accentuated and stimulated the tendency of union and civic leaders to attribute the problems to foreign manufacturers. In terms of economic theory, indeed, a demand has been created for seeing foreign imports as villainous, and so the demand has been supplied. (As it happens, there has been relatively little invocation of adjustment assistance by small business.) It is quite certain that Messrs Kennedy, Humphrey, Williams, and Eberharter, and those who supported their proposals, had no such intention—in fact, they thought of aiding, chiefly, people to get out of what anyway they regarded as dying and for the most part peripheral industries. So, aside from the failure to perceive the relevant economic theory, there was a failure to take account of the probability that in the external world conditions would change from what they were industrially in the late 1950s at the height of relative American economic strength. In consequence, the program has been not only a considerable drain on the national exchequer but has been a *counter-implementation* of the designs of those who most strongly pushed it in its formative years.

However, Congressman Thomas Jenkins of Ohio, at the time acting senior Republican on the House Ways and Means Committee, who represented one of the districts in the country most jeopardized by foreign imports at the time, said when I asked him his views of the proposal in 1955:

> Well, I don't know. I'm afraid that sort of thing can spread. Now look at social security. You know I voted for social security at first because we already had it in Ohio—and then I felt it should be extended to the blind. So, I pushed that and made a heartrending speech about it, which they still make fun of me about, but look at what we have now, all sorts of social security everywhere. (Dexter, 1970, 239-40)

He did anticipate, more or less, what happened, because like many conservative Republicans of his generation, he suspected government aggrandizement almost everywhere. But he had nothing to do with designing the measures.

There has already been pointed out the possibility of more than one reason why we have not accumulated most knowledge about legislative effects is the concentration of attention in Congressional and Parliamentary studies on process and on representation. Another (mis)direction of focus may also play a part here; most students of Congress, Parliament, etc, are interested in Congress or a given Parliament or a state legislature. Bauer, Pool and Dexter (1963) went considerably beyond the halls of Congress to see what people were doing (Dillon, 1981, i; Hayes, 1981). But we went backwards—to what was happening in the district and among the lobbyists rather than forward, to what happened among the affected people. We thus for the most part regarded Congress as defining our problem—rather than regarding the legislation, its antecedents and outgrowths, as defining one issue. That is to say, we got a little bit away from the danger of letting the data (the institutions as socially defined) define our problems; but we *did not* seek out a genuinely sociological definition of it. Until several students of Congress, Parliament, and the like, can abandon their orientation to these institutions as problem-defining, they can only out of the corner of one eye, as it were, see effects and implementations.

5. An Economic Law about Side Effects of Legislative Policy

In the preceding section, it was pointed out that the demand created by the Trade Adjustment Assistance Act created a supply. In fact, this appears to exemplify a general law.[2] That law is this: Whenever a piece of legislation creates a demand for a particular service or activity or even attitude, that demand is likely to be fulfilled. An important corollary is that: In a number of instances, legislators through legislation create demands without thinking through their creation, still less how they can be supplied. (Or even if they think it through, they are unable or unwilling to design anything which will affect the way the supply-demand situation operates.) And it follows consequently that: *many demands are supplied in ways which are either irrelevant or counterproductive to the purposes of the legislation.*

For example, I am told that in Iceland a number of houses, obviously not brand new, are to be observed with part of the scaffolding left on. This is so because the Icelandic tax laws provide different rates for unfinished houses from finished houses and a house with scaffolding left on, no matter how long, is regarded or defined as unfinished. When I happened to mention this to a colleague who had spent time in Bangladesh, he commented that he had seen exactly the same phenomenon there. Originally, I was interested in this sort of thing because of the Napoleonic Wars phenomenon reported for Britain: taxation was greater on houses which had considerable window-space. Result: gentlemen's houses were constructed with relatively narrow window-space. Further result: after the tax was changed, the phenomenon persisted because architects, builders, and/or gentlemen had become accustomed to expecting houses with narrow windows.

An illustration which has no doubt been replicated in one form or another often throughout history! A few years ago, Governor Rockefeller and other New York authorities instituted an all-out campaign against the selling of drugs; in conformity with this, penalties were vastly increased (or it was declared that they would be increased) on drug-peddlers. Result: drug wholesalers made more use of children as drug-peddlers, because, under other state statutes, they had to be treated as juveniles, and would not be likely to receive the harsh penalties threatened to adults.

Of course, there are other ways in which people respond in economic terms to legislation in such a way as to counteract the legislation or produce side effects, unanticipated or undesigned. For instance, Belgium has devoted more legislative effort than most countries to trying to insure that people can keep their jobs. In consequence, it has become even more difficult than elsewhere to lay people off (although presumably not any more difficult than for tenured university professors in the USA or civil servants in Britain). In consequence, innovators, entrepreneurs, and speculators adapt by being more reluctant than is customary elsewhere in the Western world to hire people for untested programs; therefore there are fewer innovative entrepreneurial programs in Belgium. Now, in the long run, this is presumably counterproductive and it would thwart the underlying purpose of the legislation—for in the long run, it means less employment and/or prosperity in Belgium. But it will take a long time to realize this; and many advocates and supporters of the program, such as labor unions, which are chiefly oriented to defending the present interests of their present members may not realize it at all. Another country, less law-abiding than Belgium has adopted very similar legislation—but in that nation, its efforts are in large measure avoided by the following: the law specifies that people are entitled to their jobs after working a specified number of years. But, therefore, in the last year before such a right would be created, employers take pains to discharge employees for a period long enough to prevent the establishment of the right, a month or so, then usually reemploying them.

6. Rules about Adapting to Rules[3]

Legislation may be viewed as consisting of rules for conduct, prescriptions, prohibition, permissions, addressed to officials and citizens. They look like rules to be added to the whole system of formal and informal rules by which, in fact, the life of society is carried out. Indeed, if we want to understand what is going on in a given society, we need to arrive at the rules, which the actions of its members fit. But there is a tricky equivocation here; the rules we want for this purpose are not by any means the same as rules expressed in enactments (but there is an overlapping). However, the form of legislation and the form of stating the rules, which the actions of people in society fit is the same or similar. Indeed, legislation is expressed as though it were the latter. People ask themselves "What effect do we want to have?" After argument, they adopt answers to that question. The argument, as a matter of practical reasoning persuades them that such rules are good or desirable. The practical reasoning ends with the rules. So, there is a temptation to think that the work has ended with the rules as formulated, particularly because they are of the same form as the rules which described how society actually operates, or how people like to believe it operates. But it does not follow at all that any newly enacted rule will actually operate as an effective rule. It is merely problematic—a venture—until it has been adapted to and accommodated to the existing body of rules by which people actually live. And very often such adaptation and accommodation means that it cannot be accepted as written, at all.

Another way of saying this is that rules can be and are drawn only so as to fit into the preexisting body of written rules. But in the external world they are subject to a large number of contingencies, chiefest of which are the rules of actual behavior, many of which are not formulated very well, or are deliberately misformulated, because of the sociological tendency to distinguish social reality from professed behavior. Of course, it is possible that the rules will, as legislatively written, alter the rules as practised of behavior; but this itself is one of the contingencies with which written rules have to cope to be implemented. It is indeed the subject of the controversy between Myrdal and Sumner (see Myrdal, 1944) about mores. But sometimes, and more frequently, the rules as written will be modified—or twisted.

The following examples seem to involve a particular application of the issue just stated. The application is this: rules tend to be, and often must of necessity, be stated quite generally. The law, supposedly, admits of no exceptions. But, in fact, societal practices and sociological realities do involve a much larger and more sophisticated number and sort of variations than the written law can handle. The written law, if it is to be implemented, then has to be enforced on or against the variants—persons or situations. It becomes necessary then, also, to prove that exceptions have not been admitted or to treat variations uniformly. So, the law, according to Anatole France, gives the rich and the poor alike the right to sleep under bridges; or as President Lopez-Portillo of Mexico has said, "Justice between the rich and poor cannot rest on equality between them." The variants, the exceptions, respond in some way differently to the law as written; or the effort to prove that everybody has been treated uniformly itself demands that a side effect, a new adaptation, develop.

First, equals are treated unequally where schooling is made compulsory for everyone. Stein and Susser (1963) have shown persuasively that, epidemiologically speaking, mental retardation correlates with school attendance. That is, persons are identified as retardates when they are (generally) forced to enter the schooling system—and they are less likely to be identified as retardates when they pass the age at which they are subjected to compulsory schooling. There is exceptionally strong evidence that a high proportion of those so classified are quite capable of managing their own lives in work and social situations outside school and not dependent upon artifacts of the school system such as examinations of a written sort or intelligence tests (see Dexter, 1964). It is, however, a matter of common observation (and was more so twenty years ago than now) that persons whether classified as retardates or slow learners who are defined as incompetent by the system and who do in fact do badly at what the system rewards are under a stigma. They suffer as simpletons; they are frequently treated as a social problem, and sometimes they may become such, not as a consequence of the original intellectual deficit, but either because of the stigma itself or because so much work and life needlessly requires that every one possess the ability to do somewhat decently in school. As Dexter (1964) shows, a society which chose to do so could make of clumsiness a similar source of stigma and social problems.

It is quite certain that the founders of the modern school system had no such intention; they probably were for the most part unaware that such a development could ensue, partly because the universal requirement for compulsory schooling has grown bit by bit, rather than being effectively enforced all at once. (In recent years, to be sure, some of the provisions for special education in some environments have ameliorated the stigma and handicap just described; but up until 1960 this was largely true—and it may be of significance to add that in the Western world the more democratic and egalitarian the school system, the greater the problem with mental retardation.)

Second, the United States Civil Rights program has had an effect at least in enhancing, perhaps in accelerating, the insistence upon publication or the nearest possible equivalent in regard to university promotion and tenure. People who have taken part in promotion and tenure decisions in recent years in the United States—perhaps still more in initial recruitment—learn that they must live in apprehension of appearing to have discriminated against members of those minority groups or statuses whom the civil rights laws try to help. They must show that they treated everybody equally, every applicant, every candidate. Publication of meritorious sort in quantity becomes a clear protective device when, as the statistical and social situation indicated will frequently happen, there is no clear reason to reject minority candidates or aspirants, but the feeling of the people who do the selection, their assessment of character and originality, lead them to prefer several of the candidates who are not in a minority status.

Another effect of this situation is, self-evidently, that it removes control of hiring from departmental chairmen or, in smaller institutions, the chief executive officers. Accordingly, if such persons might desire to recruit persons with a certain sort of competence and interest—say, people deeply concerned with a particular sort of general education, such as, e.g. the University of Chicago recruited in the 1930s to some extent—they will be handicapped in so doing. They might ultimately prove to the requisite authorities and courts that they had acted objectively in terms of their criteria; but the expenditure of time and money in so doing will tend to discourage such efforts.

Now, to be sure, there are other factors in modern U.S society—its increasingly egalitarian emphasis, its shuddering horror at establishments and old-boy networks, and the sheer effect of the great increase in number in the relevant professions—which tend in the same direction. But the Civil Rights program would appear to have enhanced and accelerated the effect of these other factors by interacting with them. (And, incidentally, because of the considerable influence of the United States in Canada, there has been a tendency towards such an effect, partly for these reasons, in Canada—that is partly for civil rights reasons, ironically enough most likely to be sympathized with by those Canadian scholars most apt to be suspicious of the USA.)

Yet, it is reasonably clear, as Glaser (1975) shows, that there was no design or intention or expectation by the supporters and advocates of civil rights legislation that such a development would or should occur.

7. Clarifications and Prescriptions for Further Study

Of course, this is a preliminary treatment, unsatisfactory in many ways, incomplete, demanding much criticism and analysis, if it is to prove worthwhile. It may, consequently, be worth pointing out a few considerations which may help in such further work.

First, as Iain Gow has pointed out, the time frame ought to be specified more precisely than here. Clearly, there is a difference between first-generation effects, such as those attributable above to the Civil Rights Acts, and effects spread over several generations, as in the public school example, just preceding. There is also an important difference between first-order effects, which occur because of the legislation itself, and its effect on something, and second (or third, etc.) order effects where the legislation has an effect on something, which in turn affects something else.

Second, there should be an attempt to clear up the Myrdal-Sumner debate (see Myrdal, 1944) in transactional terms (Bentley, 1954; Dewey and Bentley, 1949). The postulation is both that written law affects users and that users interpret written law. The user (typically?) looks at a statute to see how it may serve his or her purpose or be evaded if it does not appear likely to do so. But in using it, even in evading it, he is apt to adopt its rhetoric, its logic, and thereby at the least ascribe to himself motives and purposes which he would not otherwise have chosen. So, over time, the statute may change him (or a clutch of hims and hers), even though he may not see it as so doing.

For example, a few years ago the United States changed its policy, legislatively and administratively as to the categories of persons eligible for specified aid in rehabilitation treatment, and apparently this was also interpreted as affecting what kind of rehabilitation specialists would be financed or supported. A substantial proportion of rehabilitation funds in some institutions came from the Federal exchequer. So, not surprisingly, in a particular institution, the cases and the specialists were reclassified to conform to the new Federal guidelines. The people who did the reclassifying regarded this process as simply another example of constantly having to con the Feds by verbal conformity. But was it? It remains to be found out whether in adopting the new vocabulary they did or did not, over time, alter their own expectations, their own definitions of situations, their own tendency to take case x or case y, etc.

Third, it is presumably possible, and presumably desirable, to classify types of responses and types of side effects in a way, which is only hinted at in this paper. For example, the side effects of what is clearly special-interest legislation might be different from or less than those of general-purpose legislation. Or more. Many matters of this sort need exploration.

8. Conclusion

It is desirable to adopt one leading hypothesis or notion: let us as students and scholars assume that we do not know till we have studied and observed (just as physiologists would do with a new medical drug) what consequences, if any, will flow from a given legislative action. Tentatively, we can further assume that a significant proportion of such consequences will have no clear or evident relationship to the designs, purposes, and intentions of the initiators of the legislative action.

This statement, however, raises again a question which has been previously suggested; how do we define and clarify intentions and purposes or designs? People have, of course, many subconscious and unconscious intentions or purposes, which it is difficult or impossible to identify. But beyond this—how can we determine who had what purpose, design, or intention, let alone anticipation, in regard, say, to the Trade Adjustment Assistance Act above discussed? For preliminary purposes, it is well enough not to spend effort on making more precise our definition of manifest design or purpose. But, sooner or later, that will be necessary because in matters political, different persons, different interests, different institutional leaders, have different purposes and designs.

This will be necessary, but it does not cancel the value of what has been done here, or what can be done without such precision, because many side effects are clearly not part of anybody's purpose or design. Contrary to what the naive might expect, after going through this exercise, my tentative impression is that it will often be easier to trace side effects, clearly not part of anybody's purpose or design, in historical examples, where the whole development can be looked at, than in contemporary ones where the process is not complete and we may get overwhelmed by knowledge of too much detail and by the temptation to take a side or to avoid appearing to take sides (often, for scholars, a greater danger).

Finally, for the person who wants to know: What use will this be? Will it tell us how to carry out intentions and purposes, how to implement better? Maybe. I do not know. But, at a minimum, I suggest that awareness of this set of problems about side-effects will have two valuable consequences: (1) to the degree that general tendencies are clarified, as in the economic cases above, in terms of the law there suggested, gross perversion of purposes may be avoided; and (2) in general, where no clear regularities of response can be discovered, we can look at side effects as we look at demography. Few demographers have done much to increase or reduce population. But they can, in many cases, by observing birth and death rates, and correlating them with other factors, predict the most likely population distributions in the next few years—and in so doing provide something for policy-makers to consider.

Similarly, as scholars in the field of legislative or other policy become more perceptive of side effects, they will, perhaps, see them sooner, and thereby be able to suggest readjustments, which it would be well to consider.

Notes

*   I am grateful to Henry Bain, David Braybrooke, and Iain Gow, for suggesting ideas incorporated into the paper. I am also grateful to the Canadian Political Science Association for letting me read a previous draft of the paper at its 1981 meetings. (By the time this paper is printed, a third draft, focusing somewhat more on Congress, will have been read at the American Political Science Association Meeting, 1981, by invitation.)

1.   It is sometimes helpful, and frequently interesting, to indicate the broader context within which conceptions have been of importance to writers and scholars. Aside from my interest in Congressional actions:

   (a)   I became vividly aware of the subject of medical side effects, partly through the writings of Morton Mintz of the *Washington Post*, partly due to the fact that in the last fifteen years I have had an abdominal operation, been in an auto accident, which injured a shoulder, and been mugged with serious damage to one eye—in all three instances, the side effects of medical treatment seemed to me to be as traumatic or more so than the original trauma.

   (b)   The original formulation of the points in this article was in terms of organization theory and its emphasis on input, throughput, and output. Although, for several reasons (and I am much indebted again to critics at the Canadian Political Science meetings and to Henry Bain for indicating some of them to me), this introduces unnecessary awkwardness, it does have the great advantage, by analogy, of causing one to think of side-effects—pollution being as much an output of old-fashioned steel plants as steel, employment of any firm as much as whatever it produces in a certain sense, etc.

2.   Henry Bain helped me realize this.

3.   I owe this formulation largely to David Braybrooke's comments on an earlier draft.

References

Bauer, R. A., I. de S. Pool, and L. A. Dexter (1963) *American Business and Public Policy.* New York: Atherton. (2nd ed. Chicago: Aldine, 1972.)

Bentley, A. F. (1954) *An Inquiry into Inquiries*. Boston: Beacon Press.

Dewey, J. and A. F. Bentley (1949) *The Knowing and the Known*. Boston: Beacon Press.

Dexter, L. A. (1964) *Tyranny of Schooling: An Inquiry into the Problem of Stupidity*. New York: Basic Books.

Dexter, L. A. (1969) *How Organizations are Represented in Washington*. Indianapolis: Bobbs Merrill.

Dexter, L. A. (1970) *Sociology and Politics of Congress*. Chicago: Rand McNally. (Now being revised under a different title; New Brunswick, NJ: Transaction Publishers.)

Dillon, W. S. (1981) Introduction. In L. A. Dexter, *Representation versus Popular Sovereignty*, Cambridge, MA: Schenckman Books.

Dominic, R. B. (1980) *The Attending Physician*. New York: Harper & Row.

Fenno, R. (1973) *Congressmen in Committees*. Boston: Little, Brown.

Glaser, N. (1975) *Affirmative Discrimination*. New York: Basic Books.

Gross, B. (1953) *The Legislative Struggle*. New York: McGraw-Hill.

Hayes, M. (1981) *Lobbyists and Legislators*. New Brunswick, NJ: Rutgers University Press.

Majone, G. and A. Wildavsky (1978). Implementation as evolution. In H. Freeman (ed.), *Policy Studies Review Annual*, No. 2, Beverly Hills, California: Sage, 103-17.

Merton, R. K. (1936) The unanticipated consequences of purposive social action, *American Sociological Review*, 1, 894—904. (Reprinted in R. K. Merton, *Sociological Ambivalence*, New York: Free Press, 1976.)

Myrdal, G. (1944) *An American Dilemma*. New York: Harper's.

Ogburn, W. F. (1922) *Social Change with Respect to Culture and Nature*. New York: B. W. Huebsch. (Several subsequent editions by other publishers.)

Peabody, R. L. and N. Polsby (eds.) (1963, 1969, 1977) *New Perspectives on the House of Representatives*. Chicago: Rand McNally.

Pressman, J. and A. Wildavsky (1973) *Implementation*. Berkeley: University of California Press.

Simon, H. (1971) Designing organisations for an information-rich world. In M. Greenberger (ed.), *Computers, Communications, and the Public Interest*. Baltimore: Johns Hopkins Press.

Simon, H., D. Smithburg, and V. Thompson (1951) *Public Administration*. New York: Knopf.

Smith, T. V. (1940) *The Legislative Way of Life*. Chicago: University of Chicago Press.

Stein, Z. and S. Susser (1963) The social distribution of mental retardation, *American Journal of Mental Deficiency*. 67, 811-21.

Vierkandt, A. (1908) *Die Stetigkeit im Kulturwandel*. Leipzig: Dunckler & Humboldt.

Part III

Practicing Social Sciences

1

Causal Imputation and Purposes of Investigation*

There is a considerable literature about causation.[1] A great many investigators constantly employ the notion of causation in some form. But with the exception of a very few items, these investigators will find little of use in this literature.

In our culture, "scientists" possess a prestige, largely based upon the fact that they are believed to be especially skillful in discovering the "causes" of certain phenomena, and thereby providing means for controlling them.[2] One would therefore expect them to have formulated, more clearly than ordinary people, the principles of causation which guide them.

This does not seem to be the case. Usually, they content themselves with unanalyzed, intuitively-derived, ad hoc conceptions of causation, for each different problem which they encounter. There is no need to convince readers of this journal that, even in matters of scientific method, it is preferable to apply the "scientific" type of analysis. There is of course no a priori reason for assuming that ad hoc conceptions are to be deplored; but it is inaccurate to believe, as many men do, that they are acting in terms of a universal causal theory when they are not. Such inaccuracy might be and perhaps is misleading; it is entirely possible that techniques of investigation could be improved, if the underlying conception of cause were more rigorously analyzed.

Philosophers (and scientists, functioning as philosophers) have found two chief stumbling blocks in their analyses of causation. In some form or other, they put forward the argument that "reality" is too "complex" to permit any genuine recognition of causes. In other terminology, this is the argument that causation is so multiple that one might as well give up the idea altogether. (In the social sciences, this viewpoint leads to the argument that social sciences cannot be, because social happenings are so diverse, and to the adoption of a complete scepticism towards any result, obtained by a sociologist, because "you can't be sure.")

The other stumbling-block is also presented in two major ways: (1) Inevitable sequence is not distinguishable from cause; and (2) conditions cannot be separated from causes. (Exceptions are sometimes granted, if a perfect experimental situation can be obtained, but in the social and biological sciences, this is excessively rare.) Most of us have heard many times in arguments about war and unemployment, the view "O! capitalism doesn't cause war or unemployment. It just happens to be there," or "O! national 'sovereignty' would never lead to war, except for the presence of capitalism." And the kind of confusion about valid causal imputation presented in such statements is manifested by distinguished political scientists, economists, and sociologists, as well as by politicians and by hoi polloi; and, in relation to different problems, be it added, by allergists and otolaryngologists.

Some of the confusion about causes may be cleared up if we examine for a moment the assumption that an investigator "discovers" the "causes" of a phenomenon. This phrase seems to indicate a belief that causes "are" in the universe and part of its pattern. John Dewey in his latest study of logic,[3] has expressed to a considerable extent what it would otherwise be necessary to say here. He points out that the term "causal laws" is a figure of speech, and that the "category of causation" is logical, not ontological. He makes quite clear the point that any semantical discussion of cause is irrelevant in writing about scientific investigation, because the term does not designate or denote anything at all.[4] Discussions about cause, at least within the world view characteristic of modern science, are of two kinds: (a) syntactical (logical) about "cause" a term representing a verbal operation or (b) about cause$_p$ (pragmatical, sociological), that is to say the interpretation which individuals place upon the term "cause" within a given context. (A discussion may of course deal with both these levels at once.)

Our concern here is obviously not with the metaphysical notions of causation, which introduce such conceptions as essence, ontological character, first cause, etc.,[5] nor even with the statements about cause as a universal which linguistically self-conscious logicians of "science" have made, but rather with the ideas about cause, which diagnosticians in any field display when talking about the "causes" of certain more or less specific phenomena.[6]

When faced by a serious problem (i.e. a problem about which he feels something should be done), the ordinary biological organism does do something. Immediately upon determining that one course of action is preferable to another, he makes a causal imputation. (Purely random, trial-and-error actions are so rare, once human organisms have actually formulated a problem, that it is probably accurate to say that all human goal-oriented behavior is associated with causal imputation.)

For instance, many people, when afflicted with or fearful of acquiring colds or indigestion, etc., try to avoid the continuance or occurrence of these evils. They therefore alter their ordinary regimens of work, diet, and exercise, thereby showing certain causal imputations about the relationship of work, and/or diet, and/or exercise to colds and indigestion. Similarly, throughout the last twenty years, statesmen and scholars have been making causal imputations about war and unemployment. (In the latter instances, no overt change in what is ordinarily described as "behavior" took place; but the statesman and scholars have verbally advocated certain alterations, thereby indicating their assumptions about causes.)[7]

That is to say, when one wishes to prevent an unpleasant, or undesired happening, enhance the pleasure or desirability of a desired one, (or simply arrange for its repetition), one does something to achieve such a result. The basis and justification for believing such activity will be rewarding, furnished by brute sensory experience, has been so adequately discussed elsewhere,[8] that it need not be presented at length here.

We recognize then that people are acting upon causal assumptions, when we see them acting to obtain a desired goal. Cause$_p$ might then be described as precisely that which, if an antecedent, if altered, will produce a result which we wish. (The result may of course be negative, as the stoppage of some phenomenon which we consider bad.) This description is simple, but from its utilization may come the means for the solution of often-mooted problems.

First, it means that the scientist, whose concern is with the patterning of phenomena, is entirely correct, when he says that he is concerned with correlation, concomitant variation, etc., but not with causation. He is however entirely mistaken when he states categorically that Science cannot be concerned with causation. (Two interesting studies in the sociology of knowledge are suggested by these statements: (1) how far, in any given cultural context, does even the "purest" and most non-causally-minded scientist organize his problems, researches, and findings, in terms of the socially-significant in his society? (2) how often does the pure scientist, not concerned (according to his own statements) with results, in modern American culture, speak in the name of the great God, Science, about matters of politics and economics, of which, as a pure scientist, he may be profoundly ignorant?) He is not concerned with causation, because he is not planning action; but there is nothing to prevent anyone from investigating, as a basis for action.

Second, and by the same token, those individuals who deny the possibility of National Socialist science, Marxist science, Catholic science, etc. may be mistaken. Obviously, these ideologies are organized around differing sets of values; different problems will surely be investigated by scientists, insofar as they are permitted to function within societies, motivated by such ideologies. Furthermore, even where similar problems are investigated, there will be differing assumptions about what must be retained and what can be altered. Thereby, a different framework of causal imputations may grow up, and a different series of rationalizations link them together. (How far such a possibility does in fact develop, and in relation to which categories of propositions, is again a problem for research by the sociologist of knowledge. If he found that in the specific cases cited above, or in any others, such differences existed, his next problem would be to discover how the differing sciences were intertranslatable.)

A clearer example of the above point may be drawn from a controversy current in our own culture, viz. how far is war due to capitalism and/or to political nationalism? The probabilities are that it is due to either, both, both with other factors, neither. In other words, consistent action, predicated upon any of these four assumptions (provided other factors are clearly specified) might work in getting rid of war. The question to argue is: Which, in terms of other values, would you rather change, if either? If this, and other social and biological problems, were, after a certain point in investigation has been reached, regarded from this standpoint, a vast amount of argument might be avoided.

Third, the definition of cause$_p$ here employed might make it easier to distinguish a priori elements in investigation from those susceptible to modification in the light of further knowledge. If one of one's basic starting points is that capitalism is evil, and must be held responsible for other evils (i.e. war), it is at least time-saving to take this for granted and go on, rather than to spend time and effort undertaking investigation to prove the point. (Or vice versa of course.)

For purposes of emphasizing a point, which has been hitherto minimized, this article overemphasizes to some extent one position, and may seem to adhere to the conventionalist school entirely. There are of course antecedents (such as those which we classify as superstitions), which it is ridiculous to classify as causes. But on the whole common sense, or at least elementary statistics, can detect such errors; trained investigators ordinarily argue about causes, much as the blind men did about the elephant, each being within the correct field of observation. Frequently, every single one of them (within a given framework of values) is right, and the only choice which needs be made, is that of choosing from among them one to follow through to the end.

Fourth, scientists should realize that cause, when dealing with contemporary problems, such as war, unemployment, etc., has a signification very different from cause when applied to the development of the solar system or even of exogamy. For, we (plan to do something or) can imagine someone planning to do something about the two former phenomena, far more easily than about the two latter.

This distinction may throw some light on the often-heard assertion that history can not be a social science, because it is descriptive. Our analysis would suggest that historical propositions often are arranged without any goal-orientation in mind, and therefore proceed upon the assumption of multiple causation. This represents a historical method, differing from that of those scientists who wish to guide action towards the future; but most propositions of anthropology, history, and geology can be placed within a framework where they have relevance to contemplated action.

Lastly, the two stumbling blocks mentioned at the commencement of this article can be removed. Ordinary sequences can be distinguished from causative sequences within a given framework of value; the individual who is in a popular sense a sceptic, i.e. one without any ethical system (if such a one exist), will therefore be in the philosophical sense a follower of Hume, viz. a sceptic. (Many values may be biologically-conditioned, so the present insistence on values probably would not lead to chaos.)

In this connection, a further difficulty may be mentioned. In common speech, we are apt to say, "The sun is the cause of warmth," "War is the cause of depression," etc. Actually, of course, substances do not cause substances, etc. What happens is that a certain series of events causes another series of events, i.e. emission of light from the sun leads to sensations in the skin, etc. If this be remembered, Reid's suggestion that Hume must be wrong, because day did not cause night, although one invariably follows the other, is seen for the error it is. If one attempts to describe day and night in terms of actions and reactions between each other, the tangle becomes enormous; but, described in terms of the actions of sun and earth, it becomes relatively clear. This being the case, if one were to attempt to prevent night in a certain area, one would not try to do anything about eliminating day, but would rather try to control earth and/or sun.

Conditions may finally be defined as the negative of causes; factors which are present but are not (from a given standpoint) significant.[9]

Notes

*   I am grateful to Professors J. S. Bixler and T. Parsons, and to Messrs. R. Bierstedt and N. Demareth for criticisms of this paper, which have at least helped me towards clearer statement.

1.   See bibliographical note at end of this article.
2.   W. I. Thomas and F. Znaniecki, *The Polish Peasant in Europe and America*, **2nd** ed., New York, 1927, "Methodological Note," presents a conception of the scientist as one who facilitates possibilities of "social control" a role which, professedly at least, our culture often ascribes to him.
3.   J. Dewey, *Logic*, New York, esp. 442-62 "Scientific Laws—Causation and Sequence." The general theme of this work, that philosophy should be a tool for solving problems, is of course adopted in this article.

As far as Dewey's discussion goes, it is unequalled, but it does not cover most of the points raised here, nor attempt to place them formally at least within the framework of semiotic[s].
4.   From here on the discussion has been greatly guided by C. W. Morris, Foundations of the theory of Signs, Chicago, 1938, *Ency of Unified Sci.*, 1, 2, from whom the technical employment of semiotic, designate, etc. comes.
5.   Else Wentscher, *Geschicte des Kausalproblems*, Leipzig, 1921, deals chiefly with metaphysical notions of cause.
6.   Linguistically semi-self-conscious individuals, acting upon some assumption about causal imputation, but desirous to prove to themselves that they are not naive, frequently use some circumlocution or synonym for cause, rather than the term itself.
7.   Q. Wright, *American Sociological Review*, 3 (1938), 461-74, summarizes the "causes of war" series of the University of Chicago more or less.
8.   Dewey, *op. cit.*
9.   Sometimes "conditions" is used as meaning basic, underlying, "cause" as immediate, precipitating. It would seem more convenient to call the former basic causes, the latter immediate cause.

Bibliographical Notes

Dewey, *op. cit.*, and Morris, *op. cit.*, are required reading. The above article will appear more significant to anyone who is familiar with the different tenatives towards semiotic made by K. Burke, F. Schiller, H. Reichenbach, H. Lasswell, R. Carnap, I. Richards, A. Korzybski, etc. M. J. Adler and J. Frank, *Crime, Law, and Social Science*, explicitly discuss what kinds of propositions may be taken as causal and what as recording concomitant variations. H. Oliphant and A. Hewitt, Introduction to J. Rueff, *From the Physical to the Social Sciences*, Baltimore, 1929, show the relationship of causal assumptions and formal deduction in the judicial process.

J. Woodger's three articles in the *Quarterly Review of Biology*, 1930-1, "Concept of Organism" deal with the causal postulate (esp. 5; 12-21) and define cause as "the one element essential to the result observed." This definition may be coordinated with the present article; "essential" and "result observed" can only be judged in terms of some sort of purpose. See also E. Nagel, *Principles of the Theory of Probability*, Chicago, 1939, 25-6.

J. Somerville in *Philosophy of Science*, 2 (1935) 246-54, "Aims in Social Science" and M. Weber, "Die Objektivitat" *Archivf. Sozialwissenschaft*, 1904 (19) 22-78, supplement the points made above about purpose.

Several studies of the notion of cause and effect in children have appeared of which the latest is from Cornell, by J. Lacey and K. Dallenbach, *Am. J. Psych*, 41 (1939) 103-10.

Chester I. Barnard, *The Functions of the Executive*, Cambridge, 1938, presents a conception similar to the one here given. "The limiting (strategic) factor is the one whose control in the right form at the right place and time will establish a new system which meets the purpose," 202-3.

As for the rest:

In the whole of philosophy, there is scarcely any subject in such utter confusion as as causation.... Hume got it into a tangle which has been worse and worse entangled, by subsequent writers, until the latest contributors have essayed to cut the knot by denying altogether that there is such a thing as causation.... Few writers treat the subject without contradicting themselves and none without outraging common sense....

This from Charles Mercier's amusing and often pointed *Causation and Belief*, London, 1916, 1, is too true to be funny. His shafts are especially directed against J. S. Mill, *A System of Logic*, (8th ed. esp.) who is the source of most show-window quotations on the matter, and who, he claims, uses "cause" in eighteen irreconcilable ways.

More recent writings include D. Hawkins, *Causality and Implication*, London, 1937, a (not very) neo-Aristotelean refutation of Hume, H. Margenau, *Philosophy of Science*, 1 (1934) 133-48, "Meaning and Scientific Status of Causality," and N. Bohr, *Philosophy of Science*, 4 (1937) 289-96 "Causality and Complementarity" or P. Bridgman, *The Intelligent Individual and Society*, New York, 1938, esp. 33-5, who concludes that "The assumption [cause] … is not necessary because physicists have been doing valid thinking without it." (viz. statistical thinking.)

2

Role Relationships and Conceptions of Neutrality in Interviewing[1]

"The essential point regarding role relationships in an interview is that the interviewer must occupy some role, whether he wishes to or not."[2] In my experience, under normal circumstances the role assigned to the interviewer by the informant will be in terms of the informant's conception of the interviewer's group affiliations. In interviewing in which I have recently been engaged, it became clear that many of the most involved advocates of reciprocal trade expected me to be on their side,[3] and many of the protectionists expected me to be against them. Obviously, my role, therefore, in the one case was likely to be different from my role in the other; and yet, presumably, in a study of communications about the reciprocal-trade program a reasonable distribution of equivalent relationships should be established with both sides.

The expectation in itself was perfectly reasonable: I represented two academic institutions (the Center for International Studies at Massachusetts Institute of Technology,[4] and American University), and for many years past nearly all vocal academic people have supported free trade, internationalism, and the like. And, in fact, protectionists in Washington could hardly fail to be aware that my colleagues and I belong to the same group from which the State Department recruits its personnel. On several occasions, protectionist informants stated that the State Department was certainly their biggest enemy (in fact, the only other candidate for that position was "big oil"). One of the ablest and most aggressive protectionist leaders in Congress, himself a college graduate, declared that the only people supporting reciprocal trade in his constituency are some of "the educated," a term he used sneeringly to denote some people at the colleges in the state. And the favorite damning adjective of the protectionists about the State Department and reciprocal trade generally is "theoretical."

If under these circumstances I started out by saying and declaring that I am a "neutral," that we at MIT are interested only in finding out what people hear about reciprocal trade and the tariff and from whom they hear it, what will happen? Many of the protectionists will think, "He's a liar." I can, of course, declare a personal position, adding that it does not affect my objectivity in seeking the facts. But this will handicap interviewing in two ways: the most involved people will try to convince me of the correctness of their position, unless mine happens to be theirs; and the less involved will, out of courtesy, desire to avoid a possible argument or, out of respect for academic people, stress their agreement somewhat more than the facts warrant.

In several interviews I encountered the latter difficulty. Some inconsistencies in my interviews with some local labor union officials may be explicable in this fashion: they sympathize more with a protectionist position than does international headquarters; and, because I, the interviewer, came from Washington, I was to them possibly identifiable with the brain trusters of the international and CIO headquarters and might know some of them, and therefore these local officials might tend to play down their own protectionist sympathies.

This problem is not peculiar to studies of reciprocal trade. There is a wide variety of issues on which academic people regard one viewpoint or another as "enlightened" and obvious—and by their tone and manner show their sympathies. Studies of McCarthyism, for instance, by almost any academic people or professional interviewers or studies of anti-Semitism start out with a similar handicap. There are scores of proposals at present for studies of desegregation and integration—and, of those who plan such studies, how many regard the arguments against integration as intellectually admissible?

The point, even so, is not the actual sympathies of research directors or interviewers; it is the sympathies which will be attributed to them, the role that will be assigned to them, by those whom they study. The Puerto Rican terrorist, the McCarthyite, the member of the National Association for the Advancement of White People, the protectionist, will all, sensibly, define the scholar as "enemy"; and the internationalist, the economic planner, and the member of the NAACP are likely to regard him as "friend."[5]

In a study of attitudes of some Chicago businessmen toward price control and rationing regulations made in 1943, an important general conclusion was: when attitudes toward price control are cooperative, businessmen are in consequence more likely to conform to the regulations. This now seems less certain than it seemed at the time, because of the related fact that those who demonstrated "cooperativeness" tended to be more friendly toward academic research and therefore were more likely to give the kind of answers they thought the interviewers would approve. The only generally valid conclusion was merely that those who showed more friendliness to the interviewers and/or the university and/or economic research were less likely to report non-conformity to regulations[6] (the same group would, for the same reasons, have been less likely to report anti-Semitism).

So the problem with which an interviewer is frequently faced is, "On whose side shall I be neutral?" In general, the preferred solution seems to be: where possible, to accept the informant's definition of neutrality, for there is great respect, in American culture at least, for neutrality, and to be neutral in the informant's terms.

Failure to recognize this may create trouble. Early in our reciprocal trade study, for instance, I was given the chance to explain to a strategy meeting of protectionist leaders why I wanted to sit in on the meeting. A coal man objected strenuously: "We don't want any neutrals here," using the very words of the old Harlan County song: "We don't want any neutrals here; either you are a union man or else you are a ———scab." I explained that we could not take sides; and yet to at least one-third of the men the very way I spoke and the phrases I used meant taking sides against them. They interpreted what I had to say about "neutrality" in terms of their general frame of reference of suspecting academic economists of being free-traders.

Kinsey[7] met an analogous problem. He speaks of the need for using "the vernacular." "A volume could be written on the things that should be known by anyone attempting to deal with people outside their own social level.... A single phrase from an understanding interviewer is often sufficient to make the subject understand ... and such an interviewer gets a record where none would be disclosed to the uneducated interviewer." Such a phrase, essentially, suggests to the informant that the interviewer is "on my side" because he "speaks my language." It tells him that the interviewer shares his perspective on whatever he is going to describe; and, for all except a very few informants, that is neutrality.

Dollard,[8] similarly, reports: "One complaint against me: I had addressed a certain Negro woman as Mrs...." Later on, however, he said to a southern white man, "I am studying personality among the niggers." The man replied, "I am glad to hear you say 'nigger.' I see you understand about that." Dollard adds that the use of the word "Negro" is evidently "the hallmark of a Northerner and a caste enemy."

In the same way, for any given informant, one may be able to pick up the particular damning terms he uses about his opponents and use them one's self. In general, the unfavorable use of "free trader," "cheap labor," "theoretical," and of leading questions about the substance of the issue seemed to help offset the impression that, as an academic person, one cannot be trusted. Such questions as "Are you bothered by cheap foreign imports?" "Do they undersell you unfairly?" "Does the Defense Department nowadays apply the Buy American Act properly?" while not absolutely committing one, in case one has guessed an informant's views wrongly, help set the stage. Relevant reassurance, for example, that, because of a Massachusetts background, I knew how industries like textile and watches suffer from foreign competition also helps. Some of the Bricker Amendment objectors to reciprocal trade would probably have been favorably impressed by the use of the terms such as "constitutional government."

The real point is not to establish neutrality for its own sake but to create a situation in which the informant will tell what is needed. There are, of course, informants who will do this better if one argues, disagrees, or criticizes; but since, after all, one is dependent upon the voluntary cooperation of the informant, this is a hazardous approach, particularly when the informant is of higher status than the interviewer. Frequently, too, one may want to return to check up on something or to repeat an interview under changed circumstances, and this is likely to be easier if one has established one's self as a friend or sympathizer. Of course, studies are conceivable in which more would be told to an unfriend or enemy than to a friend: for instance, some Puerto Rican Nationalists appear to be more eager to convert and instruct the skeptical and scoffing enemy who will listen than to explain to a sympathizer. Also, members of cliques of female homosexuals, who regard everyone as hostile, are more frank apparently with avowed critics than with those who, they suspect, conceal disapproval. But with busy and preoccupied politicians or businessmen in the United States the tendency would be to avoid the minor discomfort of talking to an unimportant critic. Ideally, probably, many politicians or businessmen should be interviewed by several different interviewers, some definitely expressing sympathy, some adhering to rigid professions of scientific neutrality, some definitely hostile—"had we but world enough and time." In a study which focuses on processes rather than on attitudes, one other disadvantage of a failure to imply agreement with the informant is this: if he is genuinely concerned about the issue, he may try to convince the interviewer, taking up time with relatively valueless discussion of the issues.

Paul, in an able discussion of interviewing, says: "The investigator who makes an effort to remain neutral is in danger of being caught in a crossfire. He may have to align himself with one side to participate at all."[9] In a small village or a tribe, where most relationships are face to face, this is probably true; but in United States society it is remarkable how segregated the channels of communication are and how slight the communication is, even between people who know each other, on an issue where they might disagree, such as the tariff.[10] This lack of accurate knowledge about each other's positions is characteristic even of Washington; probably because congressmen and lobbyists generally have so many things to attend to that they do not know much exactly about any given one. Few congressmen, lobbyists, or businessmen are going to waste the time in scrutinizing in detail the exact phrasing used by an interviewer. They will, if they ever talk about him at all, say: "Well, I got the impression he was on my side"; and each will rest content to believe the other wrong.

Joseph Jastak, of the University of Delaware, points to an extreme case of the disadvantages of the ordinary conception of rational neutrality. He reports that the only way he could hope to establish contact with a certain psychotic was to accept the latter's frame of reference about reality. Such a course, presumably, may be necessary either for therapeutic purposes or in order to study the "nature" of psychoses.[11] To be sure, this situation poses problems considerably greater than those encountered by the ordinary academic interviewer, dealing with relatively normal people; but it provides a clue to the latter's difficulties. Children, adolescents, and the very naive refer indiscriminately to all who appear to have different conceptions of reality or value as "crazy"; the more sophisticated academic man, in resorting to Freudian or sociological explanations, may sound more neutral and may be more accurate but produces just as much resentment. Even if a particular scientist or scholar has freed himself of the attitude and the use of a vocabulary, which suggests "I want to find out why these crazy people are crazy," will hardly produce good will.

At a much more normal level, the study by the American Political Science Association of presidential nominating processes[12] necessarily forced many scholars to interview politicians and journalists. Almost certainly the role of the scholar interacted with the roles of the politicians interviewed; in the several states and parties politicians belong to different groups, so that what the scholars learned may have been a function of the social role of the interviewee and of the scholar confronted with the interviewee as well as of the intrinsic character of the data. Yet nowhere in the five volumes of reports is there a systematic attempt to tackle this issue, basic to the comparative analysis of the politics of the various states.

To establish this sort of neutrality calls for rigorous intellectual discipline. I had to put myself into a frame of mind where I felt as my informants might; I practiced getting indignant, for instance, at the "callousness" of a friend in the State Department who did not seem to care about the coal miners thrown out of work by Venezuelan oil, and of another in a purchasing agency who seemed indifferent to rigid interpretation of the Buy American Act. Then I could use terms like "cheap labor," "Buy American," etc., meaningfully and sincerely, having some idea of what they meant emotionally to those being interviewed. In the same way, actors feel that they have to "throw themselves into" a part; it is not sufficient merely to repeat lines. Not every interviewer would have to do this; and obviously it should be done only with the actor's awareness of what he is doing. One great advantage of this effort was, incidentally, that it made me more aware that my customary terms and vocal tones implied an orthodox reciprocal trade position; and I was therefore better able to avoid them. Most academic people, studying McCarthyism, would probably have to go through a similar discipline to attain neutrality in the eyes of McCarthyites but would have to make a more stringent effort.

This is not at all to argue for the establishment of rapport, if by that is meant a personally friendly relationship with the informant. Valid arguments against this have been advanced elsewhere.[13] There are various obvious disadvantages in some cases, although advantages in others, in trying to establish rapport on the basis of organizational contacts in common; informants will fear that you hold the organizational viewpoint and may then familiarize themselves with what the organization thinks in self-protection. But it is to argue for the development of a sympathetic understanding, so that the interviewer can, without strain, talk the informant's language. It is probably better, however, to make the effort to do so, even if it is not well done; Paul has again suggested a relevant point. He says[14] that the anthropologist's effort to learn native skills "will prove inept but if the effort is made with good grace and a minimum of condescension, the gesture may promote good feeling." The academically trained interviewer who starts out interviewing McCarthyites and tries to intimate his sympathy with the viewpoint that Eisenhower is being befooled and misled by the "same old State Department gang" will sound clumsy; but he is more likely to be regarded as "having the right spirit" than criticized for awkwardness or insincerity.[15]

Notes

1. This paper is a by-product of a study of business and political opinion in the United States on reciprocal trade and tariff issues, conducted by the Center for International Studies, Massachusetts Institute of Technology, 1953-56. Part of the time the author's portion of the project was under subcontract to the Bureau of Social Science Research, American University. The author is greatly indebted to his colleagues, Raymond A. Bauer and Ithiel de Sola Pool, for criticisms and suggestions on this paper, but neither they nor the universities are responsible for anything said hereinafter.
2. E. and N. Maccoby, "The Interview: A Tool of Social Science," in G. Lindzey (ed.), *Handbook of Social Psychology* (Cambridge, MA: Addison-Wesley Press, 1954), 1, 463.
3. A colleague reports that a person associated with a group favoring reciprocal trade declared she was shocked that a university should undertake such a study as ours without trying expressly to help "the cause."
4. While Massachusetts Institute of Technology is likely to sound more realistic and practical to most of those who fear "theoretical free-traders" than most universities, the Center for International Studies puts the curse on again.
5. It is even possible that some of the sharper personality distinctions reported between, for instance, anti-Semites and non-anti-Semites in the literature would be blurred if due allowance were made for the fact that the anti-Semites are much more likely to be made hostile by contact with the testers.
6. This study is reported in G. Katona, *Price Control and Business* (Bloomington, IN: Principia Press, 1945), esp. pp. 157-71; see also my comment: "O.P.A.: A Case Study in Liberal Priggishness," *Applied Anthropology*, IV, No. 1 (1945), 32-33.
7. A. Kinsey, *Sexual Behavior in the Human Male* (Philadelphia: W. B. Saunders Co., 1948), pp. 52 and 60.
8. J. Dollard, *Caste and Class in a Southern Town* (New Haven: Yale University Press, 1937). pp. 44 and 47.
9. B. Paul, "Interview Techniques and Field Relationships," in A. L. Kroeber (ed.), *Anthropology Today* (Chicago: University of Chicago Press, 1954), pp. 430-51.
10. Ithiel Pool, in a summary of the results of seven community studies, points out the low pitch of communication between industries. (To be published.)
11. See also R. Lindner, *The Fifty-Minute Hour* (New York: Rinehart & Co., 1954).
12. P. David, R. Goldman, and M. Moos, *Presidential Nominating Processes in 1952* (5 vols.; Baltimore: Johns Hopkins University Press, 1954).
13. See S. M. Miller, "The Participant Observer and Over-rapport," *American Sociological Review*, XVII (1952), 97-99; H. Hyman et al., *Interviewing in Social Research* (Chicago: University of Chicago Press, 1954), several times touch on this point, notably on p. 282, where they deprecate "excessive social skills" as useful for interviewing.
14. Paul, *op. cit.*, p. 436.
15. A. Kinsey, in *Sexual Behavior in the Human Female* (Philadelphia: W. B. Saunders Co., 1953), gives what must be an example: "The adaptation of one's own vocabulary in an interview contributes to ... bringing out information which would be completely missed in a standardized interview" (pp. 58-62). Considering the variety of types he and his associates interviewed, it is almost certain that they

often failed in getting the mot juste. Paul (*op. cit.*) suggests that the anthropologist needs to establish a role which can be assimilated by the society under study. The social science interviewer has a role with many groups in this country, but not for all; and some labor and thought devoted to the interpretation and creation of roles among unfriendly groups might be rewarding for many studies. Frequently, congressmen whom I have interviewed equated my role with that of a journalist, which led a congressman who is usually rude to journalists to refuse any meaningful answers. I might have had a better reception if I had been introduced as an economist or a historian. In general, I judge, we got more uniform co-operation from big businesses than from small; for one thing, some small businessmen were suspicious because they could not figure out what we were getting at. To overcome this, one might design a special letter of introduction and set of explanations for small businessmen.

3

A Note on Selective Inattention in Social Science*

The subjects that scholars persistently avoid studying are worth considering because such consideration may: (a) suggest a reordering of priorities for research and exposition; (b) help in determining whether certain important topics are left out of account for nonrational reasons; or (c) illuminate the ways recommendations and emphases relate to the logic of theory and diagnosis.

It is assumed that persistent avoidance by a group of scholars of pertinent topics is not purely or chiefly accidental. The key word here is "pertinent." We are not interested in the fact that social pathologists have rarely discussed frustrated romance amongst cockroaches—despite William James' remark that "the problem of evil remains in the universe in its full force so long as one cockroach is dying of unrequited love."

We are concerned with consistent inattention to fields and problems which, in terms of theory and definition, seem to fit into particular disciplines. Significant advances in science have sometimes taken place when someone has realized that a problem hitherto neglected or excluded does in fact fit into the methods and techniques of his discipline. One recent example is the "sociologization" of health, previously regarded as a purely medical and biological area.

An organized and systematic set of hypotheses about cases of avoidance could be of great value to sociologists of science—and particularly to students of social problems. The present note is a preliminary contribution to the construction of such hypotheses. It arose from the writer's experience as a research consultant, 1949-57, in the area of mental deficiency. He was particularly impressed by the fact that during 1910-25 the literature showed considerable concern by sociologists and social workers with mental deficiency, that by 1935 this concern had diminished almost to the zero level, and that by 1949 there was virtually no interest by sociologists in the topic. A real revival of general scholarly and philanthropic attention to mental deficiency during the recent past has been accompanied or followed by a fainter but perceptible sociological re-awareness of the social effects and implications of mental deficiency.

Inattention to, or lack of interest in mental deficiency by sociologists has seemed, superficially at least, to resemble the similar lack of concern by sociologists with civil defense and survival plans during recent years. On the other hand, such topics as psychological warfare, "brain-washing," limited war, suicide, and the Stevenson campaigns seem to be regarded by sociologists as more sociological or more exciting.

Inattention has not been a function of money; during 1949-54, indeed, the writer tried to find out how to spend a trust fund of $60,000 on social science research about mental deficiency; yet, if recollection serves, only two sociologists under 65 had any suggestion regarding the study of mental defectives as such. Other proposals assumed that one would take the mental defective as a given—something like a geographical fact—and, for instance, determine how his siblings reacted. Or they involved purely statistical analyses of records about defectives. But, most interesting of all, the majority of sociologists—and psychologists—whose advice was sought shifted the conversation, immediately and apparently unconsciously, from amentia to neurosis or psychosis.

It may be pointed out that, similarly, during recent years sociologists could have received considerable financial help from the Federal Civil Defense Administration for research, but few have manifested much interest in the central problems of civil defense, concentrating whatever attention they give to the field on peripheral issues of natural disaster, panic in small-scale fires, etc.

It is, of course, possible to suggest ad hoc reasons why sociologists show little interest in this or that particular problem. But we need general reasons: explanations would have to be multiplied indefinitely if we developed one to explain why prostitution and illegitimacy seem to have attracted more sociological attention than homosexuality, a second to make clear why political corruption has occupied more space in social problems texts, and probably time in social problems courses, than military or industrial espionage, a third to show why alcoholism lost and regained respectability as a sociological problem, more or less concurrently with mental deficiency, a fourth to help us deduce why divorce is much more emphasized in social problems discussions than warfare, and a fifth to make plain why sociologists very rarely, if ever, devote systematic attention to the problem of genocide.

There have been attempts to account for the characteristic emphases of social problems discussion, but they are not particularly helpful: Mills asserts that the focus of the social pathologist is "utilitarian ... in terms of community welfare," (7, pp. 168, 175) apparently implying a Benthamite concern with the reduction of unhappiness. A standard, not particularly extreme, text in social pathology, published in 1927, says of the mentally defective: "The moron constitutes a great social menace [and] furnishes recruits for those who commit brutal murders, incendiarism, rape, and assault. Most serious of all, he leaves behind a large progeny" (5, pp. 151-152). Between 1910 and 1930, many similar statements appeared in literature accessible to sociologists. In utilitarian terms, such statements should have constituted a strong stimulus to the study of mental deficiency. But actually, even then, serious attention and study were rare.

Further, taking again a utilitarian conception of happiness and unhappiness, it seems reasonable to assume that among middle-class families in recent American society, the mixture of shame and worry created by a mentally defective child is considerable; and it is often believed that the same sort of shame and worry exists among many other families with mental defectives. Nevertheless, the topic of mental deficiency was ignored throughout the 1930s and 1940s.

A third sense of "utilitarian," of course, involves the saving of money. Between 1930 and 1950, the cost of public institutions for mental defectives rose considerably; any concern with saving public moneys and taxes should have led to much emphasis on mental deficiency research.

Hobbs states that sociology text book writers "rely on other sociology texts as the chief sources of information" (6, pp. 9, 175). This seems to be true; but the sociologist of sociology will also want to know what citations in earlier writers are ignored or minimized. Presumably, the same factors tend to operate that affect memory or conversation: we edit out those matters that we find boring or unrewardingly unpleasant. At any rate, the textbook writers of the 1930s and 1940s had available to them not only the earlier sociological treatises, which did discuss mental defect, but also the original works on the Kallikaks, Jukes, etc. Mental deficiency was nevertheless de-emphasized or ignored.

Hobbs also says that sociology tends to include those subjects that are left over, "those aspects of personality not included in the principal foci of psychology, biology, or genetics." Actually, psychologists and students of genetics were concerned with mental deficiency at the same time that sociologists were—roughly from 1910 to 1930—and their interest in the topic waned as that of sociologists did. On the other hand, the Kinsey studies stimulated interest in sexual behavior in several disciplines; and alcoholism and propaganda were ignored and emphasized in the different disciplines at about the same time.

A more adequate general explanation of the avoidance of specific social problems by social pathologists would seem to lie in the following interrelated considerations:

A. The development of sociology since 1920 has in large measure been guided by considerations of the effect of socio-environmental differences upon personality and intergroup relationships. Topics which did not fit into this approach, no matter how significant per se, tended to be neglected or overlooked for at least four reasons:

(1)   They are frustrating or puzzling in themselves. Once a theory has become accepted as plausible, true, and above all "natural," we find, to paraphrase Spencer, "substantial facts exiled by elegant theories—or by theories which have all the acceptability of common usage—from respectable consideration." This process is (except where taboos are involved) rarely deliberate and, therefore, if consciously realized, could be taken into account.

(2)   A prevailing theory or point of view tends to attract into a discipline those with a particular ideological bent or focus; topics which do not seem compatible with both the methodology and its implicit or explicit ideology tend to be shunted to one side, or overtly ridiculed, by the second or third generation of scholars, if not by the first.

The interpretation of behavior in democratic, egalitarian, anti-genetic terms attracted into sociology between 1925 and 1945 people whose interests, ideals, and values led them strongly to resent any notion of inherent inequality or even of the biological conditioning of behavior. As they have grown older, their own social situation and perhaps greater maturity has made this egalitarian bias per se less significant to some of them; at the same time, immanent in the formal pattern of sociological thinking has been a bias against being influenced by one's own biases, and another bias in favor of using one's detection of one's colleagues' biases as a weapon, biases of which this essay is no doubt in part a product and which may aid in obtaining consideration for it.

A hundred years ago, economic orthodoxy left out of account the qualifications and limitations of which Adam Smith himself was probably well enough aware, because of the same tendency of disciplines to select those persons who find the central ideological implications of the methodology most attractive. Perhaps the real hatred and contempt, which some scholars feel or appear to feel, for extrasensory perception represents the same process; and the fact that there has been little attention paid, except by a few historians, students of rebellion, to the relationship of weather upon behavior or the psyche** may indicate not so much the unimportance of the issue as its incompatibility with the preferred worldview(s) of social scientists.

The ideology of sociologists in the United States involved defense of, if not identification with, the underdog. Typically, excluding a few serious followers of Sumner and Pareto, American sociologists tried to get students disembedded from "the cake of custom" so that they might become "less prejudiced" against counter-mores behavior; "to understand all is to forgive all" or at least "to defend all." But there were, of course, exceptions; even in liberal colleges, in the late 30s or early 40s, sociologists would have found it difficult to defend conservative Republicanism; by the same token, sociologists found it difficult to defend warmongers or mental defectives.

(3)   Granted the exciting possibilities, which sociological and anthropological interpretations of behavior opened up in the 1930s, it was nevertheless hard to "explain" or "explain away" differences in the mental endowment of individuals without simultaneously questioning the value and validity of the selective institutional processes by which scholars themselves generally acquire their status. That is, in an open society, sociologists acquire status because they are bright; so they receive some deference and are able to dominate some classrooms. In fact, at least until the postwar period of consultantships and research endowments, most sociologists were teachers, in day-to-day contact with students, able to maintain status in that daily environment by intellectual superiority.

To tell these students—or to say anything to them which could be interpreted as telling them—that stupidity and brightness could be interpreted in the same cultural fashion as the difference between "savages" and "civilized men" would have tended to impeach the legitimacy of the sociologists' own treatment of students.

Put another way, skill at manipulating symbols is the capital of men who have become sociologists; it is consequently no "skin off their hides" when someone attacks the sixty families of American capitalism in exaggerated terms: they are sympathetically "objective" to the attackers; but when a McCarthy threatens the possessors of *intellectual* capital in similarly exaggerated language, their involvement is considerable.

The difficulty in being dispassionate in regard to the social role of the mental defective is a related one. Perry (8) and Dexter (1, 2) suggest that, to comprehend the social origins and meanings of mental deficiency in our society adequately, one must be skeptical about the system of universal competition in manipulating symbols and a career open to the talents, with everybody *compelled* to try to manifest talent.

Sociologists, therefore, found it difficult to interpret mental deficiency in sociologists' terms. And they could not, particularly after

Hitler came into power in 1933, state that mental defect is related to inheritance; in those days this shocked the liberal conscience. And so the subject tended to be shunted to one side.

(4)   Another reason for shunting it to one side is that the exaggerations of one generation may, if detected, cause the omissions of the next. The history of the "debunking" historians and biographers could well be written in terms or this generalization. If one generation has distorted the significance of a subject, anyone who talks about the subject may be suspected—or may be afraid he will be suspected—of endorsing these distortions. In sociology and social science, in general, study of a subject is supposed to involve sympathy with a prevailing viewpoint about it; in the late 30s for example, a graduate student in sociology who studied labor unions might be automatically supposed, even by his instructors, to sympathize with John L. Lewis, regardless of his actual views.

Hence, the emphasis on "the fruit of the family tree" and the over-simplification of genetic interpretations in the 1920s (carried on by some textbook writers in genetics for another dozen years) led to a de-emphasis of genetic interpretations and of precisely those topics to which the genetic interpretations had been most dramatically and carelessly applied. Somewhat similar developments took place in the field of alcoholism; the overdramatic claims of extreme prohibitionists in the early part of the twentieth century created a climate in which scholars and intellectuals generally ignored the real and significant problems of alcoholism for about twenty years.

B. The counter-mores emphasis of American sociology generally tends to imply that the discriminated-against are not as bad as they are painted ("Slums have their own social structure," we say), are not as bad as they seem to be on first impression (we point out that higher crime rates in certain discriminated-against groups are either not correctly compared or a function of discrimination), and are really not any worse than the middle or upper classes (sociologists point out that university students usually do not get taken to court, although they do in fact perform all the offenses of which juvenile delinquents are accused). These statements are all frequently true and it is highly desirable they should be realized by ethnocentric human beings; but it is virtually impossible to argue that mental defectives are "really" as intelligent as university students, in terms of those measures of intelligence, which sociologists have been constrained to accept until very recently. It is also extremely difficult to deny that there appear to be ineradicable differences in intelligence even between persons of the same general background.***

C. Attention by scholars is in part a function of popular attention; for example, people who talk about nuclear physics have a following and a public, whereas other fields of physical study are more or less ignored. In the 1910-30 period, there was an audience for those concerned with mental deficiency. Depression and war diverted the attention of the interested and educated publics from this social problem to others. It was not until things became almost "normal" again, from the standpoint of the educated citizen, that he had time again to concern himself with mental deficiency; fortuitously, the advancement of medical research had during the 1940-53 period kept alive many low-grade mental defectives, born in middle-class families, who would previously have died; and consequently middle-class interest in mental defect has been stimulated.

In any case, from 1930-1950, sociologists, insofar as they were competing for student interest, colleague attention, and the like—and also, more significantly perhaps, insofar as they were influenced by the same factors as the intellectual public at the time—found mental deficiency a losing game, because the audience for it, real or imagined (11), did not seem impressive.

By itself, of course, this is not an adequate explanation. The present interest of some social scientists in rather complex methodological devices (such as "contact nets") stirs little public excitement. And if sociologists in the 40s had been simply following the headlines, they would have concentrated on genocide, warfare, etc. But there is a strong anti-military, anti-toughness component in the ideology of American sociologists that makes it difficult for them to believe in or tackle such topics in a comprehensive fashion. At any rate, up to the present, sociological theory does not provide particularly helpful clues to understanding the prevalence of massacre in human history.

Aside from Hitler, the savage slaughters by the Ustashi in Croatia, the communal slayings in India and Pakistan immediately after World War II, the activities of such rulers as Trujillo, Stalin, and Ibn Saud, not to mention the present conceivability of supergenocide through a cobalt bomb, lend the issue some practical relevance. But what have sociologists to say about why "man is a wolf to his fellows" even though the problem is presumably a social one? It is personally depressing and discouraging to deal with such a problem anyway; and it is still more depressing when one has nothing to contribute to its solution.

D. It may well be that criteria of involvement can be set up for any given social issue, and that study will usually follow such involvement.

These criteria may be: (1) drama (where "the good side" has some chance of winning); (2) the possibility of doing something or recommending something; (3) identification. The subject matter of mental deficiency is not, somehow, very dramatic; genocide is, in an eerie way, but the good can hardly win out. Few sociologists have any reason to identify themselves with mental defectives, and very few would care to put themselves either in the role of perpetrators or victims of genocide. And, from 1925 to 1955, sociologists had little to recommend in their professional role about either mental defect or genocide. Prior to 1925, the emphasis on heredity, sterilization, etc., did give many sociologists a platform regarding mental defect, which they could support; in the past three or four years, some sociologists may have found in the writings of Sarason (9, 10), Perry (8), and Dexter (1, 2, 3) a perspective whose adoption they may recommend, although, for the most part, this perspective is as yet lacking in concrete practical implementation. And aside from pointing out that genocide is not very nice, what can American sociologists say about it? Have we any way of making a Rosas or a Caligula, or a March of the Cherokees less likely?

The foregoing is, of course, a speculative essay with some overstatement to make a point, as is not uncharacteristic of efforts to apply the sociology of knowledge to concrete issues. In particular, it should be stressed that the references to sociologists and social pathologists are to a central tendency, to which there are exceptions; for example, although most sociologists probably do acquire their status through intellectual skill, there are some sociologists whose status and self-confidence arise rather from good fellowship, business ability, athletic prowess, religious devotion, a sense of virtue, etc. And it should also be said that whereas the writer has read most of the social problems texts prior to 1950, and much available literature on mental deficiency, civil defense, and genocide, he may have overlooked some highly relevant changes in the emphasis of sociologists in recent years.

A meaningful study of avoidance would inquire into fields other than sociology. Why, for example, have political scientists until recently avoided the study of the government of nonstate organizations? Why is the systematic comparative method so rarely applied to local politics? Why did psychologists for long steer away from such topics as hypnosis and telepathy? Why are economists generally much more interested in the management of businesses than in institutional management?

The justification for presenting this essay is that it does have serious practical implications for teaching, research, and exposition. If it does no more than redirect attention to the possibility that, despite the rationality of our techniques of research, once we have chosen a subject for study, the choice of subjects for study may itself be needlessly and avoidably irrational, it is probably worthwhile; particularly so, if some of the individual observations in the text may suggest specific ways of increasing rationality in the choice of subjects for study and in determining why avoided subjects are avoided (4).

Notes

*   This article was prepared under a grant from the Kate Jackson Anthony Trust of Lewiston, Maine, "for the benefit of God's children known as the feeble-minded."
**   By social scientists; a few physiologists have discussed weather and behavior.
***   Sarason and Gladwin have recently reviewed the literature in such a way as to indicate a way out of this dilemma, (10). The writer has some doubt as to the validity of their solution. (3).

References

1.   Dexter, L. A., "A Social Theory of Mental Deficiency," *American Journal of Mental Deficiency*, 62 (March, 1958), 920-928.
2.   Dexter, L. A., "Towards a Sociology of the Mentally Defective," *American Journal of Mental Deficiency*, 61 (July, 1956), 10-16.
3.   Dexter, L. A., two papers read before the American Association of Mental Deficiency: "Comparative Politics and the Handling of Social Deviates;" "Research Needs in Mental Deficiency."
4.   Dexter, L. A., "The Policy Sciences and Limited Warfare," *Political Research—Organization and Design*, 1 (1958), 17-19.
5.   Dexter, R. C, *Social Adjustment*, (New York: Knopf, 1927).
6.   Hobbs, A., *The Claims of Sociology* (Harrisburg, PA: Stackpole, 1951).
7.   Mills, C. W., "The Professional Ideology of Social Pathologists," *American Journal of Sociology*, 49 (September, 1943), 165-180.
8.   Perry, S., "Some Theoretic Problems of Mental Deficiency and Their Action Implications," *Psychiatry*, 17 (February 1954), 45-73.
9.   Sarason, S., *Psychological Problems in Mental Deficiency*, 2nd ed. (New York: Harper's, 1953).
10.   Sarason, S., and T. Gladwin, "Psychological and Cultural Problems in Mental Subnormality: A Review of Research," *American Journal of Mental Deficiency*, 62 (May, 1958), 1115-1307.
11.   Zimmerman, C., and R. A. Bauer, "The Effect of an Audience on What Is Remembered," *Public Opinion Quarterly*, 20 (Spring, 1956), 238-248.

4

The Good Will of Important People: More on the Jeopardy of the Interview

Specialized publics, such as Congressmen, physicians, or community leaders, are frequently subjects of opinion surveys. Their good will may be jeopardized unless steps are taken to maintain their confidence and trust in opinion research, and not to exhaust their time and patience. The author offers various suggestions, based in part on his own research experience, for dealing with the situation.

As the editor of the *Public Opinion Quarterly* (*POQ*) pointed out, "the greater part of opinion research rests on kindness and confidence: kindness in the willingness of respondents to give time to the interview ..., confidence in accepting the implicit or explicit assurance of the interviewer that ... the survey will in no way harm [the interviewee's] interests."[1] The succeeding three articles in the Spring 1964 *POQ* suggest the jeopardy of the survey interview, when kindness is abused or confidence is betrayed.

The probability is, however, that there is a more imminent and serious danger to the public opinion industry and the social science profession in the abuse or potential abuse of interviews with specialized and identifiable respondents, especially elite interviewees. And because elite interviewees can influence legislation and acceptance, abuse of their confidence and kindness may constitute a danger to the survey interview itself. There are two major respects in which the good will of elite interviewees (and, incidentally, of others who are clearly identifiable) is, or is likely to be, strained—first, abuse of time and patience, second, betrayal of confidence and trust.

Time and Patience

On the one hand, certain elite interviewees are far more likely to receive repeated requests for interviews than are choices for survey interviews; on the other hand, most members of professional and political elites are of necessity far more conscious of the value of time than the average person. Unfortunately, the concentration of research effort tends to follow journalistic and academic fashions—for instance, it is highly probable that Washington officials concerned in 1964 with civil rights will receive far more requests for interview time than officials concerned with the management of forest land or the regulation of interstate commerce. And the growth of the (in itself sound) pedagogical emphasis upon direct contact, learning through handling the data, means that inexperienced or ill-prepared students needlessly take up the time of important persons. And, in at least a few areas, the very success and popularity (they are not necessarily the same) of the interview technique are likely to make it more ineffective by destroying the willingness of subjects to be genuinely cooperative.

These points can best be illustrated by discussion of three occupational categories whose members are often asked for interviews:

1. *Congressmen.* When I first conducted interviews with members of Congress in 1953-1954, few of those with whom I talked made any clear distinction between the academic interviewer and the journalistic interviewer seeking background information for a serious piece. By 1959 some Congressmen were complaining about the frequency and the "stupidity" of academic interviews. The reasons for the latter complaint appeared to be two. First, a good many interviewers ask questions of elite interviewees when the latter have no particular feeling of expertise or even opinion about the matter but know, unlike the average member of the general public, that documentation is available or have a clear idea who are experts. Second, a good many interviewers carry over from survey to elite interviewing a bothersome insistence upon asking questions explicitly and precisely, whereas most Congressmen and many other elite interviewees prefer to handle an interview as a conversation and expect those who talk with them to be intelligent enough to know when a question has been answered implicitly. (I have not conducted congressional interviews except with personal acquaintances since 1959; but in connection with a book on Congress that I am now writing I expect to undertake some in late 1964, and I half-anticipate much greater difficulty in getting cooperation than I experienced in 1953.)

Several partial solutions to the problem of abuse of congressional time and patience may be suggested. With appropriate modifications, these may also be relevant to the over-interviewing of other elite or specialized respondents.

a. Such leading learned societies as AAPOR, American Political Science Association, and American Sociological Association might set up a clearinghouse for would-be academic interviewers and notify members of Congress that they stand ready to screen such persons. Obviously, many Congressmen, as a matter of good will or to please constituents, would continue to accord time for irritating interviews, but, nevertheless, such a clearinghouse procedure might serve to get openings for serious scholars with Congressmen who would otherwise turn them down. In fact, the next foundation considering a grant to study some aspect of legislative politics might profitably give the money to underwrite such a clearinghouse.

b. Through such a clearinghouse, and also in the planning of any study, more emphasis might be placed on consulting available documentation, whether published or unpublished. Scholars who emphasize the interview as a research technique (myself included) sometimes overlook relevant published material, or fail to explore the possibility of locating relevant unpublished written materials, such as correspondence. Generally speaking, such written material cannot be used entirely in place of the interview in political studies, but it can sometimes reduce the amount of interview time needed from a given respondent, make the questions and conversation with him more meaningful and significant to him, or reduce the total number of interviews needed.

c. Such a clearinghouse could also serve to focus professional attention upon the increasingly annoying problem created for some prominent people by the emphasis in college classes on the research interview. A year or so ago, I was talking to an instructor who told me proudly that, although he had not thought too much of the students in a particular class, during spring vacation one of them had managed to get a couple of hours' time from a Federal cabinet officer, another from a leading Senator, etc. So far as I could find out, however, absolutely no contribution to knowledge had resulted from these interviews, and the students could as well have practiced on less preoccupied individuals—with less danger that their practice would deprive serious scholars of opportunities later.

d. This is not to deny the value of student practice, but students should not acquire proficiency at the expense of the busiest targets. Studies of Congressmen undertaken by graduate students, for instance, might often, so far as the substantive problem goes, be revised to focus on state legislators; and, frequently, information solicited from Congressmen could be obtained or verified in part by ex-Congressmen (who are often pleased to be interviewed and can spare more time, make more correspondence accessible, etc.). And where it is simply a matter of practice in interviewing, the practice is just as great (though the excitement may not be) if a student interviews one of the five commissioners of a state commission instead of a Congressman. (Here, again, some care in selecting the less currently exciting fields is desirable. Probably, at present, members of state commissions against discrimination are often solicited for interviews, whereas it may be that few students of political behavior think of interviewing members of the Appellate Tax Board, a politically very sensitive and interesting agency in some jurisdictions.)

2. *Community officials and leaders in middle-sized communities.* University teachers in political science and sociology often encourage all students in their classes to interview a local official. In large cities, students may be referred to a public relations officer or the like; in small towns, if there is resentment, there will be feedback to the teachers; but in middle-sized cities, perhaps, neither of these things happens. And yet, a number of such interviews will tend to make serious cooperation more difficult if, later on, a really first-rate student or a faculty member wants to undertake a significant study.

3. *Physicians.* It is unlikely that any professional group is as much assaulted by salesmen (detail men) as physicians. Add to this the facts that several advertising agencies finance studies of the effectiveness of their advertisements and of detail men, and that these studies tend to be concentrated in metropolitan areas where competent interviewers are readily available, and it is not hard to see why some physicians are not unduly welcoming to interviewers. In any case, as members of an independent profession, their time is particularly valuable to them.

The solution in this field is not obvious to me—but at least university scholars who are employed as research consultants to pharmaceutical and advertising firms might try to see if alternative ways of answering client needs could be constructed. As I look back at my own brief experience in this field, I cannot see that the interviewing was generally worth the bother, either practically or theoretically; its main function (like that of much interviewing conducted for political campaigns) was to assuage the client's nervousness or to help the advertising agency feel it really had a gimmick. If such nonrational purposes lead to a good deal of interviewing of physicians, social psychologists ought to be able to invent equally lucrative and less bothersome (to physicians) ways of meeting these purposes.

Confidence and Trust

The imposition upon the time and patience of elite interviewees is a consequence of the publications explosion and the university population explosion. It will lead to growing exasperation but not to a sudden cata-strophic reversal of the present acceptance of social science researchers engaged in interviewing.

The situation is more perilous in regard to the abuse of interviewee trust and confidence. Here, there is a danger—a very real and serious danger—that some few dramatic cases might upset a significant number of influential people, in such a way as seriously to hurt the profession and the industry. The considerable furor in Congress about the jury-tap-ping episode indicates what may happen. Cornell University, through the Springdale study, apparently suffered something of the sort.[2]

On the whole, the academic and public opinion professions have been plain lucky that, so far, there has been no dramatic, damaging abuse of confidence. Yet, in my own observation and experience, I have seen enough instances where academic organizations as a whole do not take needed steps to protect their sources, that I have, for myself, made two decisions: (1) I will never assure any interviewee that I can protect his confidence, and, on the contrary, will tell him that I probably cannot do so except when I, personally, keep all the records of interviews; and (2) vice versa—in the role of interviewee, rather than interviewer, I will not tell any interviewer anything I regard as conceivably embarrassing or harmful to anyone I respect or like, or to whom I have an obligation, unless I know that the interviewer himself is personally trustworthy, and also that he has sole supervision over his reports of his interviews.

It happens that I am asked to give interviews because I have taken a moderately important part in several political campaigns and in state gov-ernment, etc. And, precisely because I am familiar with the way in which interviews are handled, I have decided, ordinarily, to refuse requests for help, no matter how worthy the purpose and attractive the interviewer, where any possibility of embarrassing abuse of confidence exists!

The emphasis on academic organization is central. Where one or two individuals have the only copies of reports of particular interviews, it may be possible to control confidences, and to retain the feeling of obligation to the interviewee. But the more remote the reader or archivist of a report is from the actual interviewee and interview situation, the less feeling of obligation he has to the interviewee, and the more temptation he feels to tell a good story even if that means betraying a confidence.

The following events, which I have seen (somewhat disguised so as to avoid embarrassment but retaining the basic issue), have involved the risk of betraying trust in regard to identifiable interviewees:

1. A study was undertaken in which a good deal of information was incidentally obtained about businessmen who were violating certain tax codes. During the months immediately following the writing up of the interviews several of these men were indicted. It happened that one of the research analysts, for good reason, had frequent conferences with the tax authorities in question, and the interviewers felt that he had passed on the information. But, in fact, at one time or another several other research officers of the organization, totally unfamiliar with interviewing ethics, a number of clerk typists, and a couple of editors had access to the interviews and could have gossiped.

2. In another study, state political figures were persuaded to give very freely opinions it would have embarrassed them to have known. (Also, in some instances, they reported events that might have made them liable to legal action.) At the headquarters of the project, some distance away, scholars taught courses in which they required their students to read a number of these interviews, even though the interviewers repeatedly emphasized that interviewees wanted the interviews to be confidential. The interviewers did not learn of these courses until after the field work was completed, but were not much reassured when they were told that a questionnaire had shown that none of the students had any family connection with the state in question! Who could tell, for instance, when a student might spend a weekend with somebody interested in what they knew?

3. A graduate student who had received information of considerable confidentiality on political matters was subjected to some harassment in his doctor's oral by outside, nondepartmental members of his examining committee because of his failure to name informants in his thesis. It was at least possible that these examiners were more interested in getting "inside dope" than in verifying the accuracy of the thesis.

4. A university researcher's assistant was told, apparently in confidence, in the course of an interview of the exceptionally low opinion the distinguished interviewee held of the late President Kennedy. Either to make a good story or possibly to influence my own political actions, the researcher has several times told me in detail what was said. I suspect that, if he had had the initial contact himself, he would have felt more obligation to respect a confidence whose violation could have greatly hurt the interviewee.

5. On half a dozen occasions, at least, I have seen sets of highly confidential political interviews in unlocked file cabinets, where secretaries who had no "need to know" could easily read them, and where any passerby could pick them up, with relatively little risk, if he chose his time appropriately. One study, on which I, myself, did the interviewing of certain aspects of city licensing procedures, involved specific complaints by businessmen and attorneys about the mayor and commissioners, usually given to me with adjurations never to let the authorities know what they had said. I had to write the report, therefore, without submitting the interviews or naming informants. When the sponsoring

organization asked for copies of the interviews, I asked them where they would keep them. "Oh, in our offices,' they replied. I pointed out that their file cabinets were old and unlocked, and that frequently the room in which the file cabinets were kept was left unguarded. "Oh," said they, "we trust people!"[3]

Frequently, in fact, trusting people is one of the dangers in the academic handling and recording of elite interviews. Interviews should be guarded, so far as reasonably possible, in the spirit in which CIA materials are presumably watched, not because, ordinarily, anybody will betray the trust, but because an occasional failure to keep trust may have extraordinarily serious consequences. (One simple way of making confidence easier to keep: interviewers often dictate interviews, when they could about as well type them up themselves.)

The other difficulty is, of course, that academic people do not always realize what might be embarrassing to people active in politics and the professions, who, in turn, are accustomed to journalists and colleagues who know when breaking a confidence would be dangerous. Frequently, one has to understand a good deal about a specific situation or occupation to see what would be embarrassing to the interviewee, whereas the academician's interest may be quite restricted. (For example, academics may interview a member of the House Judiciary committee about civil rights, knowing nothing of the factional fights in the Congressman's home district, and something he "lets out" could hurt the Congressman in such fights.)

In writing up reports, there is one other respect in which scholars probably could be more cautious than some of them are. I suppose that a dozen times at least I have been fairly certain which Congressman or what state official said something cited in a research study, either because he was the only one in the situation (say on the given committee) who could possibly have made the remark quoted, or because a particular turn of speech is quoted verbatim, which serves to identify quite as well as the name. There is no reason why phrasing cannot be hanged in most political studies, and considerably more effort than is usual could be made to disguise a particular informant's position. In *American Business and Public Policy*, I deliberately attributed to Senators or senatorial assistants remarks made by House members where it made no difference or, in a few cases, attributed to a male, rural Representative something said by an urban female, or quoted a remark made by an ex-Congressman in 1953-1955 as though it had been made by an incumbent—again where such switching made no difference to the point and helped disguise the source.

In the same book, I have taken similar pains to disguise businessmen in Appalachian City and the Fifty-third Openvirmarky; and, as I recollect, we similarly made a few switches among lobbyists.[4]

Notes

1. See *Public Opinion Quarterly*, Vol. 28, 1964, p. 118, and the three succeeding articles, especially Rome G. Arnold, "The Interview in Jeopardy: A Problem in Public Relations," pp. 119-123. On the same general topic, see the valuable comment by Eleanor Wolf, "Some Questions about Community Self-surveys," *Human Organization*, Vol. 23, No. 1, 1964, pp. 85-89.
2. See, for instance, the editorial on that study in *Human Organization*, Vol. 17, No. 2, 1958, pp. 1-2.
3. Although this example is not strictly in the elite field, by happenstance I have heard of "interesting" remarks made by a prominent married couple who had cooperated in a family study, even though I tried to shut the interviewer-raconteur up.
4. R. Bauer, I. Pool, and L. A. Dexter, *American Business and Public Policy*, New York, Atherton, 1963, Part V on Congress, and IV on Pressure Groups, and Chap. 19 on Appalachian City and the 53rd. I have no reason, incidentally, to think that anybody in Appalachian City was embarrassed by anything attributed to him; but, on the other hand, I could not disguise Delaware (Chap. 16) and at least two (and possibly more) remarks quoted in that chapter were apparently embarrassing to subjects.

5

On the Use and Abuse of Social Science by Practitioners*

These remarks were prepared for a group of psychiatric social workers; since delivering them, I have become aware that they are equally relevant for members of an occupational class to which I have belonged, that of state house politicians; and so far as I can see they would have pertinence to any type of practitioner, affected by social science ideas, whether public health nurse, guidance and personnel expert, forensic psychiatrist, or Madison Avenue research consultant.

The first section below discusses and explains what are probably the greatest dangers facing practitioners trying to use (or required to use) the social sciences; the second discusses one perspective, likely to be useful to practitioners, but hardly known at all to them; the third part is concerned with one of the traditional fields of social thought, which is of great, current relevance to practitioners, but which has gone almost entirely out of fashion.

I

Confronted with social science as it is today, with its complexity of theories and techniques, practitioners face a situation similar to that of Africans or Polynesians confronting Western science, technology, and law. There is much that is exciting and ego-gratifying; but whether it is relevant, useful, and pertinent is another question. There is considerable danger of confusion, waste, and disappointment. Such an apprehension may be regarded as untrue because when persons possessed of one technology have reached the level of desiring to acquire another, they are apt to regard the suggestion that the more complex technology is not appropriate as a kind of insulting condescension. Thus, nuclear energy programs and proposals for steel mills developed where such mills would be wasteful or unjustified, are defended against Western European economists when the latter argue for more sensible capital investments. The parallel is: Once practitioners have reached the stage of believing some aspect of social science is worth borrowing from, they react similarly to efforts to warn them against it, whether it be game theory, or Lazarsfeldian methodology, or overmuch emphasis on the anthropological theory of culture.

It may be desirable, therefore, to start out with some general reasons as to why and how social science may sometimes be useless or harmful to practitioners. In the first place, experts generally tend to assume that the purposes of those with whom they talk and whom they advise are the same as their own. This frequently is not true. I, myself, for instance, once wasted the time of a client who was interested in trying to organize the literature about social science interviewing to help him find out how he could use interviewing skills to validate factual information. The literature which I canvassed dealt largely with opinion, attitude, orientation, viewpoint, but not with ascertaining specific, detailed fact, and I did not notice the difference! And I wasted the time of another client by assuming that he had accepted my statement as to his purposes; he was much impressed apparently by what I said, but did not understand that it involved a redefinition of his purposes. The point in citing these bits of personal history is that I exemplified a common tendency of people who are or believe themselves to be "specialists" in a given area.

A second and even more crucial reason why social science is often harmful to the practitioner is that the practitioner falls victim to current intellectual fashion. This is because, at any given time, scholars in a particular discipline are likely to be concerned with a few particular ideas or conceptions, and to be working on and talking about these. This may do no particular harm to scholarship and, hopefully, is likely to be corrected by later developments. But for the practitioner, the applied anthropologist, the social worker, or the politician, such overemphasis on one approach or another is likely to mislead, because what is emphasized may not be what is needed for his practical purposes.

This is a way of stressing the need for countervailing intellectual power. On this point Margaret Mead has said:

> When practitioners who are committed to the well-being of human beings, attend at all to the findings of the laboratory, they attend with far too much vigor....

One of the consequences of all this is that anyone actively concerned with developing the kind of hypotheses, which promise some help to mankind has to spend a lot of time putting out fires. No sooner is a preliminary skirmish won—critics and opponents convinced of the validity of some position—then, before the grass has grown green again on that battlefield, one has to be off a pace to start a skirmish against those who have accepted the new idea too thoroughly and too well.... The new battle often has to be fought long before most people have become familiar with the last victory. A battle for the advisability of breast-feeding babies may be so over-won in a metropolitan center that it is already time to warn mothers that some babies can live on artificial food, even while in a nearby community, the local physicians and parents-in-law have not yet heard that breast-feeding is anything except hopelessly old-fashioned.[1]

"All the while, one feels more and more like the old visiting nurse who complained that after climbing stairs for years to tell those Italians to stop feeding their babies tomatoes, she now has to climb them all over again to tell them to start feeding tomatoes." Similar examples can be cited from many areas of medicine and government; and Mead indeed in the particular note quoted goes ahead to point out that, whereas in 1941, it was necessary to insist that war has psychological roots because the kind of watered-down Marxism which stresses the "forces of history" was so popular, by 1955, it became necessary to reverse the emphasis, and to point out that war is a social institution, since by 1955, the psychological approach had become so exaggerated, in its turn.

That is, any particular interpretation or technique or set of ideas, as it becomes unusually widespread among practitioners, is to be regarded with grave suspicion. For practitioners tend to use it as a short-cut, a semi-universal solvent, an answer. And in practice there are few universal answers. Overemphasis in science or research may serve a legitimate purpose; if a number of scholars pay attention to the same set of problems, probably they will work more usefully than if attention is scattered over a wide field. But, if and when, social work or even applied social work researchers start talking chiefly about Freud, or chiefly about "culture," in the sociological sense, it is time to become suspicious. Of course, Freud or Benedict are very useful per se; but there is a likelihood of carrying them too far. In the much more "objective" field of medicine we know that fashions occur, so that at one time "everybody" is suggesting (and a good many are undergoing) some operation, forgotten a few years later, or vitamins are regarded as much more significant for the patient at one time than at another. So, in 1929, a specialist in mental retardation might have avoided mistakes in judgment (and perhaps also a good deal of unhappiness for families, which he dealt with) if he were very sceptical about notions of genetic determination, then popular; but today a specialist in mental retardation would be well-advised to pay more attention to the possibility of genetic determination of certain characteristics than is widely popular. Similarly, in the general field of politics—and also in the particular discipline of social work—skepticism about Marxist ideology as it applied to practice was, in 1937, a highly valuable preservative against nonsense.

A fictional character once declared himself "the sworn enemy of sloppiness." When a detective asks him what would happen if most men were like him, he replied, "If most men were like me, we should constitute an intolerable nuisance; a necessary reaction towards sloppiness would set in and find me at its head"[2]

Of course, this sort of thing happens in all fields of knowledge and has its effects on practice. Sophisticated political scientists defend prevailing actions which "well-educated" municipal reformers and administrators bitterly oppose, and sophisticated anthropologists criticize management experts who wish to eliminate traditional methods.[3]

In each case, the well-educated practitioners learned their ideas from the previous generation of research experts!

The current (current, at least in 1962) employment of the notion "culture" in social work—and elsewhere also— supplies a good example of the exaggeration of what is in itself a valuable intellectual approach. Some social workers use the idea beyond what it will carry. As a general means of interpreting types of behavior, attitudes and institutions, it works; as a stimulant to asking fruitful diagnostic questions about misunderstandings and disputes, particularly between people of radically different backgrounds, it is often helpful. But in the realm of detailed personal reorientation—budgeting, "mental health therapy," etc.—is there any way of observing or even inferring "culture" without meticulous recording of patterns of social interaction? Is there any evidence that impressions or generalizations about cultural differences are useful in helping to solve people's problems? Probably every psychiatric social worker interested in the sociological notion of culture has an image of the relationship between particular sorts of personalities and the kinds of family, social setting, and society from which they come. If so, three questions are pertinent: (1) Are these images of any actual relevance in the decisions the worker makes about what to do?; (2) Are these images valid, accurate, correct?; and (3) Are they any more likely (or are they less likely) to be valid, accurate, and correct for workers who have learned about cultural differences or for those who have not? My guess is that, within the limits of more or less Americanized society, it is just as likely that learning about culture and personality would make workers more prone to inaccurate guesses, as the reverse. I suspect, for instance, that a person who has learned about the social aspects of feeding in Jewish-American culture or about female domination among Negroes, etc., is apt to "see" Negroes or Jews and their problems in terms of these "stereotypes," and actually ask questions or interpret answers in these terms beyond what is helpful or accurate.

Of course, questions of the sort just raised could be answered by field studies of how psychiatric social workers actually perceive and interpret the clients with whom they deal.

What kinds of inferences are made on the basis of certain backgrounds, appearances, gestures, mannerisms, tricks of speech? How are these inferences influenced by training and background? How valid are they? Is there a great difference in the validity of inferences drawn by different workers or by the same worker in different situations, or with different kinds of people?

Hopefully, we may some day be able to overcome what is perhaps the biggest single disadvantage of being aware of a particular interpretation or problem; at present, once we are so aware, we ask our questions, make our observations, and call to the attention of ourselves, our subjects, and our informants, the particular variables which fit into our way of looking at things. So, many students of political science and journalists find "pressure" because "pressure" is what they are looking for;[4] similarly, many students of the retarded, and social workers generally, find retardation and intellectual deficit significant in interpreting and locating difficulties, which in fact are not different from the difficulties the non-retarded experience.[5] One of the great needs of social practice is to discover better techniques for overcoming this tendency.[6]

II

Fashion leads to overemphasis. On the other hand, ideas and approaches of considerable pertinence and relevance are overlooked or unknown because they are unfashionable. One branch of social science of especial relevance to practitioners is almost unknown to them. This is the sociology of occupations or professions. Here, it may best be introduced by raising the question: What is the job of any practitioner?

Study tends to confirm the experience of daily life—that the ways in which people verbally describe their jobs do not tell us what they actually do and that the meaning, nature and significance of a job is not at all the same to one practitioner as to another. Considerable "insight" may be obtained into our own concerns and assumptions and those of our fellow workers by trying to work out what a job actually means for sociological and personal identity. This leads us into a sociology, which takes far more account of literature, the analysis of dramatic relationships, the moral sciences, et cetera, than is currently customary. Well-known scholars who have practiced this sort of sociology include: George Simmel, George Herbert Mead, David Riesman, Margaret Mead, Ruth Benedict, and most of all Everett Hughes of Brandeis. The appeal of Freudian and post-Freudian thought, and of the culture-and-personality approach in large measure may derive from the fact that it does retain a clear sense of the dramatic. But the Freudian dramatic model is far too limited in scope adequately to contain all the varieties of human experience. It is, for instance, as misleading to use Freudian doctrine to interpret career lines in modern society as to interpret modern U. S. politics by citation either of Shakespeare or of Hobbes.

The dramatic interpretation of careers and occupations is well-stated for our current discussion in three volumes, Everett Hughes' *Men and Their Work*,[7] Goffman's *The Presentation of Self in Everyday Life*,[8] and Kenneth Burke's *Attitudes Towards History*.[9] There are also numerous monographic studies of particular occupations or activities, which are illuminating. There have been several efforts to deal with institutions of some pertinence to some social workers (e.g., Stanton and Schwartz' *The Mental Hospital*),[10] which throw light on the institutional complexes within which some practitioners work. There are also relevant community studies; William Foote Whyte's *Street Corner Society*[11] contains a picture of a settlement house, for instance; and an extremely brilliant but neglected institutional study, John Seeley's *Community Chest*[12] shows how "insight" can be provided by "disciplined dramatic imagination." It probably will be useful to try to demonstrate the utility of this dramatistic approach to the sociology of the professions by illustration. Hughes points out, for instance, that "society, by its very nature, consists of both allowing and expecting some people to do things which other people are not allowed or expected to do."[13] What does this mean for social work and related fields? Continues Hughes: "All occupations—most of all those considered professions and perhaps those of the underworld—include as part of their very being a [social, not a legal] license to deviate in some measure from the common mode of behavior." Now, what is the permitted social license of the social worker? Do "psychiatric" social workers in their turn claim a license to deviate from standard case work behavior? Do social workers or psychiatric social workers claim or demand license(s) not recognized by their associates or clients or by the public? Are their claims different in public, private, Catholic, or Jewish organizations?

Hughes; again: "Some people seek and get special responsibility for defining the values and for establishing and enforcing social sanctions over some aspects of life. The differentiation of moral and social functions involves both the setting of the boundaries of realms of social behavior and the allocation of responsibility and power over them... " The psychiatrist has some kind of special, suspect knowledge of lunacy; and, probably, the considerable body of anecdote and humor about crazy psychiatrists, immoral behavior of psychiatrists, etc., represents in part discomfort at the feeling that they have such knowledge—and license. A study from a sociological—not a narrowly psychiatric—viewpoint of humor and gossip about psychiatrists might prove quite enlightening. Is there a similar body of gossip and humor regarding psychiatric social workers? Especially among other social workers?

Hughes further: "Most occupations rest upon some explicit or implicit bargain between the practitioner and the individuals with whom he works, and between the occupation as a whole and society at large about receiving, keeping and giving out information gathered in the course of one's work." One example: the claim of newspapermen to protect their sources. What is the bargain—not the policy statement or the formalized procedure—but the actual bargain social workers make with clients? What is there that some clients know (or think they know), which will not be recorded? Very probably, many social workers push these bargains to the back of their minds in order to avoid a feeling of discomfort; Hughes suggests, however, that they are the very stuff of professional life, and are enlighteningly recognized as such. All these questions have clear analogies for, e.g., State legislators or Congressmen.[14]

Of course, there is a problem because of the multiple responsibilities which all of us face in explicitly discussing the bargains we make—those "on the firing line" may have to make bargains which the board, or the boss, or the legislature, or the courts, would disapprove of. In every residential college, the actual dormitory head may have to make bargains which he would not wish to explain to the trustees or the Dean: but a dormitory head who self-consciously realizes his position is presumably—if knowledge is worth anything—in better case to determine the hierarchy of values in particular circumstances, whether in some flagrant instance he ought to break the bargain and can get away with so doing (in the sense that he will not spoil his future effectiveness), or whether indeed he is being maneuvered into a pseudo-bargain by some "con man" in the student body. All that has just been said about dormitory heads applies—in terms of social structure—to social workers.

An even more systematic and comprehensive treatment of the occupation of social work might be based upon Goffman's *The Presentation of Self in Everyday Life*. He, for example, discusses the problems involved in and the recurrent necessity of dramatizing one's work. He indicates how much more difficult it is for medical nurses to dramatize their responsibility than for surgical nurses[15]—and goes ahead to point out that "the work that must be done by those who fill certain statuses is often so poorly designed as an expression of a desired meaning that if the incumbent would dramatize the character of his role, he must, divert an appreciable amount of his energy to do so. Those who have the time and talent to perform a task well may not, because of this (very fact) have the time or talent to make it apparent that they are performing well." Hence the "lawyer's lawyer," or "senator's senator," for instance, a man such as Senator Hayden of Arizona is said to have been, whose legislative achievement as an appropriations expert tends to make it difficult for him to become known to the general public; vice versa, nowadays much legislative business is handled by committee clerks and legislative assistants because some senators are too busy acting like senators to function as such. I guess this happens among social work administrators, too!

The question to ask is: What kind of dramatization is feasible, possible, necessary, or inherent in the role of social worker or psychiatric social worker? In fact, one may wonder, how far such adjectives as "psychiatric" and "medical" are used because they permit some to come under the umbrella of prestige and drama attaching to medicine and psychiatry.

III

Historically, political philosophy was one of the earliest branches of the social sciences. But it has fallen out of fashion, so that practitioners are hardly aware of its tremendous relevance to their decisions and actions and policy problems. Indeed, in the social action-social policy area—and here I do not mean legislation, but social policy in practice, as carried out by the unit head or the individual worker in deciding what to do about a particular sort of deviant behavior by clients—political theory is probably the most relevant skill for increasing self-awareness about one's function and role. The particular pertinence of classic political philosophy at this moment perhaps may be shown by mentioning the fact that psychiatry, sociology, and social work have in this country at least done a great deal to spread the notion that environment is responsible for people's defects and individuals are not to be blamed.[16] As a reaction to the Calvinist idea of absolute good and bad, white and black, saved and damned, this emphasis was no doubt of considerable value. As a technical device for securing objectivity in social and philosophical analysis, it also has much to commend it. Certainly, in face-to-face dealings with one's "data," whether they happen to be political enemies, psychopaths, or perverts, many interviewers must sympathize with them to some degree, simply as a matter of interviewing technique and stance; otherwise rapport and confidence may be lost. Presumably, also for similar reasons, psychiatrists and psychiatric social workers, engaged in repeated interviewing of "difficult" persons, train themselves to feel sympathy with their clients.

But to use these technical requirements of social work and social science[17]—these pre-requisites for the acquisition of the kind of "guilty knowledge" in Hughes' terminology which our work demands of us—as justification for legal or political conclusions is indefensible. Sentiments, which enable us to perform our work well may, when applied to the administration of justice or the formulation of foreign policy, lead to dangerous actions.[18] The slowness of many humanitarian intellectuals to recognize Hitler as a danger, their reluctance to resist Stalin or to believe that Mao was a Communist or that there is such a thing as subversion, is, in part, traceable to the combination of neutrality and humanitarianism, typically found among American sociologists and social workers. In the same way, it is quite possible that some forms of crime and juvenile delinquency would be reduced if intellectual fashion were to swing away from the unwillingness to blame, the emphasis upon neutrality and humanitarianism, so that police would receive more intellectual and moral support, and judges, juries, public officials generally would be more willing to try to find out empirically if punishment does deter crime rather than rely upon deductive humanitarianism or deductive punitiveness.

It is not suggested that classic political philosophy supports a preventive war or demands capital punishment for theft; merely that on the principle of redressing intellectual balance we need to question much which is now taken more or less for granted as the "creed" of the respectable "liberal" professional. At present, psychiatrists,[19] social scientists, and social workers are often regarded almost as allies of those who perform illegal or conceivably illegal actions; this might in 1810 have been a highly desirable situation, and, even now, in regard to some few victims of prejudice may be admirable, but, in general, we should think through the philosophical, empirical, and political consequences of such an attitude and stance, rather than clinging to a set of traditional doctrines allegedly justified by questionable evidence, as to the ineffectiveness of punishment.

There are at least grave and unresolved issues in the entire area of political and legal philosophy as to the effectiveness of blame, the possibility of deterrence, the utility of punishment, and the nature of social and individual responsibility. Perhaps what we need is a clearly worked out theory, taking account of modern knowledge, on this last point, focusing not on the question "when (in terms of 'objective' sociological analysis or conventional psychiatric practice) should an individual be held responsible?" but on the political question "Under what circumstances is it socially worthwhile for the categories of psychiatric or social work practice or for the sociologist's attitude towards his 'data' to be made the basis for large political or legal decisions?" Rethinking political and legal issues in these terms would necessitate rather broad revision of widely accepted notions as to what is a "liberal," a "conservative," or a "reactionary."

Here, our discussion may seem far away from the relevance of social science to professional practice—narrowly defined; but it is still focused on the social work profession because, due to training in that and related fields, and due to selective factors, which lead "humanitarians" to enter the profession in the first place, there are characteristic differences between the way in which most social workers, etc., look at political and legal problems, for instance, and the way in which such problems are typically regarded, for instance, by engineers or salesmen. In any case, remembering Margaret Mead's nurse acquaintance: "after a century of walking upstairs to tell those Italians to stop eating tomatoes, maybe it's time to walk upstairs to tell them to start eating tomatoes." In other words, perhaps we ought now to offset the cultural relativity, the humanitarianism, and the opposition to blaming anybody for anything, which we have helped to inculcate. We have, in some areas, probably been too successful and, if so, we should correct for our own success![20]

References

*   Read at the Psychiatric Social Workers' Institute of the Michigan State Department of Mental Health at Detroit. March 2, 1961; very radically recast. I want to express my gratitude to the officers of the Department and the Institute.

1. M. Mead, "The New Isolationism," *American Scholar*, 24 (1955), pp. 378-82. Mead wrote in 1955; and fashions have changed since. One might add, of course, that there were certainly sections of the world where breast-feeding was, in '55, and is now the only conceivable desirable action.

2. E. Bramah "The Ghost at Massingham Mansions," republished in D. Sayers (ed.), *Third Omnibus of Crime*, Garden City, 1929, p. 213.
3. In Lewis A. Dexter, *Tyranny of Schooling: an Inquiry into the Problem of "Stupidity,"* Basic Books, New York, 1964, I try to show how the "good custom" of educational opportunity has now become a dogma, which interferes with some of the very values, which led to its initial formulation and creates other undesirable by-products, not because the initial approach was wrong, but became it has been carried too far.
4. See here R. Bauer, I. Pool, and L. Dexter, *American Business and Public Policy*, New York: Atherton, 1963, esp. Ch. 30, and Lewis A. Dexter, "Marginal Attention and Pressure Politics," *Int. Rev. Hist. & Poli. Sci.,* Vol. 1. 1963.
5. See Dexter, Tyranny, op. cit., esp. Ch. 6; I am now preparing a paper to be read at Northeast Regional Meeting, Am. Assn. Mental Deficiency, 1965, indicating some reasons why expectation creates perception and determines interpretation in this field.
6. A minor possible contribution to this effort in the field of interviewing technique is found in Lewis A. Dexter, "Role Relationships and Conceptions of Neutrality in Interviewing," *Am. J. Socio.,* 62 (1956) 153-7.
7. Free Press, 1958.
8. University of Edinburgh Social Sciences Research Center, 1958. Monog. No. 2.
9. New Republic, 2 vols. 1937.
10. Basic Books, 1954.
11. U. of Chicago Press, 1943.
12. U. of Toronto Press, 1957.
13. *Men at Work, op. cit.,* "License and Mandate," pp. 78-87.
14. See on this, Lewis A. Dexter, "Analogies Useful in Understanding Congress: What Does Congress Resemble in What Respect?" paper read at American Political Science Association meetings, Sept. 9, 1965.
15. *Op. cit.* pp. 20 ff., citing E. Lenz "A Comparison of Medical and Surgical Floors," mimeo, N.Y. School Ind. & Lab. Reins, Cornell U., 1954.
16. See the insightful article by A. Keith-Lucas, "The Political Theory Implicit in Social Casework Theory," Am. Poli. Science Rev., 47 (1953).
17. In fact, they are, in somewhat different ways, also, technical requirements for effective participation in practical politics.
18. As a research interviewer or as a dean of men, it might be desirable or unavoidable for me to sympathize with students who cheat in a way, which I should avoid as a teacher or dean of liberal arts, or a research student of extremist groups or an analyst of political theories must show a sympathy towards John Birch Society views, which few political scientists as citizens feel.
19. See T. Szasz, *The Myth of Mental Illness,* Hoeber, 1960, for an indication of some factors leading to this development.
20. An excellent example of how social work philosophy (and presumably practice) could be changed by some concern with traditional political philosophy would be provided by an analysis of N. Cohen's otherwise admirable *Social Work in the American Tradition*, Dryden, 1958, in fact, it would be easily possible to take the first three pages of this valuable book by themselves and write a lengthy critical commentary showing what such men as Leslie Stephen, William Graham Sumner, Aristotle, Halifax, and Edmund Burke would have said about (what they would in all probability have interpreted as) a failure to take into account relevant institutional and ethical considerations that each of them dealt with.

6

Impressions about Utility and Wastefulness in Applied Social Science Studies

The following remarks are based upon observations and impressions derived from: (1) participation in about a hundred contract efforts in social science, largely, but not entirely, as a self-employed consultant; (2) discussion and consideration of the possibility of employment on about a thousand other contracts and studies; and (3) listening to the experiences of, and reading reports by many other applied social scientists. Since the writer's experience has tended to focus on: (1) political analyses; and on (2) opinion and market research studies, his findings may be more relevant in this field than to the application of economic or psychological propositions; but it is probable that what is here said is pertinent to most efforts to use social science.

Although the hypotheses here stated have not been systematically tested, they are, in principle, testable. They could also be formulated, from the standpoint of the theory of social organizations, as propositions about the unintended purposes of purposive social action.

1. Social science research has a 50 percent chance of being boondoggling, designed to: (a) postpone a decision which it is uncomfortable to make; (b) put the onus of a decision which has already been reached upon someone outside the agency; (c) provide the satisfaction to some official of supervising and using scholars; (d) provide "scholarly" support, which can be put in rhetorical terms for a policy, which has already been decided upon.

The use of outside consultants for any of these purposes may be entirely justifiable; but is formally rational only if the purpose is recognized by those doing the hiring. It is likely that scholars or consultants will be less dissatisfied and will undertake less expensive—and from the enterprise's standpoint, less irrelevant—activities if they recognize these purposes as partially or wholly determining the procedures to be followed. But it would destroy the utility for some of these purposes of "research" if the purposes were explicitly admitted.

2. Where research is not a priori boondoggling for the reasons indicated above, it is likely to be wasteful because basic questions are not formulated. Therefore, a good deal of research is undertaken, which is not pertinent to answering the real source of concern. The difficulty here is usually avoidable if the distinction is carefully made between researchers who are employed to answer a "purely" technical question and researchers who are employed to advise management on policy issues. But there is a strong tendency to believe that what is in reality a policy question is simply a technical one and to put researchers to work on answering a seemingly technical problem, which is really a matter of policy.

A good many researchers, entirely qualified to undertake technical research on attitudes, for instance, or on management controls are not equipped to answer (or even to realize the nature of) the policy questions underlying their particular assignment. Accordingly, as a matter of long-range practice, enterprises planning to make use of consultants should first have the problem analyzed at the highest relevant policy levels with informed social scientists able to think in policy terms from the standpoint of the enterprise.

So long as consultants tend to be paid by time or effort, this approach is difficult for them, because the natural tendency is to suggest research, which is time-consuming and lucrative rather than to spend (very much less) time (usually) in trying to locate the basic policy question. Quite aside from the immediate cash nexus, scholars who often can obtain no other support and not enough prestige for their own particular area of interest tend to stress their skill rather than the needs or concerns of the client. (A "beautiful" example was the expansion of the Analysis Division of the Foreign Broadcast Intelligence Service, Federal Communications Commission, in the early stages of the war by social psychologists, much interested in content analysis, earnestly wishing to contribute their skills to the war effort, with little or no awareness of the administrative and attention problems of consumers of their reports.)

It would probably be profitable for enterprises making any long-range use of consultants to arrange a procedure for formulating the policy problems prior to any extensive field research; if outside or in-service social science consultants cannot be obtained to participate in such analysis, the mere realization that in principle somewhere between 5 and 50 percent as much time should be spent on formulating a problem as in trying to get data to deal with it would be helpful. The tendency to "do research" leads away from the formulation of the problem to the premature collection of data.

Of course, it should also be recognized that perfection is not going to be achieved—and that in many cases, an honest statement as to why a study is desired might serve to hurt morale.

3. Since, in many cases, management itself cannot or will not formulate the problem, management men might profitably remember that the ideal consultant is the one who has enough tact to know when assistance in formulating the basic problem will be welcomed and when such an effort will merely serve to reveal a sore spot; in cases where sensitiveness is present, the skilled consultant ought to be prepared to try to determine the real question but careful never to state it.

4. In some instances, the first social scientist brought in to advise or consult will necessarily offend or upset a good many people, because he will necessarily call attention to an unpleasant or sensitive situation, perhaps merely by questions which he asks. It is therefore extremely desirable, once a serious decision has been made to use social scientists on, for instance, studies of sensitive areas like management improvement, or community attitudes towards an unpopular organization to pursue the following procedure to have someone come in and ask some of the pertinent questions. Then, when he has made himself unpopular, say "Well, he was a mistake .... too bad he was so tactless ... but there is this first-rate social scientist over here who differs (in some superficially noticeable way—one was a sociologist, the other an anthropologist; one from Chicago, the other from Harvard, etc.) from that guy. Let's hire him." If the second man is properly briefed, he can take advantage of most of what his predecessor did, dress it up in somewhat different rhetoric, and obtain acceptance the second time the sensitive points are touched on.

Of course, in all fairness to the careers of the consultants and social scientists involved, their colleagues should realize that this type of situation may occur.

5. Much, probably most, social science research—certainly opinion research in crisis situations by government agencies, politicians, etc.—is contracted too late. This is partly because of the tendency to procrastinate, which most people have, but partly because few executives realize that lead time is essential for a social science project. The executive worried, for instance, about Latin American attitudes after a Dominican episode may call for public opinion polls immediately (this is purely hypothetical; I do not know whether any agency

actually commissioned such polls). But it takes time to formulate the new issues raised by such an event as this and particularly to consider whether interviewing technology has to be modified. It also takes time to recruit field staff or to determine whether a changed situation calls for an unusual type of field staff.

6. The emphasis on the real problem will lead management to realize that research will not in some instances help very much. Research does not supply the nerve to choose between two unpopular decisions.

7. One way of determining whether research is worthwhile is to try to imagine and actually write out conceivable results which might be reported and then determine what use would be made of the answers. At one time, some colleges were interested in measurement of teaching effectiveness and in evaluation of teacher popularity (or more strictly, reports on student evaluation of teachers). But there was only the vague conception that the two issues were related to justify the latter; and if a dummy report had been prepared, perhaps it would have become obvious either that what students were asked about teachers would have to be altered a good deal or that questions about teacher competence, asked of students currently in classes, could not clearly be related to measurement of teaching effectiveness. The real difficulty, probably, was that there is little clear definition of what is meant by teaching effectiveness.

The foregoing comments apply chiefly to efforts to organize research around particular problems. It may well be that firms or enterprises willing to commission social science research without reference to particular problems, over a period of years, may benefit more than those which ask for immediately applicable results.

Selected Bibliography:
Lewis Anthony Dexter (1915-1995)

Dexter, Lewis Anthony. "Administration of the Social Gospel." *Public Opinion Quarterly* (1938).

Dexter, Lewis Anthony. "Causal Imputation and Purposes of Investigation." *Philosophy of Science* (1939).

Dexter, Lewis Anthony. "The Politics of Prevention in Wartime and After." *Psychiatry: Journal of the Biology and Pathology of Interpersonal Relations* (1941).

Dexter, Lewis Anthony. "Implications of Supranational Federation." *American Sociological Review* (1942).

Dexter, Lewis Anthony. "A Note on the Unification of Sociology," *Psychology, and Psychiatry.* (1943).

Dexter, Lewis Anthony. "Be Not the First." *Journal of Liberal Religion* (1944).

Dexter, Lewis Anthony. "Analysis of Educational Programs." *School Review* (1946).

Dexter, Lewis Anthony. "Ethics and Politics III: Political Processes and Judgments of Value." *American Political Science Review* (1946).

Dexter, Lewis Anthony. "Examinations as Instruments of and Obstacles to General Education." *School Review* (1947).

Dexter, Lewis Anthony. "John Taber: Watchdog of the Treasury." *Zion's Herald* (Boston) (1948).

Dexter, Lewis Anthony. "On the Construction of Social Science General Courses." *Journal of Education* (1948).

Dexter, Lewis Anthony. "Social Psychology of Colonialism: Puerto Rican Professional Personality Patterns." *Human Relations* (Great Britain) (1949).

Dexter, Lewis Anthony. "On Teaching the Transfer of Training." *Harvard Educational Review* (1949).

Dexter, Lewis Anthony. "Sociology of Innovative Leadership," in *Studies in Leadership: Leadership and Democratic Action*, Alan Ward Gouldner, ed., 1950. New York, NY: Harper.

Dexter, Lewis Anthony. "Recent Political Science Research in American Universities." *American Political Science Review* (Claude E. Hawley, senior author) (1952).

Dexter, Lewis Anthony. "Democratic Me-tooism or Active Opposition?" *Reporter* (1953).

Dexter, Lewis Anthony. "The Use of Public Opinion Polls by Political Party Organizations." *The Public Opinion Quarterly* (1954).

Dexter, Lewis Anthony. 1955. *Congressmen and the People They Listen To*. Cambridge, MA: Center for International Studies, Massachusetts Institute of Technology.

Dexter, Lewis Anthony. "Defense Means Protection." *American Scholar* (1955). (Reprinted in Congressional Record, end of session, by Humphrey of Minnesota.)

Dexter, Lewis Anthony. "Candidates Must Make the Issues and Give Them Meaning." *The Public Opinion Quarterly* (1955).

Dexter, Lewis Anthony and David Bobrow. "Erosion and Reclamation: Situation and Prospects of the Stevenson Candidacy." An 85-page report prepared for the Adlai Stevenson presidential campaigns of 1952 and 1956.

Dexter, Lewis Anthony. "Heredity and Environment Reexplored: Specification of Environments and Genetic Transmission." *Eugenics Quarterly* (1956).

Dexter, Lewis Anthony. "What Do Congressmen Hear: The Mail." *The Public Opinion Quarterly* (1956).

Dexter, Lewis Anthony. "Role Relationships and Conceptions of Neutrality in Interviewing." *American Journal of Sociology* (1956).

Dexter, Lewis Anthony. "Towards a Sociology of the Mentally Defective." *American Journal of Mental Deficiency* (1956).

Dexter, Lewis Anthony. "The Representative and His District." *Human Organization* (1957).

Dexter, Lewis Anthony. "A Social Theory of Mental Deficiency." *American Journal of Mental Deficiency* (1958).

Dexter, Lewis Anthony. "A Note on Selective Inattention in Social Science." *Social Problems* (1958).

Dexter, Lewis Anthony. "More on Voter's Information About Candidates." *American Behavioral Scientist* (1958).

Dexter, Lewis Anthony. "The Policy Sciences and Limited Warfare." *Political Research—Organization and Design* (1958).

Dexter, Lewis Anthony. "Conventional Death or Unconventional Survival?" *Saturday Review* (1959).

Dexter, Lewis Anthony. "On Interviewing Business Leaders." *American Behavioral Scientist* (1959).

Dexter, Lewis Anthony. "Social Invention and Social Technology." *Journal of Liberal Religion* (1959).

Dexter, Lewis Anthony. "Research Needs of the Mentally Subnormal." *American Journal of Mental Deficiency* (1960).

Dexter, Lewis Anthony. "Research Problems on Mental Subnormality." *American Journal of Mental Deficiency* (1960).

Dexter, Lewis Anthony. "Where the Elephant Fears to Dance Among the Chickens: Business in Politics? The Case of DuPont." *Human Organization* (1960-61).

Dexter, Lewis Anthony. "The Sociology of Adjudication: Who Defines Mental Deficiency?" *American Behavioral Scientist* (1960).

Dexter, Lewis Anthony. "Has the Public Official an Obligation to Restrict His Friendships?: the Right to Privacy vs. the Public Interest." *American Behavioral Scientist* (1961).

Dexter, Lewis Anthony. "On the Politics and Sociology of Stupidity in Our Society." *Social Problems* (1962).

Dexter, Lewis Anthony. "The Role of the Professions in Evaluating Retardation." *Journal of Mental Subnormality* (1962).

Dexter, Lewis Anthony; Bauer, Raymond Bauer; Pool, Ithiel de Sola. *American Business and Public Policy: the Politics of Foreign Trade*. New York, NY: Atherton Press 1963.

Dexter, Lewis Anthony. "Congressmen and the Making of Military Policy," in *New Perspectives on Congress*, R. Peabody & N. Polsby, eds., Chicago, IL: Rand McNally, 1963.

Dexter, Lewis Anthony. "An International Social Anthropology Quinquennium." *Indian Sociological Bulletin* (1963).

Dexter, Lewis Anthony. "Sociology of the Exceptional Person." *Indian Journal of Social Research* (1963).

Dexter, Lewis Anthony. "What Do Congressmen Hear?" in *Politics and Social Life*, Nelson W. Polsby, Robert Dentler, and Paul A. Smith, eds. Boston, MA: Houghton Mifflin, 1963.

Dexter, Lewis Anthony. *The Tyranny of Schooling: An Inquiry into the Problem of "Stupidity."* New York, NY: Basic Books 1964.

Dexter, Lewis Anthony. "Marginal Attention, 'Pressure' Politics, Political Campaigning, and Political Realities." *International Review of History and Political Science* (1964).

Dexter, Lewis Anthony and David M. White, eds. *People, Society, and Mass Communications*. New York, NY: Free Press, 1964.

Dexter, Lewis Anthony. "Communications—Influence, Pressure, or Education." *People, Society, and Mass Communication*, Lewis A. Dexter and David M. White, eds., New York, NY: Free Press, 1964.

Dexter, Lewis Anthony. "Opportunities for Further Research in Mass Communications." Chapter in *People, Society, and Mass Communications*, Lewis Anthony Dexter and David M. White, eds., New York, NY: Free Press, 1964.

Dexter, Lewis Anthony. "Politicians, Science and Scientists." *Indian Sociological Bulletin* (1964).

Dexter, Lewis Anthony. "The Good Will of Important People: More on the Jeopardy of the Interview." *The Public Opinion Quarterly* (1964).

Dexter, Lewis Anthony. "On the Use and Abuse of Social Science Practitioners." *American Behavioral Scientist* (1965).

Dexter, Lewis Anthony. "Impressions About Utility and Wastefulness in Applied Social Science Studies." *American Behavioral Scientist* (1966).

Dexter, Lewis Anthony. "A Note on Policy Problems of Being a Consultant or Using Consultants." *American Behavioral Scientist* (1966).

Dexter, Lewis Anthony. "What the Practitioner in the Field of Mental Retardation Can Learn from Social Science." *Mental Retardation* (1966).

Dexter, Lewis Anthony. *Civil Defense Viewed as a Problem in Social Innovation,* Oak Ridge, TN: Oak Ridge National Laboratory, 1966.

Dexter, Lewis Anthony. "'Check and Balance' Today: What Does It Mean for Congress and the Congressman?" in *Congress: The First Branch,* Alfred de Grazia, ed., New York, NY: Anchor, Doubleday, 1967.

Dexter, Lewis Anthony. "Standards of Representative Selection and Apportionment," in *Representation,* J. Roland Pennock and John W. Chapman, eds., New York, NY: Atherton, 1968.

Dexter, Lewis Anthony. *How Organizations Are Represented in Washington.* Indianapolis, IN: Bobbs-Merrill Co., 1969.

Dexter, Lewis Anthony. *Elite and Specialized Interviewing.* Evanston, IL: Northwestern University Press, 1970.

Dexter, Lewis Anthony. *The Sociology and Politics of Congress.* Chicago, IL: Rand McNally, 1970.

Dexter, Lewis Anthony. "Organization Climate: A Preliminary Appraisal." *Political Methodology* (1976).

Dexter, Lewis Anthony. "Court Politics: Presidential Staff Relations as a Case in Point." *Administration and Society* (1977-78).

Dexter, Lewis Anthony. *Representation versus Direct Democracy in Fighting about Taxes: Conflicting Notions of Sovereignty, Legitimacy, and Civility in Relation to a Tax Fight, Watertown, Massachusetts, 1953-59.* Cambridge, MA: Schenkman Books, 1981.

Dexter, Lewis Anthony. "On the Use of Private Interest in Public Programs: The Administrative Difficulties." *Administration & Society* (1981).

Dexter, Lewis Anthony. "Marketers, Not Donors." *Society* (1981).

Dexter, Lewis Anthony. "Undesigned Consequences of Purposive Legislative Action: Alternatives to Implementation." *Journal of Public Policy* (1981).

Dexter, Lewis Anthony. "Intra-Agency Politics: Conflict and Contravention in Administrative Entities." *Journal of Theoretical Politics,* (1990).

Dexter, Lewis Anthony. "Complexities of Corruption." *Society* (1993).

Index